MW00990306

THE PROPAGANDISTS' PLAYBOOK

FRANCESCA BOLLA TRIPODI

THE PROPAGANDISTS' PLAYBOOK

How Conservative Elites Manipulate
Search and Threaten Democracy

Yale
UNIVERSITY
PRESS
NEW HAVEN AND LONDON

Yale University Press books may be purchased in quantity for educational, business,
or promotional use. For information, please e-mail sales.press@yale.edu (U.S. office)
or sales@yaleup.co.uk (U.K. office).

Set in New Aster with Syntax display types by IDS Infotech Ltd.
Printed in the United States of America.

Library of Congress Control Number: 2021948866
ISBN 978-0-300-24894-4 (hardcover : alk. paper)

A catalogue record for this book is available from the British Library.

This paper meets the requirements of ANSI/NISO Z39.48-1992
(Permanence of Paper).

10 9 8 7 6 5 4 3 2 1

To information seekers everywhere:
be mindful where the journey leads.

CONTENTS

PREFACE

In 2017, when I began this ethnographic project, I wanted to understand how conservative voters sought out information they felt they could trust. My goal was to better understand how Trump voters made sense of the contemporary news environment, and how search engine optimization might play a role. I had no intention of studying extremism. I had no idea that the way information was tagged and categorized would take me into a media ecosystem fueled by conspiratorial logic. I did not expect the content in which I immersed myself to influence my own mindset, and I certainly did not expect to witness the violence of the Unite the Right rally.

Quite frankly, I did not realize how bad it already was, how bad it still could get, and how vulnerable we all are, myself included.

As a sociologist and media scholar, I apply social theory to my empirical research on how communities interact with algorithmic systems in everyday life—because even if we don't think we're engaging with data-driven systems, we are, frequently and in often surprising ways. It is important to be savvy about how technology influences our decision-making at both the macro level—for example, as we collectively shape our policies and culture—and the micro level, such as when we vote or shop.[1] The interplay between these technical and social realms influences how communities make sense of themselves and the surrounding world. It also molds how we engage with and determine the American democratic process.

I started my study by seeking out what the U.S. Census Bureau calls "urbanized" city centers, those averaging between fifty thousand and a hundred thousand residents. These cities were growing rapidly, which meant a lot of construction: new roads, new schools, and new housing. But while these cities were bustling, they were also homogeneous and isolated. Along the outskirts of each city were mostly rolling hills, fast-food restaurants, and gas stations off highway exits; beyond that, miles of rural roads.

The two cities I found look similar in many ways. Both have a small downtown with walkable streets lined with mom-and-pop shops and local restaurants. Just a few blocks outside of this "main street" are larger roads lined with superchains like Applebee's, Panera Bread, Barnes & Noble, and Walmart, and after that, two-lane interstates and wide-open space.

In one city I conducted ethnographic observations of a college Republican group and in the other city, a women's Republican group.[2] In addition to participant observation, I conducted interviews and focus groups with thirty individuals: fourteen men and sixteen women ranging in age from eighteen to seventy. These people were either members or affiliates of the groups I observed, or people I met at related events. Interviews lasted approximately one hour and were transcribed by a professional service.

I centered my observations around the 2017 Virginia gubernatorial race. In the eight months between June 2017 and February 2018, I attended regular group meetings, fundraisers, rallies, tabling events, city council sessions, debate-watching parties, call center events devoted to bolstering voter turnout, backyard barbecues, Bible study sessions, church services, and an election-night gathering. I also went to events that were not directly connected to the groups I observed, including a rally for a Republican candidate during the gubernatorial primary and a winner's breakfast hosted by the Republican Party of Virginia after the primary election. Given the prominent debates over Confederate statues during this election, I took a tour of the Confederate Memorial Chapel and conducted participant observations at three rallies that were not associated with the groups I observed.

The access I gained at these events was predicated on my whiteness.[3] I am a white, cisgender, heterosexual woman and a native-born citizen of the United States. I was already familiar with the Christian rituals conducted at the meetings and events I attended. Nearly every self-identified conservative I interacted with in this study was a white, cisgender, heterosexual, Protestant, and native-born U.S. citizen.

To gain access to and cultivate trust with respondents, qualitative researchers engage in significant invisible labor. I realized very quickly that if I wanted Trump voters to trust me and share what news they believed, I needed to project a more conservative persona. I went by Fran or Franny instead of Francesca to avoid any difficulty with pronouncing my name. I bought a few outfits that projected a more modest look—capri pants in solid colors and cardigans over boat-neck blouses. I wore flats, a pearl necklace, and matching pearl studs. I put my hair up and wore more makeup than I am accustomed to wearing. Recognizing the cultural signs associated with purchasing decisions, I regularly arrived at meetings with a large diet soda in a Chick-fil-A cup rather than a Starbucks coffee when I needed to stay awake during long drives afterward. Even though I projected these outward markers, I informed everyone I spoke with that I was a sociology professor, and I was honest about my blue voting record when asked.

The goal of my research was to allow conservatives to speak for themselves and identify the kinds of news and information they trusted. Other scholars have pointed out, quite insightfully, that conservatives are not passive recipients of the powerful media apparatus, or what ethnomethodologist Harold Garfinkel would refer to as "cultural dopes."[4] Instead they are actively engaging in "deliberative intellectual exploration."[5] It is therefore critical to research how audiences interact with the media in their search for trusted information.

The impact of media in everyday life has been a rich area of study for decades. In the 1950s, in response to the direct effect

model of communication, sociologists Elihu Katz and Paul Lazarsfeld, through a series of studies, showed that the medium
itself plays a minimal role in changing audience reactions; instead
messages go through a "two-step flow" whereby influencers mediate content.[6]

In the 1970s, a cohort at the Centre for Contemporary Cultural
Studies in Birmingham, England (including Stuart Hall, David
Morley, Angela McRobbie, Paul Willis, Dick Hebdige, and Roger
Silverstone) founded a new approach to studying media that
shifted scholarly thinking about audiences from a scientific paradigm that treated and measured exposure and effects, to one that
recognized agency and cultural contexts. Their seminal work
pushed back on the traditional assumption that there is only one
way to read, listen, or watch media, and instead explored the idea
that audiences use media narratives to fit their own cultural logics rather than passively receiving the messages that producers
intend.[7]

The work by these and other earlier ethnographers paved the
way for understanding media less as a top-down force and more
as a diffuse network of agents that engage with people based on
their own life experiences.[8] Rather than searching for narrower,
more measurable media influences, cultural researchers began
examining how audiences interpret and adopt narratives embedded in media, applying them to activities in their lives. Using
sociocultural factors, these scholars have argued that religion,
geographic location, socioeconomic status, and gender all influence how audiences engage with media.[9] My findings build on
this theoretical framework of audience ethnography to consider
how epistemology shapes what audiences come to believe are
trustworthy sources of news and information.

Ethnography informed another aspect of my methodology: media
immersion. From August 2017 to December 2017, I obtained my
news exclusively from sources identified by the subjects of this
study as trustworthy or accurate. While the list was vast, primary
sources drawn on in this book include *Fox and Friends, The Daily
Wire, The Rubin Report,* Prager University (aka PragerU), *The Daily*

Signal, Red Alert Politics, One America News Network (OANN), Candace Owens (her original YouTube channel and her content produced by PragerU), Tucker Carlson, *The Drudge Report,* Breitbart, Rush Limbaugh, Glenn Beck, and Joe Rogan. In addition to the sources of news I sought out on my own, respondents would also email or share news stories from the *Wall Street Journal, Roanoke Times,* and the *Daily Progress,* as well as more obscure websites like WallBuilders.com.

By getting my news exclusively from conservative outlets, I identified patterns of information and talking points. I then used these terms, concepts, or general ideas to do more research on the subjects being discussed. When I transferred these concepts into a search query, I was able to understand how certain kinds of truths would emerge within the groups I had been observing and began to see the ways in which keywords create political silos.

I also created a Facebook account specific to this study, which allowed me not only to receive alerts and content created for a very specific audience, but also to document the kinds of news and advertising that Facebook recommended to a profile connected to conservative social groups. I also used Facebook to explore how certain kinds of public spaces were tagged in the communities I was observing. My research was reviewed by an ethical review board (the Chesapeake IRB) prior to collecting data, and all interviewees went through an informed consent process. I would issue friend requests only to those people who had consented, and I never accepted requests from people I had met at public events but who had not provided full informed consent. After the project was over, I closed and permanently deleted the Facebook account to protect the confidentiality of those in my study. Despite IRB review, informed consent, and people knowing I was a researcher, I can only assume that after a few weeks I became part of their "invisible audience," a forgotten follower, a fly on the wall at weekly events.[10]

I continually grappled with the ethical questions surrounding this alternative identity, as well as the social media account that accompanied it, which I had created specifically for this project. I was able to access and explore the various cultural experiences

I wanted to study because I blended so easily at Bible studies, political rallies, and meetings. This ability to blend in and redraw personal boundaries, however, comes with ethical challenges. I was forthcoming with my role as a researcher and as an academic, but ethnography is about fitting in. To do so, I shifted my public persona to allow the people I spoke with to make their own assumptions about who I was. During the meetings I attended, I spoke quietly, never interrupted anyone, and was careful not to ask too many questions. I often referenced my husband's military background, and sometimes I brought my children with me.

In addition to media immersion, I also worked with data scientist Leon Yin, who created a program to scrape metadata that YouTube creators used to amplify their content. Analyzing metadata alongside the content allowed me to identify the keywords that political commentators drew on to optimize their content online.

Throughout my ethnographic fieldwork and media immersion, I relied on grounded theory to identify relevant academic literature that could help guide my research. During analysis, I used comparative distinctions, coding the data for similarities and differences. After flagging particularly salient "in vivo codes," I conducted a more focused coding, determining the accuracy of the identified threads. Using these conceptual categories, I reexamined my field notes and analyzed those findings alongside the media content I was consuming as part of this project.[11] Drawing on interviews, participant observation, and media immersion, I was able to triangulate my data and strengthen the validity of my findings.

Media immersion and participant ethnography contextualized how conservatism is both a way of seeing the world and a media practice. After learning about current events from my participants, via the news I was consuming, or on Facebook, I would search on Google for more information about the topic using "incognito mode" to ensure that my existing search history did not influence my results. While this information-seeking process is not perfect and could not control for my geolocation or other personalization mechanisms, my findings exposed a pattern. Time and again, my searches documented the clear role that keywords play in shaping returns and how slight shifts in syntax can return dramatically different, even diametrically opposed, results.

One afternoon over coffee, a respondent asked me outright whom I had voted for in 2016. I was honest with my answer: Hillary Clinton. He shook his head slowly, looking into his mug. After a few long breaths, he looked back up at me, disappointment in his eyes.

"Oh Franny," he lamented. "They gotcha."

For some reason, this struck me. As I drove home that evening, I replayed the conversation repeatedly in my head. *He thinks I'm the one who got got?* To conservatives, *I* was the cultural dope. When others in this study learned about my voting record, they were equally convinced that once I started "doing my own research," I too would see the light.

In a certain sense, they were right. Once I began watching, reading, and listening to the news that my conservative respondents cited as trustworthy, it became increasingly difficult to discern the truth. This internal conflict peaked during the Unite the Right rally on August 12, 2017. After observing the rally first-hand, I interviewed respondents who claimed that radical leftists had staged the Unite the Right rally to make Trump look bad and that George Soros had paid Black Lives Matter protestors to come to town and incite violence. These paired ideas—that the mainstream media cannot be trusted and that leftists are violent extremists—were so powerful that I started applying them to my own understanding of current events without even realizing it. For example, in October 2017, when everyone was buzzing about the Mueller investigation and the forthcoming indictment, a thought struck me in the shower late one night. I knew who was going to be indicted! I turned off the water, wrapped myself in a towel, and found my husband.

"Do you think it's going to be Hillary?" I asked him.

"What?" He was confused.

"The indictment! Do you think they're going to indict Hillary?"

Then he understood me, but his face took on the same quality that those in this study had when I told them whom I'd voted for.

"No, Francesca. I don't think that's going to happen," he said quietly. "And please don't watch Fox News tomorrow."

I had been so consumed by a media ecosystem designed to distract from the transgressions of former President Trump and distort the wrongdoings of his political opponents that I legitimately thought Hillary Clinton, the person whom I had voted for in 2016, was going to be charged with breaking the law. But Clinton was not indicted, despite Trump's call to "Lock her up!" Instead Paul Manafort, Trump's 2016 campaign chairman, was. Manafort was charged with conspiracy against the United States, making false statements, money laundering, and failing to register as a foreign agent for Ukraine as required by the Foreign Agents Registration Act.

This book peels back the layers of the conservative media manipulation machine to reveal why it is so effective at exploiting constituents' worldviews and media practices. These revelations can help all of us be more mindful and savvy about our media consumption. But ultimately, my findings have much broader implications. By offering a more nuanced understanding of the keywords and processes that conservative pundits and politicians rely on to amplify, validate, and normalize white supremacist logic, this book offers practical guidance for breaking the disinformation loop. Most efforts reactively target misinformation, but to treat "information disorder" proactively, we need more ethnographic research on how the ways we use media, as individuals and communities, are exploited.[12]

After finishing this book, some might ask how search engines like Google can fix what has become an increasingly divided internet. But I believe that's the wrong question. What I observed is an ever-evolving sociotechnical issue, and to remain obsessed with a fix is to overlook the larger dynamic at play: conservative elites are leveraging cultural ideologies in order to reframe our understanding of the world around us. Without an ethnographic lens, their tactics remain invisible. Disinformation is not a bug in the code, it's a *feature* wielded for political gain, and a great risk to American democracy.

ACKNOWLEDGMENTS

This book would not have been possible without the support of the Data & Society Research Institute. Executive Director Janet Haven, along with the Media Manipulation Team, which included Robyn Caplan, Joan Donovan, Matt Goerzen, Lauren Hanson, Caroline Jack, Becca Lewis, and Jeanna Matthews, provided me with monetary resources, autonomy over my ideas, support through the ethnographic and writing processes, and most important, the time I needed to do good qualitative work. I met some wonderful people while I was there, and I feel very fortunate to have worked with such a team. I'm also grateful to danah boyd, who became both a mentor and a friend during my year as a postdoctoral scholar.

I would not have been able to take on this research if it were not for the academic training I received during my time at the University of Virginia in Charlottesville, Virginia. My academic adviser Andrea Press, alongside the rest of my committee—Sarah Corse, Allison Pugh, and Siva Vaidhyanathan—were a dissertation dream team.

Andrea Press was an amazing mentor and a central reason why I came to UVA to begin with. From her, I learned the importance of audience ethnography both as a method (there is value in qualitative inquiry!) and as an epistemological framework (media doesn't just "do"—audiences interact with what they read/

see/hear). Not only did Andrea guide my academic journey; she also advocated tirelessly for my research, and always supported my intellectual curiosity. When I first started researching the internet, many in my department did not yet appreciate the important role it would play in shaping society. As a media sociologist herself, Andrea never tried to steer my research in a different direction. Instead, she actively sought out funding that could support my inquiries, collaborated with me on papers and books throughout graduate school, and encouraged me to stay at it when it got hard. Andrea has always been a champion of my work and a true supporter as I navigated academic life.

As a central member of my dissertation committee, Siva Vaidhyanathan helped me identify case studies that would both capture my research interests and provide a competitive edge in the academic job market. It was because of his advice that I started studying Wikipedia many years ago, and it was because of his mentorship that I began examining the important role that Google plays in how we come to know what we think we know. During my last years of graduate school, Siva helped facilitate meetings with academics who were central to my professional success. Siva is the opposite of a connection hoarder; he delights in introducing people to one another in the hope that it will advance their intellectual curiosities and careers. In short, Siva's advice and support kept me going during graduate school, and his connections helped me to succeed after I graduated.

Allison Pugh taught me the importance of doing rigorous ethnographic research. She taught my qualitative methods course in graduate school, and as a member of my committee, kept my data collection and analysis grounded. As an adviser, she expects those she mentors to employ the same level of methodological rigor that she applies to her own work.

Sarah Corse was equally valuable in providing tough, but supportive, feedback. She took her job as a dissertation reader very seriously and provided amazing, thoughtful comments that helped strengthen my research and writing.

While some have horror stories of being pushed into the "mommy track," Andrea, Allison, Sarah, and Siva were all extremely supportive of my decision to have children during graduate school. In one meeting, Allison explicitly stated that she did not want to even see a draft of my proposal until after the summer and encouraged me to take time I needed to adjust to life with a newborn. When Sarah hosted graduate students in her home, my children were always enthusiastically welcomed. I vividly remember one time I arrived to find that alongside appetizers and wine, Sarah had set out graham crackers, juice, and an impressive array of dinosaur toys.

Most important, I knew it was okay if I cried in the presence of any of my mentors. Instead of making me feel like I couldn't hack it, they made space for me to feel safe voicing my doubts, provided meaningful encouragement, and even gave me a hug if I needed it. Each one of them saw in me a brilliance that I continue to struggle to see in myself, and for that, I will always be grateful.

In addition to academic mentorship, I'm very fortunate to have an expansive network of brilliant peers who bring with them an additional level of professional and personal support. I'm forever grateful to Alison Gerber for setting up the Work/Culture Collaborative while we were all going through graduate school. It's amazing to see how a small group of PhD hopefuls could eventually turn into professionals. Special thanks to Marcus Brooks, Eszter Hargattai, Rachel Sue-Tung Kuo, Becca Lewis, Alice Marwick, Sarah Mosseri, Whitney Phillips, Olof Sundin, Julia Ticona, Leon Yin, and the anonymous reviewers who read earlier drafts of this work and provided thoughtful commentary.

I'd like to also thank Rachel Durso and Leslie Jones for their unflagging emotional support and encouragement. Through our Digital Sociology Collective (un)Conference, we hope to connect, inspire, and learn from those who are still rising in their careers and sociological thinkers outside of academia. Without our daily group texts, I'm not sure I could have survived the isolation of COVID-19. Leslie introduced me to my editor extraordinaire, Joanna Pinto-Coelho. To be honest, I don't think I would have finished the book without her, and if I had, it would have been littered with passive voice.

Since starting this book many years ago, I've been fortunate to join a team of the most incredible scholars I've ever met: Dave

Ardia, Tressie McMillan Cottom, Deen Freelon, Daniel Kreiss, Gary Marchionini, Alice Marwick, Shannon McGregor. and Zeynep Tufekci. Run by Kathryn Peters, the Center for Information Technology and Public Life (CITAP) at the University of North Carolina at Chapel Hill is dedicated to understanding the growing impact of the internet, social media, and other forms of digital information sharing.

In addition to the people at CITAP, I'm honored to work with the other faculty at the School of Information and Library Science (SILS). It is such a unique and supportive environment full of intelligent, kind, and skilled scholars. The work they are doing has real-world influence, and I'm lucky to be part of the SILS community here at Chapel Hill.

I would like to also acknowledge members of the college Republican group and chapter of the National Federation of Republican Women who allowed me into their meetings. The data from this book is based on hundreds of hours of observation and would not have been possible without their participation.

Last, but not least, I want to thank my family. My husband is a true supporter—a loving spouse who recognizes the work I do as valuable and who makes space for me to write when I'm on deadline. We are fortunate to have two amazing children who bring a joy to my life I didn't realize I was missing until I met them. We are also lucky to have parental support: his parents and mine provide the "village" we need to raise the next generation of thinkers and make books like this possible. I love you all so much.

I want to end these acknowledgments by recognizing that my ability to write books for a living is a privilege. The institutions from which I earned my PhD (University of Virginia) and where I currently work (University of North Carolina at Chapel Hill) were built by hundreds of enslaved people through forced labor and sit on stolen land. I recognize that words legitimizing the rightful land ownership of Native nations and the existence of chattel slavery do not go far enough to right those wrongs. But denying the atrocities of our past is an active choice to uphold colonialism and white supremacy, and I refuse to placate the discomfort associated with acknowledging these historical legacies.

PROLOGUE

EXTREMISM ON MAIN STREET

SATURDAY, MAY 13, 2017

It was a beautiful spring day in Charlottesville, Virginia. The days were growing longer and warmer, but the inevitable humidity and bugs of summer hadn't yet settled in. My partner and I were walking from our home to the Festival of Cultures, an annual gathering celebrating the cultural and linguistic diversity of Charlottesville.[1] Designed with the goal of increasing awareness and bridging communication, the festival offers Charlottesville immigrants a way to showcase the food, art, and music of their countries of origin (at the events I attended this included Afghanistan, Columbia, Peru, and Ethiopia) in a public park at the center of town.

On our way, we passed a flyer inside a three-hole-punched sheet protector that featured a photo of the local statue of Robert E. Lee atop his horse. The statue had been commissioned in 1917 by Paul Goodloe McIntire and given to the city in 1924 to commemorate the Lost Cause narrative that Confederates were patriots rising against federal economic tyranny. The statue's unveiling ceremony was used to demarcate white-only spaces during a period of progressive desegregation.[2]

Given the statue's history, youth organizers at Charlottesville High School had recently petitioned the city council to remove it, as well as a statue of General Thomas J. "Stonewall" Jackson, and rename the parks where the two statues were located. The students' efforts

Photograph of flyer taken by author on May 13, 2017, on the corner of High Street and Park Street in Charlottesville, Virginia

paid off. On February 6, 2017, after initially denying the petition, the city council narrowly passed a motion to remove both the Lee and Jackson statues from their downtown pedestals and rename their former homes Emancipation Park and Justice Park, respectively.[3]

The flyer we saw read: "ART in PLACE: CENSORSHIP is UNDEMOCRATIC."
I was confused for a moment, then recognized the co-optation;
"Art in Place" is a Charlottesville nonprofit that commissions
sculptures with municipal funds and installs them around the city
to enhance public art appreciation. White supremacists had co-
opted their logo in this flyer to associate the Lee statue with the
nonprofit and its public works. By doing so, the disinformation
suggested that the Lee statue was worthy of protection and that
removing the statue was censorship.

My partner and I kept walking to the international festival.
Just a few blocks past the flyer, about a hundred people crowded
around the enormous bronze statue of the Confederate general
Stonewall Jackson. Again, I was momentarily confused—I even
wondered aloud if they had moved the festival to Jackson Park
that year. But as we drew closer to the crowd, it became clear they
were not celebrating Charlottesville's diversity. They were chanting that whiteness was "under attack."

At the center of this group stood Richard Spencer, white nationalist activist and a future co-organizer of the now infamous
Unite the Right rally, in a white button-down, khakis, and aviators,
his hair parted and slicked back. He stormed through the park in
black boots wielding a bullhorn and shouting at passersby. White
men in similar outfits and white women in floor-length white linen
dresses flanked him, waving large Confederate flags around the
Jackson statue. As we passed the event, pushing my young children
in a double stroller, they began to chant, "You will not replace us!
You will not replace us!"[4]

Their shouts echoed against the brick buildings of the town
square, the same town square where white people once bought
and sold Black men, women, and children, and where they used
to publicly lynch Black men.

The afternoon continued, as did the international festival, and
the police presence increased. Uneasy festival vendors decided to
put away their tables, tents, and displays early and head home.

Later that night, several dozen of the Jackson Park protestors
gathered at the Lee statue. They carried cheap, hardware-store
tiki torches that illuminated pale faces twisted in anger, chanting

"You will not replace us," "Jews will not replace us," "Russia is our friend," and "blood and soil."[5] Signaling comradery with Russia was a nod in support of the Trump presidency, and the "blood and soil" refrain was a reference to the Nazi slogan "Blut und Boden," which references a racially ideal body. Calls that whiteness will not be replaced signaled frustration with a supposed white decline (more on this later, in Step Six).

Although they brandished fire in violation of the city's open flame ordinance, chanted Nazi slogans, and failed to obtain a permit for any of the day's or evening's events, no Nazi protestors were arrested. Local law enforcement did not deploy pepper spray, tear gas, or rubber bullets to try to "control" the crowd.

SATURDAY, JULY 8, 2017

Soon after May's events, a North Carolina branch of the Ku Klux Klan (KKK), the Loyal White Knights, applied for a permit to hold a rally on the steps of the Circuit Court in Charlottesville, Virginia, to protest the removal of the statues. Leading up to the event, local government officials worked with the Charlottesville Police Department and the Klan to agree on a new location: Justice Park, previously known as Jackson Park, the same location where Spencer's May rally had taken place.[6]

Residents resisted granting the out-of-state hate group a "public demonstration" permit to "stop cultural genocide," but the city pushed back, claiming that the permit allowed for preparedness in a way that had not been feasible for the previous, unpermitted event on May 13, 2017.[7] Much of the preparedness I witnessed appeared to benefit the KKK, however. Charlottesville city officials chose to place large cement barricades around the Jackson memorial, behind which stood police officers clad in riot gear. The goal of the fencing was to keep the Klan separated from counter-protestors, but in doing so it provided KKK members attending the event an unobstructed access point to "protect free speech."[8]

For the first three hours, no KKK members were even present at Justice Park. Instead counter-protestors flew a sea of rainbow flags and rang out choruses of Black Lives Matter chants in opposition to the North Carolina KKK and its white supremacist rhetoric.

Making my way along the fringes of the rally, I noticed two men with long pepper-grey beards and Confederate flags sewn onto their motorcycle jackets. They stood with some like-minded women on the steps of the courthouse, and as I joined them there, I noticed that their location provided an excellent vantage point; it was slightly elevated so I could see into the barricaded center even while remaining on the outskirts of the crowd. I introduced myself to the men and explained that I was a researcher interested in how people validated truth in the news. They invited me to sit down with them and I listened on as they swapped stories, chain-smoked, and drank soda.

"I mean, I was raised as a son of the Confederacy," said one of the men.

"Jackson and Lee, they are my ancestors! When we start removing this, what's next?" A woman seated below him replied.

They explained how angry and frustrated they had been by the removal of the statues, and how they had decided to drive to Charlottesville because they couldn't believe the KKK was going to be there. They identified themselves as defenders of "historic preservation."

While the people I was sitting with claimed that they were "disgusted" by the KKK, they did not disagree with the KKK's choice to protest the statues' removal. They claimed they were angry that people from "out of town" were coming to protest, but then failed to acknowledge that they themselves were out-of-towners coming to protest. Collectively, they blamed the KKK's arrival on the Black Lives Matter movement.

"If *they* hadn't voted to remove the statues *we* wouldn't be in this mess!" said one of the women sitting on the grass.

Another woman agreed. "I blame the board," she said, referencing the Charlottesville City Council decision to relocate the statues in February 2017.

Perhaps in part because many white southerners grew up being taught that Black people had been content with segregation or slavery, those I spoke with that day believed that race relations in

Virginia were good and blamed "outside agitators" for disrupting this mythical racial harmony.[9] The understanding of racial justice they articulated was a zero-sum game: that is, much like white southerners of the past, those I spoke with saw civil rights *gains* for Black and brown Americans as *losses* for themselves (whites).[10]

I sat for hours in the hot sun with this group as they kept circling back to the same talking points: that removing Confederate statues was tantamount to defacing a memorial, that doing so was a liberal attempt to erase history, and that the decision to remove them was a waste of taxpayer money. But the most frequently discussed "fact" was that the Black Lives Matter movement was responsible for the KKK coming into town—in other words, that "both sides" were responsible for the violence that would ensue. All the while, those I spoke with refused to take responsibility for their own privileges, positionalities, or activities as outsiders or agitators.

The tenor and fervor of the crowd shifted all at once. A large group of people came yelling and running around from the side of the courthouse, heading toward the place where I was sitting. As the volume of the crowd swelled and intensified, I made my way from my vantage point to the blockade entrance. The Klan members had arrived.

Dressed in white hoods and robes, KKK attendees snaked their way through the protected access point into the center of the park. A man with a bullhorn tried to shout over the crowd, but no one could hear him over the din of the protestors. At around 4:30 pm, the KKK members returned to their cars, escorted by the Charlottesville Police Department.[11] Counter-protestors followed the Klan members back to their cars and refused to move out of their way. When the counter-protestors would not disperse, the police released three canisters of tear gas and arrested twenty-three of those who had gathered to block the KKK vehicles.[12]

FRIDAY, AUGUST 11, AND SATURDAY, AUGUST 12, 2017

During the summer of 2017, as my research progressed, I started hearing rumors about a "Unite the Right" rally. Using the Facebook account I had set up for this research project, I identified the various white nationalist groups planning to convene in Charlottesville for the rally, and I followed the public "Unite the Right Free Speech Rally" event page.

Jason Kessler, University of Virginia alumni and political extremist, created the event's Facebook page. Kessler's activism began with his involvement in the Occupy movement, but he gained notoriety in Charlottesville over his 2016 disagreement with then-council-member Wes Bellamy's efforts to remove the Confederate statues. In protest Kessler posted old, offensive, tweets of Bellamy's on his blog to demand his resignation from public office.[13] (That is, Kessler borrowed from the discursive accountability practices of some Black communities and tried to "cancel" Bellamy.)[14] Kessler's blog was featured by *The Daily Caller*, a conservative publication referenced later in this book (see Step Two). Soon thereafter, Bellamy was placed on administrative leave from his job as a teacher and resigned from his appointment to the state's board of education.

After that, Kessler wrote two articles in *The Daily Caller*. In an article published on May 14, 2017, titled "Richard Spencer Leads White Nationalist Demonstration in Front of Virginia Robert E. Lee Monument," Kessler wrote about the May rally I had witnessed on my way to the international festival.[15] In the article, Kessler described the collection of khaki-clad tiki-torch-bearers screaming racial epithets as "a visually striking demonstration" against the unjust removal of Confederate monuments. He also referred to the white nationalists as a "white bloc," explaining that their white polos and white dresses were meant as a response to the "black bloc" uniforms of "anarcho-communist group Antifa." (See Step Seven for how blaming "Antifa" is a disinformation tactic.)

In the article, Richard Spencer was quoted as saying, "We are here to say no; no more attacks on our heritage, on our identity; no more attacks on us as a people," and it featured a photo of Spencer and others standing behind a flag that read "You Will Not Replace Us—Identity Evropa." Identity Evropa is an American neo-Nazi and white supremacist organization established in 2016. As we will see, this fear of white decline is not exclusive to extremists like Spencer and Kessler.

After the May rally, Spencer and Kessler joined forces to organize the August Unite the Right rally. On Facebook, Kessler posted the location of the rally ("Lee Park") and an RSVP function to track how many people were planning on going or interested in attending on its scheduled date. As the rally drew nearer, Kessler served as a central point of contact and used Facebook to post "rules" for August 12, 2017. These rules

- encouraged people to show up early so they could be "on-site" by 12 pm,
- warned attendees to be mindful of their appearance and behavior as representatives of "our movement,"
- discouraged *starting* physical violence, but urged attendees to come armed and "stand their ground," and
- suggested that people travel in groups because of "Antifa" threats.

The Facebook event also helped interested attendees to coordinate ridesharing and to finance GoFundMe campaigns to help "independent journalists" attend the rally. These independent journalists promised to livestream the rally and hold the mainstream media accountable for what "really" happened. Note, too, Kessler's use of "stand your ground" language, evoking the law that expands legal justification for the use of lethal force against a perceived threat. Doing so both posits Antifa as dangerous and sets up the possibility for attendees to claim self-defense later.[16]

In other public Facebook groups devoted to white supremacist communities, users posted flyers for the event that boasted live music and an "all-star" lineup of white supremacist speakers including Mick Enoch, Jason Kessler, Baked Alaska, Augustus Invictus, Christopher Cantwell, Matthew Heimbach, Johnny Monoxide, Pax Dickson, Dr. Michael Hill, and Richard Spencer. The content posted was littered with white supremacist symbols: swastikas, images of Pepe the Frog, and Confederate flags. One meme adapted the "Join or die" serpentine symbol to represent the various white nationalist groups joining forces for the Charlottesville event. The tail segment was labeled with a "K" and filled with an image of the Kekistan flag, an alt-right symbol of chaos discussed in more detail in Step Six.

The originations of the severed snake symbol trace back to a cartoon published by Benjamin Franklin in the *Pennsylvania Gazette*. Franklin's depiction was designed to promote cohesion among the colonies with the goal of uniting colonists against France, the British government, and Native Americans.[17] Organizers' adaptation of this colonization symbol signals a need for alt-right groups to identify as part of a larger polity or risk losing their notion of "American identity" (read: white, Christian, heteronormative).

A few days before the event, Kessler held a live Q&A session on Twitter that he recorded and made available on multiple platforms for followers to access later. Kessler confirmed that the rally would take place and that it was probably better for people to leave their children at home.[18]

At around 2:00 pm on August 11, 2017, I saw a group of white supremacists in McIntire Park, about three miles away from the planned event. I was leaving the YMCA with my family when I noticed a line of cars and people surveying the premises. We hung back against the door, and I held my son's hand tight.

"They're already here," said a woman next to me.

We got in our car and locked the doors, watching from afar as a small group formed around the baseball field. They pointed in different directions, taking note of the adjoining parking lot.

That evening, another researcher with the Data & Society Research Institute who had come in from New York met me at the downtown mall. The park where the protest was scheduled had already been barricaded for days. "No Parking" signs lined the main roads. As we walked, the police presence intensified, and we learned that a large group of white supremacists had already gathered on the University of Virginia campus and were making their way through the town with lit torches chanting phrases similar to those I had heard on May 13, 2017: "Blood and soil," "White lives matter," and "Jews will not replace us."

The next morning, I watched hundreds of cars file into McIntire Park's lot. A man directed traffic, and I could see groups of people, mostly men, park and then board shuttle vans for transportation downtown. Some of them flew Confederate flags while others wore clothing with swastikas.

I picked up my colleague from their hotel and we snaked through downtown traffic back to my house. At one point, a group of about fifteen white men in jeans and black leather vests emblazoned with Nazi symbols marched through the street, surrounding the cars driving on High Street, including my own, and stopping traffic as they made their way to the Lee statue. Hours before the rally was set to begin, downtown Charlottesville was swarming with people. It was only 9:00 am and hundreds of people had already gathered around the Lee statue.

We got back to my house and parked the car, deciding to head back to Lee Park on foot. As we got closer to the Jackson statue, which is approximately two blocks from the Lee statue, two people walked past us. One pressed a white rag to his forehead, blood streaming down his face, holding on to the other's arm. The chaos had already begun. Law enforcement was starting to close the streets.

At 10:00 am, the governor declared a state of emergency. We tried to get closer to the Lee statue, but the National Guard had blocked the roads. Other members of the National Guard were already escorting out crowds of counter-protestors. Some armed protestors gathered around the Stonewall statue in Jackson Park chanting for Unite the Right protestors to "Go home!" Among the counter-protestors were armed members of the Redneck Revolt, an anti-racist, anti-fascist community group that believes in advancing equality through armed uprisings.

After the governor declared the rally an "unlawful assembly," members of the National Guard marched through the pedestrian mall. When they reached the street that James Fields would later use to plow down residents of Charlottesville, the National Guard formed a human barricade to keep residents out. Looking down an alleyway, I noticed an even larger group of people walking in the opposite direction of the National Guard along Market Street, one street away from the pedestrian mall. White supremacists came into closer contact with counter-protestors there. Tensions intensified and started to get violent. People began throwing objects and a civilian set off tear gas.

I took cover beneath the awning of a wine bar underneath the parking structure on Market Street. While I hid, Alex Michael Ramos of Georgia, Jacob Scott Goodwin of Arkansas, Tyler Watkins Davis of Florida, and Daniel Patrick Borden of Ohio surrounded DeAndre Harris, a Black resident of Charlottesville, and beat him unconscious in that parking structure. Although Harris suffered a head laceration requiring eight staples, a concussion, fractures, internal injuries, and a spinal injury, a local judge issued a warrant for *his* arrest.[19]

The National Guard was nowhere in sight at that point. I noticed Unite the Rally attendees gathering to head west on Market; they were going to walk back to McIntire Park, where their cars were parked. We decided we should make our way back to my house and check on my kids, who were in the care of a good friend.

After we arrived at my home, the other researcher and my partner rode bikes back to McIntire. Once there, they photographed men dressed up as knights and people flying the Kekistan, Pepe, and Gadsden flags. (The Gadsden flag, a yellow field featuring a coiled black rattlesnake ready to strike and the words "Don't Tread on Me," was created as a symbol of liberty by American colonists seeking separation from England, but recently social and fiscal conservatives have co-opted the symbol.)[20] On their ride back home, they also saw a large van covered in epithets equating Jewish men and Black men with pedophilia run a red light and make an illegal U-turn.

A siren went off in the distance. Kentucky rally-goer James Fields had just run his car into a crowd of counter-protestors, injuring several people and murdering Charlottesville resident Heather Heyer.

Afterward, Fox News claimed that radical leftists were to blame for the day's violence.[21] According to conservative pundits and politicians, it was because of liberal instigators that the Unite the Right rally had turned deadly. Both the conservative media I consumed and conservative respondents I spoke with for this study were convinced that these protestors were "out of towners" paid by philanthropists such as Jewish billionaire and humanitarian

George Soros, who is a common villain in conservative conspiracy theories. But none of this matched what I had seen with my own eyes. I had witnessed local organizers call on the Charlottesville City Council to remove the Confederate statues, and I had watched as Nazi protestors invaded McIntire Park the day before the rally and scoped out their parking prospects and rendezvous points.

After the rally, I listened as Trump condemned the violence but refused to denounce white supremacists. After asserting that the violence had come from "many sides," Trump doubled down on his criticism of the leftist protestors, insisting there was "blame on both sides."[22] Trump's strategy of condemning civil rights leaders as "outside agitators" and aligning social fears with white displacement is reminiscent of arguments that conservative elites have used since desegregation became law in the 1960s.[23]

An independent commission the city later hired to investigate the events of August 12, 2017, found that the Charlottesville Police Department had been ill-equipped to handle the events and had not solicited enough feedback from experienced personnel with advanced training.[24] The report also blamed the city for waiting too long to elevate the chief of police's request for assistance from the Virginia Department of Emergency Management, and further criticized city leadership for not warning the public early enough of the dangers of the situation. More transparency and communication before and during the event had been needed, the commission insisted, among city, county, and state officials and law enforcement.

THE AFTERMATH

Over the course of three months, I witnessed three white supremacist rallies in my hometown. Extremists organized all of them around the removal of two Confederate statues, which these groups used as "proof" of white genocide.

My state of mind was put to the ultimate test when the city of Charlottesville summoned me to serve as a potential juror in the criminal trial of James Fields. Sitting in the courthouse, I listened to attorneys claim that James Fields's decision to run his car into a crowd and kill Heather Heyer was an act of "self-defense." For most in the courtroom, his plea seemed like a shocking distortion of reality.

After leaving the courtroom on that cold November day, I revisited my interviews and field notes. Though nonsensical and dissonant to others in the courtroom, James Fields's defense aligned perfectly with broader themes I'd begun to identify in my research. This idea that conservatism is under attack and requires protection fits a broader pattern of media manipulation. Claiming that Fields was only trying to defend himself is predicated on the racist law-and-order frame that posits nonwhite, non-citizen, non-Christian "others" as threats to conservative ideals. Conservative politicians and pundits routinely draw on this narrative to justify violent acts, by Fields and others, and to normalize white supremacy as a necessary balance to what they refer to as "leftist extremism." That the Left, referred to by many names such as BLM, Antifa, or Social-Justice Warriors, is dangerous, and that Fields was acting in self-defense are cornerstones of the propaganda that conservative elites regularly feed their audiences.

As data reporting by Leon Yin and Aaron Sankin for *The Markup* reveals phrases like "white power," "blood and soil," and "you will not replace us" help advertisers find videos and channels sympathetic to white supremacist messaging, even years later. Their research shows that while Google blocks nefarious keywords like "KKK," "Nazi," or "white genocide," in 2021, the tech giant still hadn't blocked other keywords associated with the white nationalist rallies I observed firsthand. The persistence of these phrases to target audiences with hateful content is important. As my research demonstrates, media manipulators have a remarkable understanding of how keywords are connected to worldviews. They routinely and effectively curate, optimize, and monetize unique phrases to amplify and organize social movements.[25]

Hateful and violent extremists are not the only ones profiting from white supremacy. By knowing the concerns of their audiences, building an insular network of information, tapping into contextual media practices, and exploiting the way the public confirms the truth, conservative politicians and pundits wield the power of information seeking to make extremist events like the Unite the Right rally and the Capitol insurrection seem like normal and necessary reactions to the emotional, irrational, and dangerous Left.

Framing the Left as the "real" danger not only distracts from the acts of terrorism that took place on August 12, 2017, or years later on January 6, 2021; it also is meant to purposefully mislead the public. Steering the conversation away from the wrongdoing of white supremacists also encourages conservative audiences not to trust mainstream media's accounts of what transpired in Charlottesville or the Capitol. This discord deepens their resolve to seek out so-called alternative facts, and "do their own research." By emboldening their audiences' more extreme ideas and behaviors, it also creates plausible deniability for powerful politicians and media personalities. They can normalize violence as a necessary part of retaining power, but absolve themselves from the fallout because they do so by encouraging individualistic exploration.

Over the course of this project, I experienced many bouts of cognitive dissonance. My direct observations conflicted constantly with the attitudes, behaviors, and beliefs of the conservative media and constituents I studied. Despite white supremacists using the removal of the Charlottesville Confederate statues as "proof" of white genocide, and violently attacking counter-protestors, my research shows that conservative elites sought to manipulate the public in the aftermath, blaming the violence on the supposedly hysterical Left. Conservative politicians and media personalities used this and other acts of domestic terrorism as opportunities to spread disinformation, creating an alternative set of concerns.

The strategies that conservative elites deployed after the Unite the Right rally keep resurfacing. To take just a few examples, during the first impeachment of then-president Trump, as Black Lives Matter protests proliferated after the murder of George Floyd, while COVID-19 ravaged the world, and when rioters tried to storm the Capitol, conservative politicians and pundits repeatedly tried to steer the conversation away from topics that might damage their political brand, such as Trump's criminal wrongdoings, police violence, inadequate public health infrastructure, and an in-

surrection. Conservative pundits, senators, congressional representatives, members of Trump's cabinet, and the former president
himself all leveraged the power of how people seek information
in order to promote alternative facts and alternative realities that
could advance their political agenda, no matter the cost to truth,
our collective understanding of the world, and democracy itself.

INTRODUCTION

Political polarization defines the United States today.[1] In 2020, access to health insurance and health care, immigration policy, police brutality, and the nation's response to COVID-19 were just some of the many issues that were debated along deeply entrenched partisan lines. But a divided public is not new, and it is not limited to belief systems. A closer look reveals an equally split and historically entrenched difference in how people with various political beliefs describe their views.[2] This semantic difference often means that voters are unable to make sense of political others' experiences and concerns.

Political fissures are connected to what some scholars refer to as *filter bubbles*.[3] These academics theorize that social media platforms and the algorithms that run them influence the democratic process. The limited academic attention paid to this issue so far has focused on customization, personalization, and the notion that platforms fuel some of this divide. Little work thus far has explained how information-seeking practices and search engines also tailor information silos.

Search is a ubiquitous part of everyday life. Want to know where the closest pizza place is? Google it. Can't remember the name of that song? Google it. Want to verify if that tweet is true? Google it. Need more information on the candidates in an upcoming election? Google it. Google handles billions of searches from around the globe daily as individuals track down information to help them in their daily lives, using computers, phones, and various other devices. How they do this—which platforms they access, what search terms they use, and how they share what they learn—plays an important role in shaping collective identities around the world. A nation's media, for example, produce the meanings and messages that together form a common national language, attachment, and solidarity.[4] Without media-facilitated connections, regional dialects vary such that people who live in the same country might be unable to communicate effectively with one another.[5] *Ideological dialects,* too, shape how users seek out information, and influence the kind of content search engines return. Phrases like "illegal aliens" and "undocumented workers" may both reference immigration, but these keywords are bound by different worldviews and return content that affirms these diametrically opposed positions.

How voters engage and interact with search engines is key to understanding the growing divide within the United States. Search returns have become so fragmented that the conservative internet is incoherent to progressive audiences, and vice versa. Yet little sociological research has sought to understand how meaning-making and information-seeking processes are intertwined. Some research has explored the connections between political language and media, demonstrating that politically charged phrases impact the way people consume information.[6] More work is needed, however, to understand how relevance as an algorithmic function can unintentionally confirm politically biased thinking and increase the likelihood of encountering misinformation.

Similarly, many scholars have addressed how different news formats like podcasts, websites, social media, smartphone apps, television, radio, and newspapers inform democratic processes in the United States.[7] But only a few have considered how users' political worldviews affect how they interpret and interact with the news they seek out to confirm their beliefs.

For many years now, scholars have sought to understand the way that nefarious actors actively politicize and weaponize the media to undermine democratic participation.[8] That research opened up opportunities to explore how manipulators connect to their audiences' "deep stories," use sophisticated marketing tactics, and exploit loopholes in information systems—all to successfully shape public opinion and threaten the democratic process. It also led to the realization that how voters access the information that they need to make informed electoral decisions depends on the news sources they trust.

In this book I connect the dots and bridge together existing research to examine how self-identified conservative audiences seek out information and decide what news is true and which politicians to trust. To be sure, companies like Facebook, Google, and Twitter—commonly referred to as "Big Tech"—influence the information that audiences receive, but I use an active-audience paradigm to consider the other side of this algorithmic equation: how our own biases are coded into keywords before they hit the browser.

My research demonstrates that conservative elites, politicians, and media pundits wield the power of search in order to promote narratives that fit their own agendas and steer public attention away from news that might hurt their campaigns. To some, this media manipulation strategy might seem to be simply spreading lies, since whether problematic content is "mis" or "dis"-information is connected to the intent of those who create it, spread it, and evaluate it.[9] In this book, I call deliberate, systematic information campaigns that leverage the power of multiple forms of mass media (including print, broadcast, digital, and live events) what they are—propaganda.[10]

Propaganda is designed to link together brands, people, and nations with the goal of influencing ideas and attitudes. Successful propaganda campaigns typically include various forms of information, both truthful and deceitful, and try to cultivate a certain attitude or provoke a specific action in their target audiences. While we often associate the term with wartime practices in earlier eras, it still applies to "selective presentations of information, persuasive framings, and use of emotional appeals" by "a range of government and nongovernmental actors."[11]

Successful propaganda campaigns appeal to the core tenets of conservatism, or what I describe as the *five f's*: faith, family, firearms, the armed forces, and a free market. Conservative ideology manifests as both a way of seeing the world and a way of interacting with various kinds of media. Specifically, conservatives engage in *scriptural inference,* close readings undertaken to find truth in the words of sacred documents like the Bible or the Constitution. As we will see, conservative elites can and do exploit these practices to advance their political candidates and causes.

In setting out to better understand how conservatives validate truth in what has been described as a post-truth era, I came to understand how important the written word is in their quest for knowledge. Conservatives trust "the words" they read more than the words that come from journalists, professors, and government officials. Yet conservatives also believe truth to be self-evident, rarely considering the hidden, latent, or subtextual meanings of what they read.[12] Conservative media presents news and information in the same way.

Immersing myself in news media that my respondents identified as trustworthy, I saw firsthand how widespread and integrated the conservative information ecosystem is. Pundits and legislators use scriptural inference to legitimize their messaging. Conservative elites speak to their audience in a way that mainstream media figures do not, encouraging them to distrust "the media" in favor of doing the research for themselves. When these constituents are challenged to question their leaders' word for it and seek out "the truth" for themselves, they end up considering these arguments to be their own.

Encouraging conservative voters to do their own research is not necessarily nefarious, but it is a key component of conservative propaganda. Belief systems shape search engine queries, and keywords can lead users into algorithmic rabbit holes without their knowledge. As my research reveals, conservative elites understand how information flows and they use particular tactics both to distract the public's attention away from topics that could damage conservative interests, and to normalize extremist rhetoric. This communication strategy opens audiences up to conspiratorial content that legitimizes and promotes white supremacy, and viewers take the bait. As my ethnographic data show, conservative voters who rely on the right-wing information ecosystem and describe themselves as "moderate" or "mainstream" come to articulate more extreme beliefs. At the same time, propaganda is multidirectional. Information seekers can themselves reinforce partisan silos, and the historical legacy of some ideological dialects facilitates the cycle of disinformation. For example, many phrases popular among conservatives today (such as *law and order, tuition vouchers,* and *privatization*) are decades-old creations of earlier conservative spin doctors working to maintain segregation.[13]

There is another commonality: a recurring pattern of rhetoric that not only frames the Left as dangerous and the media as biased, but also draws on more racist tropes like race realism or white decline.[14] As I make these connections, my goal is not to label conservatives as extremists, but rather to note the pervasiveness of white supremacy and racism in the mainstream appeal, scope, and spread of this insidious propaganda.

Understanding how search works allows us to push back on the belief that those who voted for Trump were incapable of discerning real information from Russian propaganda and complicates the idea that political power depends on galvanizing an extreme base. In fact, the efficacy of the conservatives' strategy is its mainstream appeal. For example, conservatives have cultivated dog-whistle phrases to frame the advancement of equal rights as an attack on the traditional, conservative way of life. This messaging resonates with the kind of Evangelical Protestantism in the United States that mixes Christianity, patriotism, and politics, and is predicated on fear of "the other"—what Anthea Butler, associate professor of religion at the University of Pennsylvania, describes as a "powerful, pungent mix of Christian populist and patriotic racism" that delineates who gets to belong.[15] Racism is the common thread woven through disinformation campaigns, which rebrand old concerns in order to resist new calls for equality.

STEP ONE

KNOW YOUR AUDIENCE

Nestled in the back room of a family restaurant, members of the Ravine Roads Republican Women's Group sit around large rectangular tables organized in a horseshoe.[1] As the mostly white women make their way in, they collect copies of this week's agenda, last week's minutes, and candidate flyers from the table along the back wall before taking a seat next to their friends. A server assigned to the group takes meal orders, and over dinner the women chit-chat about local musings and upcoming events. Some opt for casual clothes and red "Make America Great Again" (MAGA) hats, while others are dressed more formally, adorned in expensive jewelry and patriotic brooches. Next to me, a woman shows the table a photograph of herself with then-president Trump and then–vice president Mike Pence, excited to share the details of her meet-and-greet. As the meal winds down, the president of the organization rises and comes to the podium. The meeting is called to order and a member leads the group in prayer. We fold our hands and bow our heads.

> Dear Lord, please bless our food in order to nourish our souls and watch over those who could not be here with us today. We also ask you to bless our politics and watch over us during these months leading up to the election.

Following the prayer, the women rise and turn toward the back corner of the room, where the flag usually sits. It is then that the group realizes the flag is missing. Flustered, the president turns and exclaims, "I can't believe the flag isn't here! Does anyone have one?" The women spring into action, looking in their purses for a hand-held flag, and I overhear a woman telling her friend that she has been thinking about keeping extra flags in her car for just this reason. Suddenly, the leader of the group has an idea. She pulls out her smartphone and finds a GIF of a waving American flag. Holding the phone up with her left hand, she covers her heart with her right and in unison we begin:

> I pledge allegiance to the flag of the United States of America, and to the Republic for which it stands, one nation, *under God*, indivisible, with Liberty and Justice for all.

We continue to stand as the Republican Creed is read aloud. "We believe," the president begins,

> that the free enterprise system is the most productive supplier of human needs and economic justice. That all individuals are entitled to equal rights, justice, and opportunities and should assume their responsibilities as citizens in a free society. That fiscal responsibility and budgetary restraints must be exercised at all levels of government. That the Federal Government must preserve individual liberty by observing Constitutional limitations. That peace is best preserved through a strong national defense. That faith in God, as recognized by our Founding Fathers, is essential to the moral fiber of the Nation.[2]

The prayer, the pledge, and the creed recited, we sit. The meeting is called to order and business begins.

Every event I attended began this way, with a prayer and the Pledge of Allegiance, whether it was a political fundraiser, a local barbeque, or a group meeting. In fact, the president of the college Republican group I observed aptly named the routine "the prayer and the Pledge" and used the phrase to indicate that the meeting was about to begin. While the content of the prayer varied depending on if food was served, it always mentioned politics—asking God to watch over the election process, help guide voters to make the right choice, or protect candidates running for or already in office. The emphasis on God and country I witnessed at event after event is key to understanding why the propaganda that conservative elites create resonates with their audience: it allows politicians and pundits to unite a large group of otherwise disconnected individuals in a common conversation. It is no accident that Protestant religious practices and biblical references dominate conservative media practices. The connection between Protestantism and Republicanism runs deeper than simply pandering to voters.

Not all conservatives are people of faith in the traditional sense, and my findings should not imply that all Christians are conservative or that all conservatives are Christian. Nonetheless, the concept of faith, whether it be in God, in country, in the police, or in a free market, creates an ideological dialect that resonates with conservative voters across the country. Propagandists leverage this dialect to seem relatable and trustworthy, using technology and organizational infrastructure to weave seemingly independent groups into a tight network.[3]

CONTEXTUALIZING CONSERVATISM

After Donald Trump was elected president of the United States in 2016, some researchers argued that geographic isolation, socioeconomic decline, and feelings of neglect in white, rural communities helped to explain his success.[4] Unpacking the "deep stories" of the Louisiana bayous and analyzing the political conversations of Wisconsin coffee klatches foregrounded the power of white antipathy to galvanize the voter participation of the Republican base. These researchers found that feelings of abandonment and distrust in government help ultra-conservative candidates, like former governor of Wisconsin Scott Walker and former president Trump, to win elections.

Recent sociological work, however, indicates that the influence of Christian nationalism in American political life is a better explanation for Trump's rise to power.[5] These scholars argue that the presence of a cultural framework that advocates fusing Christianity with American civil and political life and the degree to which Americans want to institutionalize their conservative "Christian" cultural preferences are the greatest predictors of Trump's success. Other sociologists argue that Trump's win was predicated on earlier shifts within the Republican Party—grassroots activists, billionaire fundraisers, and right-wing media manipulators have steadily moved the party further and further to the Right.[6]

Historians of the American Right look back much further, describing modern American conservatism as the melding of three previously distinct modes of thought:

- Traditionalism—the belief that truth comes from divine revelation,
- Free-market libertarianism—the belief that federal regulation of commerce should be limited, and
- Anti-communism—the belief that capitalism is necessary for freedom.[7]

Historical accounts of conservative social movements explain many of the themes in modern conservatism. For example, the desire to privatize public services, the drive to cut taxes for the wealthy, and the hostility toward the federal government are all rooted in initiatives designed to push back against desegregation efforts.[8] These historical accounts of whites' reaction to the Civil Rights Act created a "new conservatism" predicated on the language of "rights, freedoms, and individualism."[9]

Despite the rich work describing the complicated ways in which those who voted and aligned with the Grand Old Party (GOP) shifted their views over time, few studies acknowledge that the term *conservative* is frequently used interchangeably with *Republicanism*, despite conservatism being its own complex worldview. Those I interviewed and interacted with explained that conservatism is not necessarily bound to political identity; being conservative is not the same thing as being Republican. Even though my fieldwork was conducted inside groups explicitly associated with the Republican Party (a women's group and a college group), many in those groups refrained from identifying as a Republican.

When I asked how they identified politically, an overwhelming majority of those I observed and interviewed favored the conservative label. In order to clarify their use of the term, I would ask them to elaborate, questioning the meaning behind the term and why they chose this label over another.

Michael, a retired veteran in his mid-fifties who now does contract work for a local company to help pay the bills, described that conservative and Republican "used to mean the same thing, but now they don't." Sitting together over coffee, he explained:

> Now there are a lot of Republicans out there that don't
> act according to being conservative. They call themselves
> Republicans, but they don't seem very conservative. They
> tend to spend our tax dollars pretty quickly without tak-
> ing something else off the table. They don't do things
> within a budget. They just want to raise the debt ceiling.

Tom, a past leader in his faith community and current leader in the city's Republican Party, had a name for those Republicans who ran on a conservative platform but whose political decisions failed to reflect conservative values: "RINOs," or "Republicans in name only."

The frustrations my respondents shared are not unique to this study; Tea Party candidates propelled their campaigns and won seats in Congress on promises of keeping other Republicans "on the conservative straight and narrow."[10] The RINO term was also popular with disenchanted college students. It was this perceived difference between their political party and their personal values that led young women like Olivia, a junior in college, to claim that she too was "more comfortable saying [she was] conservative, rather than Republican."

As my respondents described time and again, being conservative is not about party affiliation but rather is a set of ideas and ideals, a way of seeing the world.

THE FIVE F'S OF CONSERVATISM

Using what is known as *grounded theory* in sociological research, I identified five sets of beliefs commonly held by my conservative respondents.[11] This method provided a systematic yet flexible way to collect and analyze data simultaneously, allowing me to move beyond description and construct new concepts as they emerged.[12] During my interviews, respondents repeatedly drew on the same categories of faith, family, firearms, the (armed) forces, and the free market, or what I call the "five f's" of conservatism.

1. *Faith.* Support for religious liberty and for laws that protect the church and promote faith-based leadership. Faith should inform political decision-making.
2. *Family.* Devotion to preserving the heterosexist institution of marriage, maintaining traditional gender roles, and criminalizing abortion, even if it's not "politically correct."
3. *Firearms.* Protection—and celebration—of the right to bear arms. Policies that oppose background checks, gun registration, gun-free zones, or regulation on concealed carry.
4. *Forces.* Reverent support for national security, the military, and the police. Allocating government funds to protect freedom.
5. *Free Market.* Dedication to limited government oversight of the economy and corporations, underpinned by a belief that consumers should regulate the market.

While conducting my research, various iterations of these core values popped up repeatedly in interviews, at formal and informal events, and in politicians' speeches and platforms. The five f's were also regular themes on nationally syndicated television series like *Tucker Carlson Tonight*. Their widespread use indicates that they are meaningful to a much broader group than simply the people I observed, and suggests that they act as a bridge between conservative politicians running for office and the voters they need to get elected.

Of course, there are various strains of conservatism. Some conservatives may identify as more socially conservative, while others are passionate about fiscal conservatism. There are also many politically conservative subgroups (for example, the Moral Majority, John Birch Society, and Tea Party). While not everyone in these different groups thinks or acts the same, the entrenched two-party system—which usually offers only a Democrat and a

Republican as voting options—means that successful politicians must focus on similarities and find ways to reach broad audiences.

To paraphrase the wisdom of David Lane, a strategist who worked to increase the political strength of the Christian Right, conservative politicians understand that campaign success is about *multiplication,* not subtraction or division.[13] Conservative activist Phyllis Schlafly, for example, was able to stop the ratification of the Equal Rights Amendment in the 1970s by uniting Catholic, Evangelical Protestant, and Mormon women with white middle- and working-class women.[14] By knowing their audience, conservative politicians and pundits routinely call on the five f's to galvanize a historically curated voting bloc like the Silent Majority.

Political success is about defining both the Right and the nation in a particular way, emphasizing boundaries that clearly demarcate who is included and who should be excluded. A central component of this unification strategy centers around the idea that the country must be taken back and that American values must be preserved.[15] Compounding this fear and distress over being underdogs in their own country is a feeling documented by other scholars: that conservatives tend to think about social change and civil rights progress as a zero-sum game: if liberals are gaining power, conservatives must be losing ground.[16]

Understanding this fear of cultural displacement is particularly important when it comes to circumventing political propaganda. As long as white workers have been voting, conservative elites have used a fear of "others" (Black people, immigrants, Muslims, members of the LGBTQ+ community, feminists) to make white workers worry about their job security; churchgoers fret about waning faith and the loosening of moral values; and "real Americans" worry that more change would mean more loss.[17] Repeating these narratives over and over legitimizes the idea that whites are dispossessed, despite their retaining an overwhelming majority of powerful positions and land wealth in the United States.[18]

Such a historical understanding of the roots of conservatism also explains how the ideology is not party-specific. George Wallace, for example, who vowed to uphold segregation to the delight of his constituents, won one election after another in the 1970s as a Democrat from Alabama.[19] Wallace prioritized conservatism over the Democratic Party, making him a "DINO" of his time. The enactment and enforcement of the Civil Rights Act in many ways strengthened the politics of white resistance in the South, bonding together people who "both rejected the goals of the civil rights movement and the means that the federal government used to reach them."[20] Soon after Kennedy famously sent the Civil Rights Bill to congress, airing a televised plea to the American people to stop segregation on moral grounds, many voters who agreed with Wallace left the Democratic Party, creating the Republican Party as we know it today.[21]

The five f's shape the way conservatives see the world and influence how they seek out information and validate truth. For conservative voters in particular, the five f's play a foundational role in determining who will best serve their political interests.

CONSERVATIVE POLITICAL PARTICIPATION

Even though my self-identified conservative respondents were wary of RINOs, they voiced support for the two-party system and specifically the Republican Party as the most reliable vehicle for conservative views and policies. The people I observed were heavily involved in trying to get Republican candidates elected as a way to ensure that their interests would be supported in local, state, and national legislatures. If a respondent's candidate of choice lost the Republican primary, they still actively campaigned for the Republican candidate who won.

This was the case for candidate Trump. Only a few actively supported or voted for Trump during the primary season, but all those I interviewed had campaigned for him in the general election. Most people I spoke with preferred Texas senator Ted Cruz at the beginning of the 2016 Republican primary season, with Florida senator Marco Rubio coming in second. These constituents felt uneasy with the remarks that Trump had made about women and worried that he would not uphold their values. Their faith in

Trump was strengthened, however, when he selected as his running mate Mike Pence, a politician who describes himself much like those in my study did—that is, as a "Christian, a conservative, and a Republican, in that order."[22] Regardless of their personal feelings for Trump, my conservative respondents believed that his election would further the conservative agenda because he would appoint conservative leaders.

They were right. Two months after Trump's inauguration in January 2017, after a tense confirmation battle over former President Obama's appointment to the seat, Trump filled the late Justice Scalia's open seat on the U.S. Supreme Court with Justice Neil M. Gorsuch.[23] Gorsuch quickly established himself as one of the court's most conservative justices, supporting then-president Trump's travel ban on Muslim-majority countries, upholding his prohibition of active transgender military members, and voting to amend the U.S. Census to add a citizenship question (which many speculated was an effort to reduce the response rate and redistricting efforts in heavily Latino states).

In addition to his conservative positions on social and religious freedoms, Gorsuch approaches the Constitution with what he defines as an "originalist" method of study. As I explain in Step Three, this way of making meaning from textual documents and returning to "the words" is a practice I refer to as *scriptural inference*. This practice has also been documented in other sociological studies of conservative groups, where it was noted that conservatives would regularly return to sacred texts like the Constitution or the Federalist Papers.[24]

Those involved with this study characterized their involvement in politics as critical for furthering conservative values. Local, state, and even federal Republican candidates seeking election also recognized their voting power. Representatives on the ballot regularly came in to speak with both the groups I observed to ask them what issues mattered most and to highlight how they could advance conservative ideals if elected.

Some have argued that younger voters are less likely to identify with any party.[25] This was not true of young conservatives I studied. The president of the college association I observed regularly stressed the importance of going to the polls to vote for Republican candidates, reasoning that "turnout on this campus can have an impact on both the local and the state-wide elections." Using the crowded quad on campus, members of the Young Republicans would volunteer much of their personal time to try to register students to vote between classes. They also knocked on doors in the surrounding neighborhoods and made phone calls on behalf of political candidates in order to raise awareness and fundraise.

Similar grassroots campaigning is the focus of Turning Point USA, a nonprofit organization committed to educating youth on conservative values and encouraging youth participation in elections. The college Republicans I observed also socialized around important political events. During each of the debates, they hosted a watching party at their headquarters, served pizza for the attendees, and made calls to get out the vote during commercial breaks. This involvement within the group not only built camaraderie but also allowed attendees to "earn points." The groups used this system of point allocation to determine who would receive transportation, hotel accommodations, and registration to the annual Conservative Political Action Conference (CPAC) hosted by the American Conservative Union (ACU).

Since the late 1970s, CPAC has been a way for young Republican groups like the one I observed to learn from rising conservative leaders. During CPAC, attendees participate in a "straw poll" contest to determine whom the group favors as the next Republican presidential candidate. While this poll sometimes yields candidates who veer in and out of the GOP—such as Ron or Rand Paul—usually the frontrunners are established Republicans like George Allan, George W. Bush, or Ted Cruz. Mitt Romney, for example, holds the record for most CPAC straw polls won. CPAC is an essential part of the conservative network that brings media personalities, influential politicians, and young voters together in an annual renewal of conservative ideals (more on this network in Step Two).

Even though Republicans don't all think and act the same way, at the core of the party are voters grounded in conservative values framed as under attack. At stake are not just the military, the family, and the economy, as was believed in Reagan's time, but rather the five f's: that is, faith, family, firearms, the forces, and a free market.

FAITH AND RELIGIOUS FREEDOM

It is no secret that Christianity has played a central role in shaping American politics. In the United States, evangelicalism has become shorthand for whiteness, Christianity, and conservatism.[26] Over time, the Evangelical focus on segregation, patriarchy, and militarism has embedded itself into the Republican Party.[27]

Many, however, have an inaccurate understanding of the history of Evangelical involvement in politics. While most consider *Roe v. Wade* (1973) to have been a defining moment for galvanizing faith-based voters, American historian Randall Balmer explains how *Green v. Connally* (1971) was in fact a greater driver of Evangelical political participation. In this important case, the U.S. Supreme Court affirmed that private schools that practiced racial discrimination were ineligible for the school tax exemption.[28]

To put this ruling in context requires looking back a few more years, to the era following *Brown v. Board of Education of Topeka, Kansas* (1954), a case that outlawed racial segregation in public schools. In response to *Brown*, Evangelical leaders had established private academies for white children only. But because of *Green v. Connally*, most of these segregated parochial schools were forced to close because they could no longer afford operating expenses or property taxes. Segregationist Evangelicals saw this decision as a reason to fear government outreach and began to frame the state as an enemy.[29] As my research shows, conservative elites regularly connect with this legacy of racism to influence public perceptions of current events.

Democratization in the United States also played a central role in the development of American Christianity.[30] A fundamental tenet of politics in the United States is that any person can potentially run for office and become a representative of the

people. This modern democratic value helped prevent elite trans-
fers of power and nepotism in politics, and when applied to houses
of worship, emboldened everyday individuals to start their own
churches and religious followings. While the Protestant Reformation in Europe posed a religious and political challenge to the
powers of the Catholic Church, in the United States it assumed a
more populist vision; it associated "virtue with ordinary people
rather than with elites, exalted the vernacular in word and song
as the hallowed channel for communicating with and about God,
and freely turned over the reins of power."[31]

Those whom I observed ranked their faith as one of the most
important parts of their identity. By reading the Word of God in
the Bible, they engaged directly in a search for Truth. Yet centrality of faith is not exclusive to those I observed. Starting in the
1980s, national and state Republican parties learned to work with
activists in the Christian Right in order to tap church networks
and engage socially conservative voters.[32] In her study of a Tea
Party group, sociologist Ruth Braunstein noted that religious
discussions typically dominated the discussions, and that nonreligious members would often yield to overtly religious members
to avoid conflict. Even though the conservatives she studied did
not identify as Christian, the idea of faith was woven into many
of their mission values. For example, a pamphlet distributed by
one of the groups referenced Christian beliefs, specifically noting
faith "in the Lord God Our Creator."[33]

I noted a similar pattern in my own observations. "One nation
under God" was often spoken at a louder decibel than the rest of
the Pledge of Allegiance, an act of resistance also documented in
other studies and seen as a way of asserting a core value of
American conservatism.[34] In fact, during one of the luncheons I
attended, a heated discussion between two older couples broke
out after the Pledge, regarding how to properly say "under God."
Shaking his finger sternly, one man said that the other had paused
incorrectly. "It's gotta flow," he said. "*One nation under God.*" The
other couple shook their heads, responding that the pause added
emphasis. "One nation, *under God*," the wife of the other couple
retorted; "you've got to emphasize the *God.*"

After a great deal of back and forth, the organizer of the meeting interrupted. She believed that they could agree to disagree on where to pause, and should focus instead on the shared understanding that "under God" must be included. Everyone in the room nodded in agreement. This emphasis on "under God" taps into the religious symbols that bind conservatives together. Indeed it was a Presbyterian minister who, in 1954, convinced President Eisenhower that it was important to add the phrase to the Pledge, because to omit the phrase would be to deny "the Christian ethic that defined the American ideal."[35]

In many ways, ideas of "religious liberty" that were articulated during my observations are connected to the Christian Nationalist belief that the very fundamentals of democracy are rooted in biblical knowledge. This is the central argument of *The 5000 Year Leap*, a book written by W. Cleon Skousen, founder of the National Center of Constitution Studies, which was repeatedly referred to by respondents in my study and by others who observed conservative groups.[36] Although Christian Nationalism is different from other forms of conservatism, other studies of conservative politics have found that Christian Nationalists often "set the tone" of the Tea Party groups they observed and that "in practice, social conservatives make up a vocal majority of many tea parties."[37]

It was clear that many I engaged with would qualify as what sociologists Andrew Whitehead and Samuel Perry refer to as "ambassadors" of Christian Nationalism.[38] They wholeheartedly believe that the United States has a special relationship with God and that the federal government should declare the United States a Christian nation and advocate for Christian values. Not only was faith a central part of the rituals I observed in the form of prayer and activism; those I interviewed also used faith to justify the belief systems of the Founding Fathers and other famous figures associated with the creation and defense of their central beliefs.

For example, Juliette, a wealthy woman in her sixties who regularly donated her time and money to conservative causes, described for me how she was "waking up" to the ideals that she believes are being "taken away" from our society. She used the metaphor of awakening to justify her involvement in local politics and the state's decision whether to remove Confederate statues. "General Robert E. Lee. *He was a Christian man!*" she exclaims. "He was a family man, he was in the middle of a war, Lee was a fine man. He had slaves because everyone had slaves."

The idea of "waking up" connects to the New Testament verse "I was once blind, but now I see" (John 9:25). After John Newton used the line in a sermon in the late 1700s—"I once was lost, but now am found, was blind, but now I see"—it became a line in the Christian hymn "Amazing Grace," which became an important part of the Second Great Awakening during the early 1800s and was commonly played at the services I attended as part of this project. Drawing on this "civil religious discourse," many of my respondents described how their use of faith and "waking up to the truths of the Bible" helped shape their involvement in political activism.[39]

Other studies of conservative groups have noted how the idea of the "red pill" from the *Matrix* film series has been used as part of this faith-based model of awakening, to describe how participants now have their "eyes wide open."[40] As I note in Step Six, using phrases like the "red pill" connects mainstream conservatism to more extremist groups. Interestingly, this is a misinterpretation of the intent of the writers of the first three *Matrix* films, Lana and Lilly Wachowski, who wrote the movie about transgender acceptance and understanding.[41]

By actively putting their faith to use, those in this study described how faith in God was part of the "moral fabric" that made America great. Skousen also makes the argument that a government without religion cannot be maintained and argues that schools should teach religion and morality as part of their standard, mandated curriculum. While the book goes on to describe how "religion in schools" is not exclusive to any one religion, the book outlines "five fundamentals of sound religion" indicative of Christianity. (As this book details time and again, persons of other faiths are often connected to fears of cultural loss, and are typically not included in a positive way in faith-based narratives put forward by the Christian Right.) Skousen then uses this

framework as the bedrock for understanding the remaining foundational principles of the United States. As such, protecting "religious liberty" was among the most important concerns of those
I studied.

Sometimes, too, the interests of whites and "the South" are
defended over those of America more generally. As Anthea Butler
explains, individualist exceptionalism has been used to absolve
feelings of personal wrongdoing associated with slavery and to
buttress the Lost Cause narrative, which has long been used to
recast the Civil War as a defense not of slavery but of the South.
In doing so, the Lost Cause became a kind of civil religion supported by the clergy, thereby "cementing the structures of morality and civility" as distinctly white and explicitly Christian.[42]

FOCUSING ON THE FAMILY

My conservative respondents supported political candidates who
would "protect the family." Based on my interviews and observations, the core issues surrounding "the family" included restrict-
ing access to or eliminating abortion; denying marriage equality
for homosexual couples; banning access for transgender individuals; and preserving traditional gender roles. While it is easy
to attribute this logic exclusively to clergy, it is important to note
that at least one conservative leader, James Dobson, founder of
the conservative organization Focus on the Family, was not a
pastor or even an Evangelical.[43] It was still through his alleged
commitment to scripture, however, that he quickly turned his
media influence into political influence.

Of the topics surrounding familial preservation, abortion
stands out. Many of my respondents described themselves as
"single-issue" voters when it came to abortion. Hannah, a middle-
aged litigator considering a run for local office, walked me through
this issue over lunch. We sat at a crowded counter talking about
myriad topics, but when it came to abortion the tone changed.
Wiping her mouth with her napkin, she stopped to consider what
she might do if she found herself pregnant as a result of a sexual
assault.

"Some people are one hundred percent against the exceptions," she says. "If I were raped, would I want to keep this child? Would I have love for this child? I've never been placed in that situation, thank God, nor with incest, and these stories do break my heart. It's like, this is a life, but this life was brought upon somebody else not of their own free will. What would I do in that situation?" Hannah pauses as she considers the depth of the circumstances. "Again, there is always adoption. I always go back to that, that there are people out there that can't have children."

For most people I spoke with and at rallies I attended, the conservative position on abortion was clear and unwavering. On many occasions, the college Republicans would devote time during their meeting to discuss what they referred to as "infanticide." During one meeting, a representative from the Christian Broadcast Network came in to talk about the lack of real journalism surrounding what he described as the "greatest genocide" of all times. As part of his speech, he drew on statistics used by many anti-abortion organizations: "in the United States there are three thousand abortions a day and over 60 million lives have already been lost to infanticide." Before concluding the meeting, the speaker somberly reminded the crowd that "during this minute, a life is lost." He then stood before us for a full minute of silence with his hands crossed in front of him before the meeting ended.

It was this strong anti-abortion conviction that drove many of the college students I observed to travel together to attend the March for Life rally in Washington, DC. Joining tens of thousands of others on the National Mall, respondents shared their videos on Facebook and garnered hundreds of likes for their participation. In June 2020, Trump became the first president in history to attend a March for Life rally.[44]

While the enthusiasm surrounding pro-life legislation was palpable, so too were discussions around preserving the "sanctity" of heterosexual spaces. According to the Pew Research Center, public support of same-sex marriage has grown steadily over the past fifteen years, from 30 percent to about 60 percent.[45] Yet the same study notes that conservatives are much less likely to support the issue (only about 36 percent). And while there may be growing support for homosexual marriage, an overwhelming majority of persons who lean Republican, regardless of generation, believe that one's gender is determined by the sex they were assigned at birth.[46] Based on my observations, interviews, and media analysis, many conservatives didn't necessarily have a "problem" with people of the same sex marrying or people transitioning genders, but they took issue when these personal choices impeded on their "space."

Consider a conversation I had with Randy, a man in his mid-forties who used to work for the armed services. Standing outside the event with a few others, Randy described how "he's fine with people disagreeing with him" on issues regarding homosexuality or transgender rights as long as it doesn't "interfere" with other issues. When I asked him to clarify, he described how he doesn't want LGBTQ+ issues becoming

> a dominant issue, because I think the family structure is the most important and the integrity of the family structure must be preserved. People who are strong advocates for gay or lesbian issues and push that as being [an] equal thing in schools and other things, tends to eat at the family structure.

The others in the group nodded their heads in agreement. In particular, "the school thing" my respondents were concerned about—specifically, whether transgender students should be allowed to use the bathroom that aligns with their gender identity as opposed to the sex they were assigned at birth—has been a critical flashpoint.

The political fight over transgender rights in schools started in 2014, when the U.S. Department of Education revised Title IX to protect individuals who do not conform to stereotypical notions of masculinity or femininity. President Obama and Secretary of Education Arne Duncan sought to prohibit discrimination against transgender people in federally funded educational programs and activities. In response, the Republican National Committee (RNC) issued a public statement following its 2016 annual meeting, stating that "a person's sex is determined at conception, identified at birth, and can be confirmed by DNA testing." As such, Republicans argue that allowing

> any students to use the restrooms, locker rooms, or other facilities designated for the exclusive use of the other sex infringes on the rights of privacy and conscience of other students; and therefore be it resolved, The Republican National Committee calls on the Department of Education to rescind its interpretation of Title IX that wrongly includes facility use issues by transgender students.[47]

Moreover, the RNC encouraged state legislatures to enact laws that would prevent transgender students from accessing restrooms, locker rooms, and similar facilities designated by sex.

Shortly thereafter, North Carolina legislators acted on the RNC resolution, signing into law North Carolina's House Bill 2 (HB-2). The law was divisive. As *Charlotte Magazine*'s Greg Lacour and Emma Way write, the legislation forces transgender men to use women's rooms and transgender women to use the men's; allows private businesses to discriminate against gay and transgender people; prohibits local governments from preventing such discrimination; and nullifies every nondiscrimination ordinance ever passed by any local government.[48]

Relying on traditional gender roles and stereotypes, those in my study described HB-2 in positive terms, framing it about protecting women and children. This mirrors findings by sociologists Laurel Westbrook and Kristen Schilt that when a transgender person wants to use the bathroom or join a sports team of their newly assigned gender category, cisgender persons can feel that the segregated space is being "threatened." This may be why cisgender individuals use explicit and officially defined criteria of what constitutes gender to police the space. Westbrook and Schilt argue that this process not only restricts transgender access to public spaces and athletic competition, but also perpetuates the belief that women are inherently vulnerable. These "imagined interactions" with what their respondents conceive of as transgender "predators" stoke fear and maintain the status position of women as inferior in American society.[49]

The origins of the current fears surrounding trans youth date back decades. Consider Schlafly's campaign to stop the ratification of the Equal Rights Amendment, which focused on the vulnerability of women.[50] Or the racist undertones of rhetoric that tries to prevent the creation of unisex spaces or activities. Just like the fears that swirled around desegregation, conservatives' focus on the "family" continues to center around the patriarchal effort to protect the "purity" of white women.[51] While abortion was and continues to be a driving factor of Evangelical involvement in politics, race hatred played a fundamental role in creating a "color-blind" gospel that could provide cover for racially motivated organizing against the federal government.[52]

FIREARMS: A CONSTITUTIONAL RIGHT

On August 3, 2019, a mass shooting occurred inside of a Walmart in El Paso, Texas. Afterward, Walmart began asking its customers to refrain from openly carrying firearms and publicly claimed that it would revise its policies on gun sales. This announcement came about a year after Dick's Sporting Goods decided to pull assault-style rifles off its shelves and limit the purchase of firearms or high-capacity magazines to anyone under the age of twenty-one.[53] Yet Field & Stream, a subsidiary of Dick's, is still a retail powerhouse when it comes to selling guns in America. The outdoor recreation retailer devotes an entire section to "shooting supplies" and boasts "unmatched expert advice and service" for customers who go to the store to buy a gun.

When I made my way to a Field & Stream, I was surprised by the number of options available to me. The back of the store was lined with hundreds of guns, including handguns, assault rifles, and semiautomatic weapons, ranging in price from hundreds to thousands of dollars. Gun sales are so popular on the weekends that they use a deli counter system, complete with a red "Please Take a Ticket" dispenser, for taking orders. I took advantage of a slow Monday and talked at length to a sales representative.

"What are you planning on using the gun for?" he inquired. "Hunting or defense?"

"Self-defense," I answered.

"Are you planning on getting a concealed carry?"

I said I wasn't sure—I had never purchased a gun before.

He offered me a warm smile and steered me toward the Glocks: "You really can't go wrong with name-brand recognition." Taking a few out of the case, he walked me through their specs, invited me to feel their weight, told me how many rounds each one would hold, and described what the kickback would be like, advising that if I purchased a smaller gun, it would have a bigger kick.

In the end, he recommended a handgun that was on sale; if I bought it today, I would save a hundred dollars. "If you give me your license, we could have you outta here in less than thirty minutes. There's no waiting period if nothing comes up on your background check."

I told him I needed more time to think about it, and he nodded. "Don't worry," he said. "There's a sale every other week; no rush."

Much like the gendered spaces of bathrooms, lockers, and dressing rooms, I noticed a women's gun section. Pink rifles and pink camouflage were marketed toward what the sales rep described as "fashion-conscious" hunters, never mind the impossibility of hiding in foliage while wearing bubblegum and neon pink. Like issues that focus on "protecting" the family, gun sales also allow men to negotiate their position as "protector." As sociologist Jennifer Carlson explains in her research, marketing campaigns around guns often claim that women need to protect themselves from a masculine portrayal of crime (strangers hiding in the bushes), which marginalizes many women's actual experiences of domestic violence.[54] Carlson demonstrates that even when women own guns, a woman's gun is described as an extension of masculinity, that is, as a stand-in for a male protector. This link between protectionism and masculinity is perpetuated institutionally in organizations like the National Rifle Association (NRA).

The importance of guns in the United States cannot be understood without referring to the Second Amendment of the Constitution. Second Amendment purists have been integral to stopping basic restraints on gun rights that even the NRA favored. As Martin Durham writes, "the rivalry between these groups and the NRA has been an important, and neglected, dynamic in gun lobby politics."[55] The organization frequently worked with conservative groups, even to the extent of providing gun registration information as a way to target voters.[56]

These efforts seem to have worked. The constitutional right to bear arms has continued to be extremely important to conservative voters, even in the wake of tragic mass shootings. Young conservatives in a focus group of college student respondents, for example, described how legislators need to "check their emotions at the door" before tackling these issues. Said one young man in the group,

> I think a great example of that would be the shooting that happened in Las Vegas. When that happened, the very first thing that you saw, everyone wanted to get rid of guns, because everyone was so freaked out. And that happens every time there's a shooting like that. And so, I think it's very important to check your emotions at the door, wait until . . . If you're really fired up about an issue, that's good, because you have passion about an issue. But at the same time, don't let that kind of fog your sight of what's important and what you're actually trying to accomplish.

Likewise, many conservatives used mass shootings to frame the debate as one of mental health, leveraging the age-old saying "guns don't kill people, people kill people." The conservatives I interviewed also described guns as the solution to the problem of mass shootings, claiming that armed schools are safer. Between meetings with clients, Henry, a white man in his early seventies who owns his own business, described how he used to bring his gun to school with him so that he and his friends could go hunting on the way home. "You'd put your gun in the cloak room. Look at the old yearbooks from back then. There's the Marksman's Club, the Rifle Club, whatever, ROTC. Guns, loads of guns, and decades without any incident."

As a way of proving their point that guns save lives, many talked about the shooting that had taken place in Sutherland Springs, Texas, during my fieldwork. Twenty-five people had died, including a pregnant woman, making it one of the deadliest shootings in an American place of worship.[57] Yet the people in my study often framed it as a reason for why more people should be armed. Much like the Fox News coverage I saw after the event, respondents focused on a man who lived near the church, Stephen Willeford, who confronted and shot gunman Devin Patrick Kelley.[58]

Standing around chairs with desks attached to them, conservative college students lamented that "the media" had failed to really cover the story. In a back-and-forth discussion, they agreed that because the shooter was a former NRA instructor and the event demonstrated the positives of gun ownership, the media was trying to "bury" the story. (In fact, CNN and NBC News had covered the event the day before Fox News did, labeling the man a "hero.")[59]

PROTESTANT PATRIOTISM AND THE ARMED FORCES

While conservatives laud cuts to federal funding, they also believe that the government should fund police officers and military personnel. This reasoning again falls under notions of protection. Tiffany, a college sophomore at the time and an active member of the college Republican group on her campus, explained perfectly this support for government subsidized defense:

> I really appreciate what Trump is doing. Because, you know, military defense really is the only thing the government has to do for us. It's the only real responsibility that they have—to protect us, and that's the military's job.

Tiffany's views represent a larger national trend when it comes to military spending. According to the Stockholm International Peace Research Institute Military Expenditure Database, the

United States spent $40 billion more on defense in 2017 than the next seven countries combined; that is, the United States spent just under $649 billion, while China, France, Germany, India, Russia, Saudi Arabia, and the United Kingdom together spent slightly less than $609 billion.[60] When I discussed these figures with respondents, they overwhelmingly agreed that funding the military was of utmost importance, often using the phrase "freedom isn't free" to both justify military spending and assert that the servicemembers who fought for our freedoms did so at a cost.

This reverence for the military played out on a national level during my study when former San Francisco 49ers quarterback Colin Kaepernick began kneeling during the U.S. national anthem prior to his team's games. He made this gesture to protest racial injustice and the systematic oppression of Black Americans in the United States.[61] As the movement began to gain momentum and players took a knee across the nation, then-president Trump intervened, claiming that the protest was ruining the game. His solution: owners of National Football League (NFL) teams should fire those players who chose to kneel, and spectators should walk out to show their lack of support. In line with his boss, Vice President Pence left an NFL game between the Indianapolis Colts and the San Francisco 49ers on October 8, 2017, when players knelt in protest.[62]

The conservatives in my study echoed Trump's position, describing the protest as disrespectful to the United States and to the armed forces who protected "our" freedoms. A sophomore in college whose family members had died while serving in the military said:

> Oh, you don't want to stand for the flag? Well, sir, if you don't believe in standing for the Pledge of Allegiance, people died for your right not to do so. You're welcome.

Those I interviewed who had personally served in the military, like Michael, also found it offensive:

> I was reading something about the Cleveland Brown football players kneeling at the football game during the

national anthem and being a retired military person, I just find that completely disrespectful to the U.S., not just the flag or the anthem.

Others in my study became even more animated when discussing the topic. Some gave up watching the sport altogether as a form of counter-protest. When I was talking with some of the women in the Republican group and asked if anyone was going to watch the game that weekend, one woman began furiously shaking her head, interrupting another woman who was saying she might watch the game.

To take a knee during the national anthem has nothing to do with racism! It has to do with support of our country and the blessings and freedom that we have. The isolated incidents of perceived racism, whether they are or not, do not warrant taking a knee during our national anthem. I'm disgusted. So, what do I see on Facebook? People burning their jerseys, and I'm delighted. I'm done watching. I'm done playing with fantasy football.

The protest that Kaepernick started focused a great deal of attention on systemic racism in police departments across the United States. And despite conservatives' unwavering support for the police, few understand the historical legacy of the institution they fervently support. In 1793 and 1850 Congress passed the Fugitive Slave Acts, which criminalized the act of escaping enslavement and sought to ensure the return of Black people to their slave masters. The patrols that resulted from these acts were among the earliest police forces in the American South and so can be considered precursors of today's law enforcement system. That is, the earliest police forces in the United States were designed to control enslaved humans and protect the interests of slaveholders.[63]

The troubled history of American policing continued during the Civil Rights Movement and beyond. Take the famous confrontation between civil rights marchers and state and local police on March 7, 1965, on Pettus Bridge in Selma, Alabama. As the trail of peaceful marchers tried to make their way over the bridge, they were assaulted by club-wielding troopers and canister after canister of tear gas. As Dan Carter writes, those who listened to the live broadcast could hear "Sheriff Jim Clarke's voice: 'Get those god-damn n*****s!' . . . his posse charged, whooping rebel yells, swinging bullwhips and ropes; one [police officer] wielded a length of rubber tubing wrapped with barbed wire."[64] Over sixty years later, law enforcement in the United States and the criminalization of Blackness is still "killing the Black body."[65]

WORSHIPPING A FREE MARKET

The idea that the state's only role is to safeguard individual and commercial rights is intrinsically tied to the belief that the government should not regulate the market—unless, of course, those regulations safeguard the rights of American companies, consumers, and workers. Therefore, it is not surprising that conservatives I spoke with who support federal spending for military expansion also champion a system that limits the government's role in economic growth.

This was the central message of a guest speaker I saw when visiting a group of conservatives who meet every second Saturday of the month in a large backroom of a buffet-style restaurant. A high-ranking RNC official resplendent in her business suit and pearls charmed the crowd by drawing on Skousen's argument for how you find balance between "Ruler's Law" (tyranny) and "No Law" (anarchy). Speaking to a rapt crowd for nearly forty minutes, she stressed the importance of restraint by both the self and the government.

"When we have high government restraints and low self-restraints, we have slavery," she said. "But when we have low government restraints and high self-restraints, we have *liberty.*"

The speaker flashed a large white smile and a man in the back murmured "Amen."

"That's the problem," she continued. "We have lost our moral restraint and our ability to restrain our own actions and so now we depend on the government to do it for us." By turning to the government for aid, she argued, we enable immorality.

Chrissy, a woman in her mid-forties who champions limited government in all aspects of life, agreed:

> I believe that the best way to take care of people would be to grow the economy for the free-market system. I believe that providing good-paying jobs that then in turn provide insurance. I think that the more that we can rely on non-government organizations and companies to provide, and community organizations, I think . . . I have a huge, I don't want to say "dislike," but apprehension to hand over more power to the federal government.

Limiting federal oversight and lowering taxes was also a central concern for a political advocacy group that many members of the groups I observed volunteered for. One day, I accompanied a man I met at a rally to the organization's local office and participated in a telephone campaign. I was given a script, a headset, and some small candies to snack on. After an orientation that lasted less than ten minutes, the group had a Skype call with headquarters during which we were told how important our work was for educating voters about conservative candidates. Condemning the Democratic candidate's decision to raise taxes on gasoline and auto sales was central to the script, as was an outline of how these and other state sales taxes would have disastrous effects on our local economy.

After making calls for three hours, the volunteers were given lunch, and I used the break to ask what drew them to support the organization. While most of the volunteers were older, one woman still in college described how higher taxes are a top priority for her when it comes to supporting conservative candidates. "I learned very quickly this summer that taxes are a terrible thing," she laughed. "And I don't want to pay taxes that I shouldn't have to. Taxes that really aren't going anywhere besides putting us in some more debt. If I'm paying taxes, I want to see it put toward something useful, not every day seeing the debt go further and the stock market going down."

The conservatives who took part in this study believe that government regulation and intervention should be limited to militaristic endeavors. Yet much of this insistence on corporate rights again can be traced back to the federal passing of the Civil

Rights Act, which denied business holders the "right" to refuse Black customers. While upper-class whites were largely unaffected by the early integration efforts to desegregate public parks, pools, and schools because they had the means to pay for private, segregated alternatives, they still had to fight the "tyranny" of the federal government when it came to the integration of their businesses.[66]

CALCULATIVE COMMONALITIES

To be sure, it would be impossible to lump all conservatives under one ideological umbrella. Yet a comparative analysis of studies from the fields of sociology, history, and political science indicates similarities between the different "strains" of conservatism, and there were clear commonalities between those whom I observed and other ethnographic accounts of Christian Nationalists and other conservative groups. Embedded in the five dimensions of conservatism, freedom operates as a through line: religious *freedom*, a *free* market, *freedom* of speech, the *freedom* to own a gun, and the military and police as a mechanism for protecting those *freedoms*.[67]

Conservative strategists use the same connections. Through focus groups with conservative voters, they found that five key issues are most likely to get voters to the polls: abortion, same-sex marriage, U.S. Supreme Court appointments, limited government, and religious liberty.[68] Each of the five f's might be promoted by a different kind of organization: for example, Evangelical megachurches focus on faith and family, the NRA stresses the importance of firearms, police unions galvanize support for the armed forces, and Americans for Prosperity emphasizes a free market. Nonetheless, much of their efforts are designed to protect and promote the freedoms of white, Christian, native-born residents. In particular, the themes of Protestantism, patriotism, and protection that I witnessed support symbolic practices that reify racism in American politics and center belonging around the emulation of whiteness.[69] After all, Francis Bellamy wrote the Pledge of Allegiance in 1892 in an effort to define "true Americanism" as something that did not include the southern and eastern European immigrants then "pouring over our country."[70]

Leveraging the five f's, conservative elites continually discuss the preservation of "freedoms" in campaign rhetoric and media coverage, a play designed to engage otherwise indifferent voters and get them to the polls. By capitalizing on faith, family, firearms, the armed forces, and a free market, owners of apps like uCampaign "gamify" conservatism, allowing supporters to connect with each other on a playful platform and making it easier for politicians to target them with advertising.[71] Data harvested from these geolocative services fuel the central talking points for politicians and pundits, all with the goal of unifying a voting bloc.

Propaganda is about connecting groups and people under a common cause with the goal of initiating action. By knowing and understanding the concerns of their audience, conservative politicians and pundits routinely filter the news through these five dimensions, framing everyday events so they resonate with conservative values. Effective messaging that a target audience can relate to is an important first step, but effectively linking and cross-linking people and brands requires a network.[72]

STEP TWO

BUILD A NETWORK

In their study of discourse around the 2016 election, researchers Yochai Benkler, Rob Faris, and Hal Roberts at the Berkman Klein Center for Internet & Society at Harvard University mapped the U.S. media ecosystem. This social network research included a unique analysis of nearly four million messages and news media in digital and broadcast form.[1] They found that most mainstream media outlets create an interconnected web of content that adheres to secular and objective standards of journalistic integrity. But their work also revealed a separate network fueled by conspiracy theories and by fringe personalities who rejected normative journalistic practices. Terming this distinct network "the right-wing media ecosystem," Benkler, Faris, and Roberts demonstrated that messages originating in further-right outlets like *The Federalist*, Breitbart, or *Gateway Pundit* bounced with ease to more widespread news outlets like *The Daily Caller, New York Post, Washington Examiner*, and Fox News, which in turn routinely amplified conspiracy theories, disinformation attacks, and unsubstantiated political rumors.

The central takeaway from their book is that there is an asymmetry between the sources that media producers on the Right deem worthy of citation and those sources that the rest of the media landscape consider credible. The right-wing media ecosystem draws from conspiratorial sources that do not rely on the

same professionalized standards of journalism to create and
maintain their extreme and partisan coverage. This network
strategy effectively isolates conservative consumers and outlets
ideologically, socially, and culturally reinforcing a central "brand."[2]

Getting a grasp of the right-wing media ecosystem is an important part of understanding how (mis)information flows. Politicians rely on media systems to get elected, and on the Right this
relationship emphasizes partisan-confirming news over truth.[3]
Working in tandem to maintain political power, the right-wing
media, conservative politicians, and conservative voters create
what Benkler and his colleagues refer to as the "propaganda
feedback loop." They argue that this closed circuit of identity-
confirming ideas creates a perfect environment for peddling
propaganda (that is, the manipulation of public beliefs or attitudes
for political gains), because disputing or disbelieving content that
flows out of the network is framed as taboo. Their comprehensive
data visualizations provided an amazing overview, and invited
further study of the messages being spread within this network.
The question I asked was *why* the messaging is believable.

As my analysis demonstrates, conservative politicians act as
indispensable bridges to power when they serve as guests on
conservative outlets and tweet out stories designed to vilify "the
Left," or frame mainstream media as "fake" or "biased." Since
political viability is contingent on media support, this feedback
loop galvanizes the voting public but also serves to recruit new
political leaders and train them in the art of signaling conservative
values. In fact, some of the most prominent conservative politicians got their start in radio broadcasting. For example, from 1994
to 1999, former vice president Mike Pence was a conservative
radio host, self-described as "Rush Limbaugh on decaf." It was
through this radio show that he networked into politics.[4]

Since 2008, there have been discussions regarding the failure
of the Republican Party to adapt to the times, with a warning that
it is likely to shrink into nonexistence.[5] Yet this vision of a static
party fails to consider how networks of power are constructed.
Ideology is about a multidirectional flow of power. Effective political ideology is the top-down adoption of the dominant classes'

ideas by the masses. Rather than forcing people to believe what they say, conservative elites manipulate the architectures, infrastructures, and fundamental beliefs that shape their audience's information environment.[6] Their goal is to convince conservatives to subscribe to the values and norms of an exploitative system. By making their opinions appear to be "common sense," conservative elites guide constituents into a view of the world that is "inherited from the past and uncritically absorbed."[7]

A successful counter-ideology must build conflict with what is framed as "mainstream." Such tensions add shape and legitimacy to conservatism, helping to create a sense of ideological unity. For example, conservative elites regularly identify "invisible disengaged groups of potential voters" and then rile them up with targeted media that claim hot-button issues are under attack. Part of this unity is formed through media messaging, but the other part is through facilitating interactions in on- and off-line gathering places frequented by these voters. By connecting these groups to each other, this network reinforces "groupthink" in a way that appears individualistic.[8]

For all of these reasons, I consider this network as more than a media ecosystem. The goal of this network is to influence biases and assumptions while hiding the inherent social dynamics behind what legitimizes it. The network advances bias but claims to spread "facts." Based on my analysis, I argue that what Benkler and his colleagues initially uncovered is more precisely defined as a *right-wing information ecosystem.* To understand the depth of this information environment, and how intertwined it is in decades-old propaganda, we must look back at this network's roots in radio.[9]

MEDIA IMMERSION AS ETHNOGRAPHY

Because our media ecosystem is so divided, I had never heard of most of the sources that conservatives I spoke with relied on for news and information. To get up to speed quickly about these information sources deemed trustworthy, I decided to use a methodological technique I refer to as *media immersion:* for a full four months, I replaced my usual sources for news and cultural information with conservative podcasts and radio programs, news sites and blogs, and television shows. Monday through Friday I woke up at 5:30 am, made coffee, and started my day with *Fox & Friends*. While watching the program, I paid attention to not only the news coverage, but also the promotional content (Ford trucks, medical interventions, weight-loss solutions), and lifestyle segments (for example, what to serve on game day). I noted the kinds of clothes that the hosts and their guests wore and how they styled their hair. I also subscribed to popular conservative YouTube channels and signed up for daily email alerts. I spent a minimum of two hours a day listening to podcasts, reading stories online, or googling topics I was unfamiliar with.

For example, during my fieldwork, Fox News, *The Daily Wire*, and *The Federalist* ran stories on Florida Democratic representative Deborah Wasserman Schulz's IT staffer being arrested, implicating that person in the Democratic National Committee (DNC) email leak. Through this process "Wasserman" (and her connections to Hillary Clinton) became a code word for DNC fraud and nefarious activity. What I immediately noticed was that news coverage about Wasserman was being discussed only in the communities I was observing. My progressive family, friends, and colleagues had no idea what I was talking about when I mentioned Wasserman's IT staffer.

In addition to direct consumption, I read and watched news stories that my respondents liked, shared, or commented on over social media. When I started a video on YouTube, I would allow the platform to continue playing videos in a steady stream of "up next" content. The websites I clicked on typically featured other stories and I would follow those hyperlinks, noticing what the internet offered up as information that best matched my queries. These media consumption practices often led me into algorithmic rabbit holes where I would spend hours watching or reading content that ranged from why I should trust the electoral college to "why leftists were ruining America." Later in my study I would sift through these programs' transcripts as part of a thematic content analysis, but during this first level of immersion I avoided this sort of deep inquiry. Instead I let myself sink deeply into the right-wing information ecosystem and avoided reading, watching, and listening to alternative points of view so that I could more genuinely understand and identify the central arguments being spread.

TRUSTED SOURCES

During our interview, Tobias, a junior majoring in political science, was eager to share all the sources he turns to for news. Scrolling through his iPhone, Tobias showed me the podcasts he subscribed to, from Ben Shapiro to The Young Turks, and his phone buzzed repeatedly during our interview with news alerts from CNN and Fox. He was aware that the sources he subscribed to are not all the same, and described the difference between those he classified as "provocateurs" (such as Milo Yiannopoulos or Ann Coulter) and people whose reporting he respects:

> So, Ben Shapiro, he . . . I just love him so much. *He just says what's true.* He says it firmly, he doesn't yell it, generally he doesn't add in profanity or vulgarity just to get your attention. I like Andrew Klavan although he's not nearly as well known. I like Dennis Prager, he's really intelligent, really articulate. Of mainstream conservatives, the thing that appeals to me in Dennis Prager, Steven Crowder, Andrew Klavan, Michael Knowles, Ben Shapiro, that crowd, is that they deal with culture too and not just politics, not just news, they talk about how, as Andrew Breitbart said, "Politics is downstream from culture." So, I like how these conservative commentators and just entertainers or comedians or authors, speakers, whatever, I like it when they deal with issues of culture.

By immersing myself in this culture, I came to identify a central group of sources that seemed to repeatedly refer to one another. While I had read the *Wall Street Journal* and watched Fox News before starting this project, I had never heard of PragerU, Dave Rubin, or Candace Owens. Much of what I discovered via word of mouth overlapped with the media network mapped by Benkler, Faris, and Roberts. Some of the most frequently cited and shared included:

- **The Federalist:** A conservative web-based magazine and podcast created in 2013. Until October 2017, it had a "black crime" tag that aggregated articles related to criminal activity by African Americans.[10] During the COVID-19 pandemic, it published several stories that contradicted CDC recommendations and spread false information.[11] After it suggested that the medical community should intentionally infect people at "chickenpox parties" to help slow the spread of COVID, the account for the website was temporarily blocked from Twitter.[12]

- **Fox & Friends:** A conservative news/talk program that airs on Fox News Channel every morning starting at 6:00 am EST. *Fox & Friends* is the highest-rated morning show in cable news.[13] The series was also a central part of Trump's presidency. Not only was *Fox & Friends* a part of Trump's media diet, he also regularly called in to speak on the live program, and frequently supported the show on his Twitter feed. This attention attracted more viewers, making it one of the most influential shows in media in 2017.[14]

- **The Daily Signal:** A product of The Heritage Foundation. This digital-first news organization covers a wide range of topics, including the economy, education, politics, and healthcare from a conservative perspective. Most of my respondents who cited *The Daily Signal* as a source did not listen to the podcasts but did subscribe to their email newsletter—which delivered morning and afternoon summaries of the news every weekday ("The Morning Bell" and "The Capitol Bell").

- **The Daily Wire:** A website run by Ben Shapiro, one of the most prolific conservative commentators of the twenty-first century. In addition to *The Daily Wire,* Shapiro, a Harvard-educated lawyer, has a regular *Newsweek* column, a daily podcast (*The Ben Shapiro Show*), a radio show (also named *The Daily Wire*), and ten books. Before starting his media empire, he was editor-at-large at Breitbart News.

- **The Joe Rogan Experience:** An audio and video podcast hosted by Joe Rogan. On the show he hosts a wide range of guests including technological ethicists (like Tristan Harris), members of the "intellectual dark web" (including Christina Hoff Sommers), and conspiracy theorists (such as Alex Jones). While the podcast hosts guests from a range of ideological positions, it has been described as the essential platform for "freethinkers" who hate the Left.[15]

- **One America News Network (OANN):** A news channel launched in 2013 by Herring Networks, Inc. While the channel is accessible via cable broadcasting, it also streams its content through its website (oann.com) and has its own YouTube channel. Conservative political commentator Tomi Lahren gained widespread exposure through the viral circulation of her segment on OANN called *On Point with Tomi Lahren*. After Trump lost the 2020 presidential election, OANN became a central source for spreading false allegations of election fraud.

- **Prager University (PragerU):** A multimedia organization started in 2009 by writer and talk show host Dennis Prager. Prager's media productions, which include eight books, a nationally syndicated radio talk show, weekly newspaper columns, five documentaries, and the Prager University website, regularly reference traditional Judeo-Christian principles. The mission of his nonprofit organization, colloquially referred to as "PragerU," is to spread "conservative Americanism through the Internet" with "Five Minute Ideas."[16] Over the past eight years, PragerU (not a university) has produced and distributed over 250 "Five Minute Ideas," regularly releasing two to three videos a month since 2016. When YouTube demonetized some of PragerU's videos in October 2017, the channel filed a legal case on the grounds of "ideological discrimination."[17] In addition to using YouTube, PragerU distributes its videos through its own website and now has a separate section devoted to content purportedly "Restricted by YouTube." In 2020, it started PragerU Resources for Educators & Parents (PREP) to provide curriculum that teaches children about "America's blessings and limitless opportunities," and to combat what the organization refers to as educational indoctrination.[18]

- ***The Rubin Report:*** A YouTube production that is in part subsidized by the libertarian Institute for Humane Studies, a Koch-funded organization. While Dave Rubin first hosted *The Rubin Report* as part of The Young Turks, a progressive news and opinion channel on YouTube, he has since denounced "the Left" for being too radical.

- ***The Rush Limbaugh Show:*** A program created, produced, and hosted by the late conservative commentator Rush Limbaugh, and syndicated on radio stations nationwide. Prior to Limbaugh's death in 2021, new content was readily available as a podcast and livestreamed on his website (archives of these episodes are still available on Spotify). In addition to his long-running radio program, Limbaugh also hosted television shows and wrote many books.

- *Wall Street Journal:* With its focus on business and economics, "the *Journal*" is one of the largest newspapers in circulation in the United States. Although not technically part of Benkler et al.'s right-wing media ecosystem, it is owned and run by Rupert Murdoch, former owner of Fox News. While its news reporting is generally objective, its editorial page focuses on limiting government regulation, lowering taxes on the wealthy and corporations, and denying global warming.

My respondents' trusted news sources were not limited to conservative networks, publications, or programs. They also included specific conservative media personalities, including:

- **Candace Owens:** Originally known as "Red Pill Black" (Black refers to her race, while the red pill is a symbol of the men's rights movement discussed in Step Six), Candace Owens is a conservative vlogger whose series was picked up by Turning Point USA, a conservative grassroots organization on college campuses. During my ethnographic observations, Owens was Turning Point's communications director. In 2019, Owens teamed up with Dennis Prager, and she currently hosts *The Candace Owens Show* for PragerU. In March 2021, she premiered a new show produced by *The Daily Wire*.
- **David Horowitz:** David Horowitz is a conservative author and founder of the David Horowitz Freedom Center, an organization created to improve the position of conservative writers and producers in Hollywood. The organization also monitors what it views as hostility toward conservative scholarship and ideas within academia and hosts an annual "Restoration Weekend," a four-day event where conservative thinkers speak to guests who have each paid over $1,500 to register and attend.
- **Glenn Beck:** Respondents in my study spoke at length about Glenn Beck and were familiar with both his radio programming and his books, much as they were with the work of Ben Shapiro. Throughout his career Beck has hosted television programs,

radio shows, and podcasts centered around conservative ideals. From 2009 to 2011 his program was a central part of Fox News programming. Shortly after leaving Fox, Beck launched The Blaze, a radio and television network owned by Mercury Radio Arts (which was also founded by Beck, who has continued to play leading roles there). The Blaze network hosts podcasts of other revered conservative personalities including Steven Crowder, Dave Rubin, *Duck Dynasty* stars Phil and Jase Robertson, and Allie Beth Stuckey.

- **Jordan Peterson:** A professor of psychology at the University of Toronto, Peterson writes books, gives public lectures, and regularly appears as an expert guest on other conservative podcasts and conversational series. Peterson's central mantra— that people should stop whining and take control of their own lives—resonates with young, white, male conservatives who perceive civil rights initiatives (including those that advance gender, racial, and LGBTQ+ equality) as complaining.

- **Tucker Carlson:** Respondents of all ages regularly tuned in to watch *Tucker Carlson Tonight,* an hour-long program that typically begins with a monologue by the host followed by a series of interviews with guests. In July 2020, the show broke the record for the highest-rated program in cable news history, averaging close to three million viewers a night and drawing audiences from across the age spectrum.[19] While his messaging is written for a mainstream audience, it resonates with white supremacists, who watch the show to get tips on how to advance their cause.[20]

A MODERN INFORMATION ECOSYSTEM

Key personalities inside the right-wing information ecosystem work in tandem, build on each other's ideas and arguments, and appear on each other's programs. In doing so, they extend the reach of their images and ideas to more consumers and across multiple media modalities (including radio, print, video, and social media). By creating a network infrastructure to support their programming, conservative elites can leverage their information landscape and sociopolitical factors in tandem. For example, podcasts and radio shows are important for reaching audiences with unreliable wireless connections, but clips from these shows are frequently circulated on social media platforms to increase exposure.

Part of this influence structure is created by circulating a set of key ideas across platforms. By cross-pollinating guests between shows while simultaneously increasing their networks' modes of production and distribution, conservative elites have created their own trove of preferred information: a self-referential, adaptable library of content that helps them to circulate claims and piggyback on the reputations of other famous conservative leaders.[21] Much like influential conservative programs of the past, these shows revolve around an enigmatic leader (think Ben Shapiro, Dennis Prager, or Tucker Carlson), but also feature other leaders as guests.[22] When new figures outside the ecosystem are converted to conservative ideas, they too are often featured on the conservative talk-show circuit. These rising stars are typically everyday people with a vivid anecdotal story that supports the "five f's," and they quickly become celebrities when their name and story are repeated in mutually reinforcing ways throughout the network.

In July 2017, for example, a computer programmer named James Damore was fired from Google after an internal memo was leaked to the public. In the memo, Damore claimed that diversity initiatives defy the "natural" differences between men and women and between races or ethnicities, and he suggested that Silicon Valley discriminates against conservatives. After the memo was released, Damore published an op-ed in the *Wall Street Journal* defending his memo, and soon thereafter landed interviews with Tucker Carlson, Dave Rubin, and Ben Shapiro, among others. In the summer of 2017, Damore, along with Candace Owens and Dave Rubin, took part in a David Horowitz Restoration Weekend panel, "How the Left Creates Conservatives." As Damore made his way through the network, he stressed a central set of talking points: that Big Media, including Google, silences conservatism, and that diversity initiatives are biased against conservative ideals and white men. By cross-promoting his ideas throughout the network, the conservative media encouraged audiences to galvanize around Damore.

This strategy—taking the story of a "real person" and using it to weave a mutually beneficial narrative throughout the information ecosystem—is one copied from conservative media activists of the past. Take the story of Herbert V. Kohler Sr., a staunch opponent of organized labor and chief executive in control of the Kohler Company, a manufacturing corporation best known for plumbing products. In October 1957, Clarence Manion, then a prominent conservative radio show host, interviewed Kohler about the ongoing strike at the Kohler Company. During contract negotiations, Kohler had refused to grant union demands, framing union supporters as bullies in line with conservative ideology. When the national radio network carrying Manion's program pulled the interview, the idea of media bias got a big boost in conservative circles, where the accusation was transformed from a "vague claim of exclusion into a powerful and effective ideological arrow."[23] After his interview was pulled, Kohler became a celebrity in conservative media circles. In addition to describing Kohler as being correct for resuming production with non-union labor, conservative publications began featuring editorials penned by Kohler, the *National Review* provided steady coverage of the controversy, and two books were published about the strike that promoted an anti-union stance.[24]

LEVERAGING TECHNOLOGY

Key to the effectiveness of the right-wing information ecosystem is the use of *technological affordances*, that is, additional access and influence made possible by various technologies. As conservative leaders mobilize everything from political action committees (PACs) to grassroots organizations to think tanks in order to improve access to their ideas, they have consistently leveraged the power of digital tools.[25]

The theory of affordances, first proposed by James Gibson in 1977 and then supplemented with work by Don Norman in the 1980s, is rooted in the ecological sciences and considers the way that both inanimate and animate objects are adapted by users to better meet the needs of their environment.[26] Affordances are opportunities for action that are constrained by the properties of the object and the abilities of the observer.[27] Social scientists have since applied Gibson's and Norman's theories to study the relationship between information infrastructure (technology) and people's uses of information communication technology. A key focus is how social structures are formed in and through technology.[28]

Yet focusing exclusively on *new* technology can usurp attention from earlier media technologies that laid the foundation for today's right-wing information ecosystem. Although social media and other digital-first sources do influence electoral success, research shows that "radio has the biggest reach of any media" and it continues to remain an important part of American life "in the home, the workplace, and the car."[29] Indeed, the success of today's conservative information ecosystem is explained in large part by the foundational legwork of early media activists who built up large audiences through radio programming and alternative publications.

Since the late 1920s, conservatives have dominated the radio waves and been early adopters of "read/write" media.[30] Among the earliest adopters were Evangelical Christians who used VHS recordings of sermons and direct mailings to reach a larger audience. These methods of distribution quickly took over the airwaves, paving the way for what would soon become the rise of televangelism.[31] One of the largest of these broadcasting networks was Salem Radio, founded by Stuart Epperson and Edward Atsinger, both members of the Council for National Policy, an elite conservative umbrella organization devoted to strengthening conservatism from within the Republic Party.[32] Christian programming via Salem Radio reaches audiences of as many as 1.5 million people during a single broadcast.[33]

Today, 100 million Americans nationwide tune into Christian radio stations at least once a month. Yet most of radio airtime is controlled by conservative interest groups. Right-wing radicals have options for their content, including the Christian Broadcast Network, Salem Communications, or talk shows syndicated via Clear Channel. Liberal personalities have less freedom when it comes to where they can voice their opinions on the radio.[34] Moreover, news that airs on these conservative channels is not

based on widely accepted professional practices, like those followed by National Public Radio (NPR), but rather emphasizes
"biblical values." And it has much greater reach: Salem's programming reaches about four times the weekly audiences of NPR.[35]

While small radio stations had once been owned by, and held
accountable by, members of their local communities, the Telecom-
munications Act of 1996 loosened regulations and facilitated
corporate buyouts of over a quarter of the nation's radio stations.
This burgeoning radio empire gave rise to corporations like Clear
Channel Communications—which by 2000 owned one in every ten
radio stations in the United States.[36] Similarly, Salem Radio began
acquiring "clusters" of channels around the United States until, by
1999, it was the eighth-largest broadcaster and largest religious
broadcaster in the country. It soon extended its reach beyond religious programming to offer conservative talk radio on its stations.[37] While all of this was happening, local newspapers were
disappearing at a staggering rate, being bought out by larger corporations or closing because they could not sustain the advertising
revenue model.[38] These shifts in the news-media landscape meant
that residents in the middle of the United States became increasingly reliant on radio broadcasting as their only source of news.

From the start of American conservatism, the idea of biased
mainstream media has been a central rallying point for conservative elites.[39] In the 1930s and 1940s, as journalism became more
professional, terms like "accurate, fair, impartial, independent,
and responsible" came to define reporting.[40] But when conservative media activists felt that this journalistic standard of objectivity failed to report their interests, they sought to attack the very
notion of what objective means: the fact that conservative concepts
were not given "equal" airtime became "proof" that journalists
were not "objective." In other words, conservatives reimagined
objective coverage to mean *balanced* coverage. By fostering this
new idea of objectivity to mean equal coverage of "both sides,"
conservative media activists soon remade American journalism—
and redefined the very nature of what it meant to be informed.[41]

At first, the asymmetry that originated in radio broadcasting
was unable to influence listeners outside of its platform. Broadcast
access was tightly bound to just three distributors, and the robust

network of local daily newspapers made it difficult for conservative media to establish a stronghold like it had in radio. It took a combination of technological, institutional, and political changes to give rise to today's lopsided information environment. The emergence of televangelism, regulatory decisions that allowed religious programming to fulfill television stations' public-interest obligations, and the repeal of the fairness doctrine as "inconsistent with the First Amendment" led to today's information ecosystem, which is fueled by distrust and is highly susceptible to disinformation.[42]

SPEAKING THE SAME LANGUAGE

One of the most powerful ways the right-wing information ecosystem appeals to its audiences is by speaking their ideological dialect. A conservative dialect uses keywords and phrases that resonate with the five f's of conservatism. An early example of this centered around anti-unionism. Since unions were popular at the time, conservatives crafted a language of "rights and liberty," framing the "union boss" as a bully who forced workers to join so they could get rich from the dues. Creating phrases like "compulsory unionism" or "right-to-work" filtered labor organizing through a free-market perspective.[43]

Research demonstrates that many of these "dog whistles," speaking in code to target an audience, conjure racialized stereotypes meant to convey a steady drumbeat of racial grievances wrapped up in color-coded solidarity.[44] In the now infamous speech by Reagan's campaign consultant Lee Atwater, he explained how the GOP captured racists' votes by using more abstract language, so as not to alienate moderate voters. In lieu of explicit racism, Atwater suggested language like "forced busing," "states' rights," and "cutting taxes." He noted that "by talking about the economic things, the byproduct leads to the desired outcome: racial inequality." Signaling to the conservative base by evoking the family, the Reagan administration conjured the misogynistic image of the "welfare queen," painting public-aid recipients as lazy yet manipulative Black women taking advantage of a feckless bureaucracy, when in fact whites are the biggest beneficiaries when it comes to government assistance programs.[45]

Keywords laced with racism are still in play. One of the central ways that former Alaska governor and vice-presidential candidate Sarah Palin was able to push misconceptions about President Obama was by cultivating terms like "small towns," "real America," and "pro-America" to delineate who was part of Christian, white America, and who was not.[46] George Wallace and other conservative politicians drew on the language of "states' rights" to reframe the Civil War, or created phrases like "freedom of choice" or "neighborhood schools" to make segregationist policies seem more palatable to whites living inside the city.[47]

In 1994, the Republican "Contract with America," co-created by Republican strategist Frank Luntz, sought to unite the Republican congressional majority against a popular Democratic president with what Luntz called "a new language" to win back disenchanted voters.[48] In an effort to restore "the faith and trust of the American people in their government," the document aimed to cut the number of congressional committees, open congressional committee meetings to the public, and introduce a comprehensive set of bills in the House within the first one hundred days of the 104th Congress. Among the legislative proposals on the agenda were five that aligned closely with the five f's: the Fiscal Responsibility Act (the free market), Taking Back Our Streets Act (firearms), the Family Reinforcement Act (the family), and the National Security Revitalization Act (the forces).

Three years later, Luntz personally distributed to GOP lawmakers a two-hundred-page (or so) document entitled "The Language of the 21st Century." He designed this summer reading assignment to give Republican members of Congress some linguistic tips, including a lesson in strong letter-writing. He outlined word choice when wooing undecided or historically liberal voters and detailed what language resonates best with fellow Republicans. The phrases that Luntz highlighted included values, morality, spirituality, and faith in God, which map neatly onto the five f's still in play today.[49]

Luntz recommended, for instance, that when faced with a question about Social Security, Republican members of Congress avoid sharing conservative solutions like cutting benefits in favor of privatization. He suggested instead to turn questions like this back around on constituents, asking if they could "trust" the government, or if they would rather be "in control" of their retirement. Doing so spoke to conservative voters' mistrust of government and beliefs in limited government intervention and spending. Other examples of this sort of reframing include renaming the estate tax the "death tax"; referring to offshore drilling as "energy exploration"; and calling crime "law and order."[50]

Perhaps Luntz's greatest accomplishment was recasting the global warming conversation of the early 2000s. Luntz posited that the American public had not yet come to a consensus about what global warming even was, much less if it was a human-driven phenomenon; therefore, there remained a window of opportunity to challenge the science and reframe the debate. It was Luntz who gave us "climate change," the less frightening term.[51] These new words and phrases—like "partial birth abortion" instead of the previous moniker "late-term procedure"—can then take hold outside the conservative network, too, becoming normalized as everyday terms used across the political spectrum.[52] As Luntz himself states, "words that work are powerful because they connect ideas, emotions, hopes, and (unfortunately) fears."[53] By carefully crafting words that resonate strongly with their audiences, conservative strategists filter current events and topics through the five f's of conservatism, thereby laying the groundwork for another important part of their agenda: making conspiracies seem credible and absolute.

TWO CENTRAL CONSPIRACIES

During my ethnographic immersion in conservative media, I noticed and tracked two central conspiracies:

1. The Left is run by emotional appeals and lacks facts. As a result, the Left is not only dangerous, but increasingly so.
2. The media is an extension of the Left and lacks objectivity. Mainstream reporting is dictated by "feelings over facts," and actively seeks to silence conservative voices who disagree with them.

I dissect these themes separately, but it is important to understand that they are not mutually exclusive; they intersect to create a broader narrative of distrust. During the Trump administration, for example, it was imagined that radicalized leftist agents lurked inside the government, undermining President Trump's agenda and conspiring with the media to report only those stories that make Trump look bad.[54]

The Dangerous Left

The right-wing information ecosystem argues that leftist claims are subjective, illogical, and based in emotions, not facts. Conservatives, therefore, seek to arm themselves with "the facts" to undermine the Left's emotional appeals. This "feelings over facts" idea positions progressives as incapable of hearing or supporting "diversity of thought." This is how the right-wing information ecosystem vilifies the Left as the "party of intolerance."[55]

In December 2017, for example, Heritage Foundation Executive Vice President Kim R. Holmes published a piece entitled "How the Left Became So Intolerant" on the foundation's website. In it, Holmes uses his credentials as a historian and former assistant secretary of state to warn readers that "intolerance comes in all political shapes and sizes." He goes on to argue that while we associate the word "liberal" with being open-minded, people who call themselves "progressive liberals" only abuse the rules and the Constitution to get their way through emotional appeals. Ultimately, Holmes characterizes the Left as a "zero tolerance regime" that co-opted traditional progressive liberalism and "mixed it" with radical egalitarianism to produce "the radical cultural left—namely, sexual and identity politics and radical multiculturalism." Not only does his racialized frame denote an idea of soiling the "sanctity" of liberalism, which Holmes notes is rooted in "a set of ideas about individual liberty and constitutional government inherited from the moderate Enlightenment"; it also implies that efforts to promote egalitarian policies are radical. The stock photo accompanying the op-ed features pro-LGBTQ+ protestors at a New York City demonstration carrying an oversized rainbow flag that reads "Stop the Hate."[56]

On his nightly broadcast, Tucker Carlson joins in this effort, regularly claiming that "the Left is spinning completely out of control." Using a variety of examples, including Black Lives Matter or the firing of James Damore, Carlson asserts that the Democratic Party's "extreme rhetoric" is "getting scary." Alluding to the same argument that Holmes outlined in his Heritage Foundation commentary, Carlson promotes the idea that what used to be considered "liberal" is now associated with "pure authoritarianism."[57]

Dennis Prager and his PragerU empire (including spinoff programs like *The Candace Owens Show*) frequently reiterate the same claim: the radical Left appropriated the word "liberal" so that it no longer means what it used to. While liberal used to represent a pro-capitalist, free-market mentality, multiple PragerU videos imply that the Left twisted the term to instead represent ideas that are immoral, repressive, and anti-American.

Repeated discussions of "purity" evoke Mary Douglas's work, which examines how ideas about who is dangerous are tied to symbolic expressions of symmetry or hierarchy.[58] The idea that women, immigrants, and nonwhite residents spoiled "classical liberalism" implies that the "new" liberalism is dangerous because it is no longer controlled by white men.

The notion of a dangerous Left crops up regardless of the platform or the mouthpiece. Jordan Peterson gave a talk at a live event hosted by The Heritage Foundation entitled "On the Impact of the Radical Left," which was then uploaded to YouTube in the spring of 2019. In the talk, Peterson argues that our society doesn't know how dangerous leftist ideologies can be because we were never taught about "the radical Left." Drawing on North Korea and Venezuela as "good bad examples," Peterson explained why people are "emotionally drawn to the ideals of socialism or the left."

The threat of the Left and leftism is also featured prominently in PragerU content, which seems to appeal to conservatives of all ages. Everyone I interviewed for this study referred to a PragerU video during our interview or shared PragerU content on Facebook over the months that followed. When having casual conversations at events, I often noticed that people I spoke with used the same talking points that I had heard on PragerU videos. For example, many explained that the electoral college is important for preventing "the tyranny of the majority" or "mob rule," a key talking point from PragerU's most popular video, "Do You Understand the Electoral College?" Given their widespread appeal, I would also ask about PragerU videos in my interviews and focus groups, which drew enthusiastic responses from all my respondents, many of whom then pointed me toward some of their favorite content.

During one of the monthly meetings co-organized by the women's organization I observed, a spokeswoman told the audience that PragerU is an excellent resource for preparing students before they go off to college. The speaker explained how she would watch them with her kids every night to help them resist the "institutional indoctrination" that happens in schools from pre-K to university campuses. After the meeting was over, several guests had already pulled up PragerU on their phones and one was installing the app. They loved how the Five Minute Videos could be used as a resource to help ensure that their children or grandchildren did not turn into what one woman described as "stinking liberals."

Some of PragerU's most widely circulated videos promoting the idea that the Left is dangerous also feature other prominent figures inside the right-wing information ecosystem:

- "Facts Don't Care about Your Feelings" (May 11, 2017), featuring Ben Shapiro (5.3 million YouTube views, 13.8 million PragerU website views): One of the most popular PragerU videos, and also one of Shapiro's book titles, suggests that emotions, not intellect, run the Left. He also claims that liberal concerns like white privilege, patriarchy, and homophobia are not real; they are just meaningless terms used to provoke emotional outrage from an uninformed liberal base. Shapiro posits that patriarchy isn't real, for example, because women make up the majority of college graduates, and because "young, single women without kids already earn more than their male counterparts." "These are the facts," Shapiro repeats, "and facts don't care about your feelings."
- "Why I Left the Left" (February 6, 2017), featuring Dave Rubin (14.2 million YouTube views, 28.8 million PragerU website views): In this video, Rubin begins with a fairly benign argument: people should be able to disagree, and openly.

Rubin says he used to identify as a progressive but grew tired of the Democratic Party's "regressive" fixation on "identity politics." By the end of the video, Rubin says that terms like "racism, bigotry, xenophobia, homophobia, and Islamophobia" are "meaningless buzzwords."

- "Who Is Teaching Your Kids?" (June 11, 2018), featuring Jordan Peterson (6.5 million YouTube views, 13.2 million PragerU website views): In this popular video, Peterson urges taxpayers and parents whose children attend elite liberal arts colleges to watch out for postmodernists. Why? Because they push a progressive activism that results in "violent mobs that violently shut down campus speakers."

- "Jordan Peterson Debunks White Privilege" (June 19, 2020) featuring Jordan Peterson (1.1 million YouTube views, 7.8 million PragerU website views): In a casual conversation, not a professionally curated Five Minute Video, Peterson claims that there is "absolutely nothing more racist" than the notion of white privilege. He also posits that a "collectively held guilt" is "dangerous, and precisely the sort of danger that people looking for trouble would want to push."

- "Playing the Black Card" (May 20, 2018), featuring Candace Owens (5.5 million YouTube views, 11.9 million PragerU website views): Owens describes how the Left "pushes" identity politics to justify moblike behavior: "You can call yourself a 'civil rights leader' and shake down multinational corporations, or you can torch your own neighborhood because you didn't like the outcome of a grand jury verdict."

In a focus-group discussion about what counts as radicalism, conservative college students drew on the same arguments as those expressed in the PragerU videos. They felt that the Right was usually depicted as "crazy," but it was really the Left that was more radical and dangerous.

ABRAHAM: Most of the major liberal issues, especially social issues, are incredibly emotional. And because of that, they're stronger to react, stronger to condemn. And it makes it even harder to try to present a perspective, because like, "What? You don't support homosexuality? Do you hate gays?"

LEE: In my opinion, I think that's why Bernie Sanders had the run that he did. Because if you would watch any of the debates

or any kind of talk show that he went on, they would ask
him an opinion related to, let's say, welfare, social welfare or
something like that. And his answer would just be something
like, "Kids shouldn't go hungry." The crowd goes wild.
And—

ABRAHAM: We all agree with that.

LEE: And if you go on Bernie Sanders' Twitter, I don't see his
Facebook, I just see his Twitter, he'll tweet out things like this
that don't really have any kind of . . . They're relevant to
policy, but, at the same time, it's just an emotional appeal.
So, he'll tweet out something like, if it's with regards to abortion, he'll tweet something like the classic, "A woman should
control what she does to her body." And no one is saying
that she shouldn't. Like the whole center of the abortion
argument is if it's part of her or not, you know what I mean?
But then, something like that, like an emotional appeal, would
just get out there, and people would say, "Wow, Bernie gets
it, you know? He's this great guy."

Key players inside the right-wing information ecosystem
actively create and reify a collective enemy when they repeatedly,
almost circuitously, return to and coalesce around this central
messaging. It enables conservative thought leaders to claim that
their ideas are "under attack" while simultaneously discrediting
their critics as hysterical. Such a strategy successfully positions
conservative talking points as "hard" and objective "facts," while
also stoking conservative fears that the nation has become too
soft.[59] By deriding the Left as a party of "feelings," it demeans
progressive arguments as feminine, symbolically associating
conservatism with logic and rationality—that is, with supposedly
white, male virtues.[60]

The Dishonest Mainstream Media

Despite their stated interests in seeking truth and avoiding
bias, many of my respondents noted that their preferred news
outlets were also subjective. They argued that seeking out this
subjective news wasn't hypocritical because a conservative bias
was necessary to combat mainstream misinformation. Since the

mainstream media is part of the Left, so the argument goes, it too is driven by feelings over facts. Hannah, a middle-aged woman and prominent figure in the Republican women's group I visited, and someone who occasionally toyed with the idea of running for office, reasoned:

> Fox *has* to be pro-Trump. CNN, MSNBC, ABC, NBC, CBS, all of them are anti-Trump. I would like to find a neutral source, but to a certain extent Fox has to be pro-Trump because all of them are so anti.

The notion that Fox has to be biased to combat mainstream media ties back to much of the same logic by which conservative media outlets were created decades ago. Some of the originators of conservative media content pledged to report factual stories that other outlets missed because they were biased. Since the conservative elites believed that their ideological worldview was correct, they could embrace the bias in what they covered, even as they sacrificed accuracy, because it helped them to maintain ideological consistency.[61]

In the 1920s, journalism moved away from partisan opinion and began fostering norms of objectivity.[62] Since the beginning, conservative elites have primed voters to think that all media *not* dedicated to the five f's is biased, and have positioned conservative content as the balanced alternative. This strategy also opened up the opportunity for conservative media outlets to be considered somehow "both objective and biased"—that each outlet "should be trusted because it was right, and because it was right-wing."[63] It also effectively forces mainstream media to air at least some conservative content and positions, because if they fail to report on "both sides" it makes them seem culpable.[64]

PragerU has three widely circulated videos that support the idea that mainstream media is biased:

- "Can You Trust the Press?" (October 3, 2016), featuring former *New York Times* reporter Judith Miller (1.2 million YouTube views, 3.2 million PragerU website views): Miller frames media distrust as a bipartisan issue and blames it on the twenty-four-hour news cycle and deteriorating journalistic standards. The

video also focuses on the role that social media and the blogo-
sphere have played in the "decline in reporting standards,
decline in revenue, and increase in bias."

- "What Is 'Fake News'? " (June 29, 2017), featuring conservative crime novelist and podcaster Andrew Klavan (900,000+
  YouTube views, 4.1 million PragerU website views): In this
  video, Klavan asserts that "mainstream American news is all
  fake" because it is controlled by biased liberals with political
  interests. To simplify his argument, Klavan creates a set of
  "rules" that "prove" how mainstream news is equivalent to
  leftist propaganda.
- "Why No One Trusts the Mainstream Media" (November 5,
  2017), featuring American journalist and former CBS
  news correspondent Sharyl Attkisson (1.4 million YouTube
  views, 3 million PragerU website views): Here Attkisson
  argues that the news has become increasingly editorialized.
  She claims that reporters cherry-pick stories that confirm liberal
  beliefs.

These three videos effectively convey the same argument: the
mainstream media has become rife with opinion, and it can no
longer separate "facts" from "feelings."

The accusation that the media is dishonest goes beyond
traditional forms of journalism. The so-called biased media
now includes Big Tech—social media sites like Facebook, video
sharing sites like YouTube, and search engines like Google—which
supposedly block conservative content at a disproportionate
rate.

On May 28, 2020, this claim made it all the way to the
Oval Office, where President Trump signed an executive order
titled "Preventing Online Censorship." His decision to do so
was predicated on a series of events that framed social media as
being biased against conservatism, including two Senate Judiciary
Committee hearings in which I served as an expert witness.
Senator Ted Cruz (R-TX) presided over these hearings and opened
each with statements asserting that Big Tech routinely silences
conservatism. These baseless claims are provocative, but my data
suggest they are merely anecdotal allegations, a manipulative
strategy designed to make the public think that conservatism

is "under attack" when, as my research demonstrates, it thrives online.[65]

Working in tandem and building on each other's ideas, arguments, and fan bases, the right-wing information ecosystem reaches across multiple modalities (radio, print, broadcast, streaming, and social media) to center news stories, stump speeches, and political platforms around the five f's. Rewriting the meaning of objectivity to mean equal coverage of "both sides" on an issue, this information network slowly eroded one of the core tenets of American journalism while employing strategists to make global warming seem less terrifying and unionizing more so.

By taking a deep dive into the sources that my respondents trusted most, I was able to more thoroughly understand the central narratives that create and sustain the right-wing information ecosystem. These intertwined narratives go something like this: those on the Left are increasingly radicalized and dangerous, unwilling to compromise with anyone who disagrees with them. Since the mainstream media platforms are an extension of the Left, they fail to show the truth and air only those stories that position the Left in a positive light.

Each of these arguments has bounced throughout an information ecosystem meticulously built over nearly one hundred years. Through lax regulatory restrictions, conservative elites were able to buy up local radio stations at the same time that local newspapers were dying, which offered them a way to not only reach a wide audience but also learn about conservative voters' concerns when those voters called in to their radio shows. Having this network is key to building successful propaganda campaigns. Far from depending on a fixed ideological form, conservative elites routinely rely on a dynamic information system of reusable talking points to resonate with otherwise different audiences, including libertarians, gun rights activists, and fundamental Christians.

Recognizing that this conservative information system has normalized the ideas of "the Left is dangerous" and conservatism in America is "under attack" is critical for understanding how, for example, Trump was able to maintain a high approval rating among Republicans throughout his presidency. He was able to satisfy his supporters, for example, by proposing and pushing through Congress increases to military and police spending as his solution to the problem of "the radical Left" and "the dishonest mainstream media." As folklorist Bill Ellis explains, the real power of these ideas is not just their logical flow; it is that they are "unfalsifiable"—efforts to fact-check or make fun of the conspiracy only provide further support for its false claims.[66]

STEP THREE

ENGAGE IN THEIR FORM OF MEDIA LITERACY

If the goal of conservative propagandists is to influence constituents' attitudes and get them to the polling stations, they must rely on the same meaning-making processes as those they are trying to reach. To legitimize their messaging and gain audience trust, the right-wing information ecosystem leverages rhetorical and hermeneutical media practices. This means identifying certain texts, like the U.S. Constitution, as "sacred" and encouraging deep analysis and individualist interpretations of these documents through the close reading techniques traditionally associated with Protestant readings of the Bible—that is, through *scriptural inference*.

Central to this media practice is the assumption that real truths—even divine truths—exist and can be discovered by doing your own research and "returning" to the facts. But while this hermeneutical practice of returning to and leveraging a personal dissection of authoritative documents is rooted in Evangelical Protestantism, it is not bound to the pulpit, nor does it require biblical literacy.

PROTESTANT INDIVIDUALISM

The Protestant Reformation of the sixteenth century was centered on the idea that the Catholic Church's sacramental rituals and sermons obscured the centrality of scripture as the word of God. In the early 1800s, John Nelson Darby extended this vision, encouraging the Christian faithful to participate in a "deep reading" of the Bible themselves, rather than trust a priest's interpretation of the text.[1] This new way of interacting with the Bible freed believers to dissect the text on their own terms and was central to the launch of large numbers of Christian denominations throughout the United States after the American Revolution. That is, the belief that one does not need a higher power to understand or interpret scriptural documents is foundational to a unique brand of Protestantism created in the United States.[2] This popular theology inverted the traditional idea that truth, especially divine truth, could come only from the elite and ordained few at the top, and went hand in hand with an "intensely egalitarian reading of the New Testament" that emphasized Joseph as a carpenter, Christ's followers as poor, the Apostles as uneducated, and the elite as behind the crucifixion of Jesus.

The new Christian movement focused on three central tenets in the 1790s and early 1800s:

1. Clergy members and parishioners are equals,
2. Inquiry and innovation are welcome, and
3. Each person has the right to interpret the New Testament for themselves.[3]

The idea that these new Christians were expected to "discover the self-evident message of the Bible without any mediation from creeds, theologians, or clergymen not of their own choosing" was perhaps the most enduring legacy of the Protestant movement.[4] As clergy members in the United States began blending liturgy with patriotism and nationalism, the ecumenical reading style was applied to nonreligious texts.[5] And as populist churches proliferated, so too did the idea that it was the individual's responsibility to seek out and learn as much as possible on their own.[6]

GUARDED INERRANCY V. EMPATHIC LISTENING

Evangelical Protestantism was not always aligned with American politics.[7] Originally its focus was "evangelizing," or spreading the word of the gospel to unbelievers. It was not until evangelical

Protestantism became more mainstream that its priorities shifted from proselytizing religious doctrine to promoting a broader idea of conservatism—what Butler describes as a "nationalistic political movement" that is designed to give white Christian men power over the flourishing of others.[8]

But the use of religion or the Bible to drive political change is not a strategy that only conservatives use. Progressive faith-based groups also leverage faith to organize people around populist concerns.[9] Many Black ministers have built racial justice into their life's work and professional mission.[10] Since church is a place of shared values, it is an environment ripe for political organizing.

Research has shown that both liberal and conservative groups believe that religion can help solve the country's most pressing problems, but they rely on faith in different ways.[11] Liberals promote religious inclusion through "the sacred value of listening," and include the author's context with their interpretations of texts (a process called exegesis).[12] As such, progressive groups use the Bible as a tool for broadening communities' "social imagination," urging readers to see themselves in relation to the historical milieu.[13] Conservative groups take on more of the eisegesis method, reading the Bible in order to prove a preexisting opinion or concern.[14] That is, conservatives focus on preserving religious liberty through "deep reading," engaging with the Bible in a literal way and using their understanding of the text as a form of "protection from" those whom they believe are trying to erode foundational values.[15]

How one reads and engages with the Bible has been shown to be tied to epistemology, a finding like what historian and educational scholar Samuel Wineburg observed in his research on how historians and high-school students engaged with texts about the American Revolution. When historians read, they don't look only at what the text says; instead, they try to understand the purpose of the text at the time it was written. For example, was the text used to support slavery or its abolition? Historians' interpretations are bound not to the literal text, or even the inferred text, but rather to what Wineburg refers to as the subtext, "a text of hidden and latent meanings."[16] This form of analysis sees textual artifacts as human, and considers how an author's assumptions, worldviews, and beliefs may have shaped what they documented. This method of reading also relies on an understanding of the secondary literature—in other words, a historian's understanding of one document relies on knowledge of other documents.

Conservative interpretations of the Bible assume an "absolute certainty in the inerrant truths of the Bible."[17] Much like how high-schoolers engage with history textbooks, my respondents approached sacred documents as unquestionable "facts," or as "straightforward information," without taking into account the context in which the texts were created.[18] Such an engagement with the Bible fails to acknowledge that it is a *human* text, one written, collated, and edited by human beings whose biases and assumptions are embedded in what they created.

As Cain Hope Felder explains, biblical scholars have often been white Europeans or white Americans, and their perspectives have changed how the Bible has portrayed Black people over time.[19] Different racial, cultural, and gender presuppositions shape different versions of this very sacred text. Felder points out that many new translations of the Bible surfaced during the post-Enlightenment period, when white, western Christians were colonizing, evangelizing, and/or enslaving Black people. Using a historical-comparative methodology to study the differences between versions of the Bible, Felder demonstrates how the authors of the New Testament focused on the Greco-Roman world, completely de-Africanizing it to the extent that modern readers of the Bible take for granted that New Testament maps exclude the entire African continent. By trivializing the contribution of Africa in shaping the cultures of today, these translations mold "a modern ideological set of hermeneutical assumptions that suggests that nothing good has ever come out of Africa."[20] Modern Eurocentric translators and interpreters of the New Testament can build on this ideological presupposition to advance their own self-interests in both religious and secular contexts.

Direct translations of the Bible that are devoid of contextual awareness can lead to what Anthea Butler refers to as a "color-blind gospel." To whitewash racism, Evangelicals started using biblical scripture to affirm that everyone was equal, regardless of race, propagating the message that race no longer matters. This direct translation of the text failed to account for the fact that segregationists had used the same scripture to justify slavery and oppose the advancement of civil rights. The result was a narrative whereby true followers had to conform to whiteness and accept white, male leadership as both the religious and social norm while glossing over the role the Bible had played in justifying segregation, violence, and racial proscription.[21]

When people try to contextualize sacred documents, they are quickly marked as anti-conservative. For example, Hillary Clinton was raised Methodist and could read and recite biblical passages with ease. But Clinton often veered away from inerrancy and used contextual interpretations, which made her use of the Bible suspicious to conservatives.[22] When the conservatives I observed perform literalist readings of documents like the Constitution and other sacred texts, they feel empowered by their positions and confident that they have done the reading for themselves. Distrust in translation also explains why the debate-watching parties I attended tended to show the debates on C-SPAN instead of on networks with pundits. They did not want someone else to tell them who "won" the debate; instead they were listening for Trump's words, hoping he would reassure them that the five f's would be protected.

SCRIPTURAL INFERENCE BEYOND THE BIBLE

I first witnessed the importance of this individualized attitude toward truth and knowledge when I met Emily, an active college Republican group member, for a regular meeting of her Bible study group. It was a rainy day in late winter and the roads were slick. Despite the weather, the parking lot was overflowing, and cars idled patiently in lines as parking attendants directed traffic. People held open the doors and welcomed me into the building as I made my way inside the megachurch. I grabbed a free copy of the King James Bible to my right at the entrance, then headed down a long corridor lined with small, numbered rooms. Emily had texted me the room number, and when I found it, I opened the door to three rows of approximately ten chairs each, with an aisle in the middle. They all faced a podium set up in front of a chalkboard.

I had arrived fifteen minutes early, and the room was nearly empty. I chose an aisle seat in the middle of the room. Along one wall with large windows that faced the parking lot, on a long rectangular table, were a crockpot keeping homemade sausage-and-egg muffins warm and a large percolator of hot coffee. The room filled up until latecomers were standing against the wall. While we sipped coffee, we spent an hour studying approximately three lines of biblical text:

> The earth mourns and dries up, and the land wastes away and withers. Even the greatest people on earth waste away. The earth suffers for the sins of its people, for they have twisted God's instructions, violated his laws, and broken his everlasting covenant. (Isaiah 24:4)

After each line, the pastor would provide time for those in the group to consider how the holy passages reflected their own lived realities. How had their earth suffered for their sins? The pastor then encouraged participants to share their personal reflections and passage interpretations with the rest of the group.

Following this period of contemplation and communal sharing, the pastor shifted his focus. Standing before the group, he called on each of us to apply a close reading to the new tax reform bill. He noted that the bill's passage had "real world implications" for the group and that we should read it ourselves instead of trusting the media coverage. Reading aloud a few choice lines from the bill, the pastor considered how the act's provisions might benefit someone who works for a large organization but hurt a local farmer. Was this tax bill also something that would cause unnecessary suffering?

As the Bible study wound down and members in the group met up with others who had participated in other church study groups, we all made our way to the sanctuary for the main service. While we walked, the pastor continued to stress to us the importance of knowing and understanding tax legislation in the same way that we were called on to know the Bible. He encouraged everyone to go home that day and obtain a copy of the bill online, essentially instructing them to "do their own research."

POLITICAL TEXTS AS SACRED TEXTS

This fusion between faith and patriotism that I witnessed is not exclusive to my study.[23] In their study of the American Tea Party movement, sociologists Theda Skocpol and Vanessa Williamson describe how their respondents believed that the text of the U.S. Constitution is "immediately accessible and obviously clear," able to be "understood by each person without the aid of expertise or intermediaries."[24] Throughout their book, they describe how the reading practices of Bible study groups were applied to the Constitution, and how families often read excerpts from the "two holy texts"—the Bible and the Constitution—before mealtimes.

Sociologist Ruth Braunstein's research backs up this finding that American conservatives apply the same close reading techniques they use for biblical passages to other texts. As Braunstein notes, originalism did more than amplify the historical significance of documents like the Constitution; it allowed members of Tea Party groups to treat "the Constitution like a sacred text."[25] It is the melding of this "strict adherence to the Constitution and a restored commitment to the Judeo-Christian values" that brings conservative groups like the Religious Right and the Tea Party into a common conversation with one another.[26] Much like the way conservatives treat the Bible as the word of God, without considering how different translations were influenced by the sociopolitical position of the translator, they endow the Constitution with the same infallible and incontrovertible quality. In this way, scriptural inference is like the constitutional philosophy of originalism. Since both documents are deemed sacred by conservatives, they come to embody obvious truth.

The act of privileging simplistic and direct interpretations is connected to the broader cultural and political issues at play. Accusing progressives of introducing needless complexity to inherent truths elevates conservative literacy as an approach that is supposedly quick to grasp the obvious, and unlikely to be misguided by human intentions.[27] It suggests that those who use scriptural inference are guided by facts, not feelings.

As I demonstrate throughout this book, elevating historical and political documents to the same sacred quality of the Bible is a strategy used by many conservative media producers to connect with their audiences. This was also an approach used by the college Republicans I observed when they were organizing a promotional table for the group during a university-sponsored event. Dressed in suits and ties, the male members of the group arrived hours before the speakers. The president of the group laid a blue tablecloth over the plastic folding table and began unpacking boxes of promotional materials. Alongside posters printed by the Young American Foundation asserting that "Socialism Kills," buttons proclaiming "Confirm Gorsuch!," and a handful of bumper stickers for local officials running for office were dozens of pocket-sized copies of the Constitution. "These will run out fast," a member of the group told me, explaining how they rely on organizations like Turning Point USA or The Heritage Foundation to help them restock their inventory. Twenty minutes after people started lining up for events, all the copies were gone.

Through ethnographic observations and in interviews, I witnessed conservatives eschew journalistic, academic, or otherwise professional interpretations of history, science, and current events in favor of reading original documents on their own—applying practices they had learned in Bible study to other documents deemed sacred.[28] By doing so, conservatives have come to very particular, shared points of view regarding government practices such as the separation of church and state, the role of the electoral college, and the need to build a wall around the United States.

SEPARATION OF CHURCH AND STATE

Public institutions in the United States emphasize a government-centered model of the separation of church and state, preventing the church from unduly influencing policy. This model comes from an interpretation of the First Amendment in the U.S. Constitution in which the Establishment Clause and the Free Exercise clause are understood as necessary to keep government and religious institutions separate.

By contrast, the conservatives in my study defended a church-centered version, where the separation is about protecting the church from the government. Members of conservative groups assert that the way the courts have ruled on issues surrounding the separation of church and state has "been perverted from the founders' intent."[29] To support their perspective, they often refer to a textual analysis of the Constitution and a letter that Thomas Jefferson wrote to the Danbury Baptists.

I first saw this connection when I interviewed a key member of the men's Republican group who conducted joint events with the women's group I observed. We met for coffee to talk more about what he described as an erosion of the moral underpinnings of the U.S. government. I challenged him on his viewpoint that politicians should be guided by the Bible. I explained how I had learned in school that government officials should not mix religion with politics, because to do so would be a violation of church and state. When I said this, Tom's eyes widened. Much like the ambassadors of Christian Nationalism identified by sociologists Andrew Whitehead and Samuel Perry, Tom quickly launched into an extensive lesson about the role that Christianity, and a belief in God, played in the creation of our nation.[30]

"They believed that God had revealed himself and they believed that God was involved in the battles of the Civil War, Washington was a man of prayer, he knelt on his knees, he prayed, he wrote in his letters, divine providence guided us in our victory today. They did not believe in a God who was distant from people," Tom said.

I nodded but pushed back. "Why then," I asked him, "did they write about the separation of church and state?"

My statement was met with a small pause, while Tom looked down at the table, crossed his hands, and shook his head. When he looked back up, he took a deep breath, and started up again, his voice elevating slightly.

This whole thing, I'm sorry, but you got me wound up here, but this whole lie regarding the role of separation is one of the most ridiculous frauds. You talk about *fake news*, how the American people have bought into the lie that this "wall of separation" is in the Constitution, I challenge you, do a research project, you ask your students, where would I find the language of the law of the separation of church and state in the Constitution? They might say, oh First Amendment, Second Amendment. The words, Franny, they are not there. The words come from a letter that Thomas Jefferson wrote to some Baptists in Danbury, Connecticut, who were afraid that we would go back to what they had in England, a national church . . . It had nothing to do with opening up the doors to the Muslims, all this kind of stuff. It was a Christian nation.

Tom took a moment to pull out his smartphone and find the letter from the Danbury Baptists. While he searches, he continues to talk, describing how the notion of a separation comes in a return letter from Jefferson where he writes, "I will defend your right as a Baptist to maintain your faith and there should be a wall of separation." We take a moment and I look at his phone. He's right, the text about separation is not in the Constitution. It is in the letter from Jefferson to the Danbury Baptists.

Using a direct quotation from the letter and comparing it to the absence of a mention in the Constitution, Tom applied scriptural inference to come to his own understanding about the separation of church and state.

He was talking about keeping the state out of the church, that's what the wall was about. It's a wall to keep the state from overreaching into the church or the community. But the liberals and the progressives believe the Constitution says that the church should keep its mouth shut and there should be a total separation. That's the biggest lie.

In a video released on May 25, 2020, conservative media producer PragerU makes a nearly identical claim. The host, John Eastman, an American law professor and constitutional law

scholar at Chapman University School of Law in Orange, California, relies on scriptural inference to make his argument. The Five
Minute Video features text from Jefferson's letter to the Danbury
Baptists, highlighting the phrase "building a wall of separation
between Church and State" to "prove" that Jefferson intended to
prevent the government from interfering with religious matters.[31]
The video also uses scriptural inference to draw a line from George
Washington's farewell address to claim that a separation of church
from the state did not imply that the government had no interest
at all in religious teachings. Rather, the video aims to establish
that the "Founding Fathers" were followers of the Christian faith.

Understanding how scriptural inference is used to interpret
sacred texts helps explain what may seem like contradictory
standpoints. For example, conservatives regularly express a need
to limit government intervention in the marketplace yet are uni-
fied in their desire to pass legislation to limit abortion. Applying
scriptural inference to Jefferson's letter to the Danbury Baptists
provides conservatives a path to rectify those contradictions.
Consider, for example, how *Masterpiece Cakeshop v. Colorado Civil
Rights Commission* sought to limit government intervention in
the market so that conservatives could act according to their faith
in God, while *Roe v. Wade* is used as a glaring example of politicians enacting "Godless" legislation.

Nonetheless, white Christians have also used the same method
of biblical inerrancy to try to justify their exploitation of human
beings. The two most cited biblical scriptures used to support
slavery are Genesis 9:18–27, the story of Ham the "cursed," and
Ephesians 6:5–7, which states that servants should be obedient
to their masters. By interpreting scripture in this way, slavery was
framed as a blessing for white people and a "cure" for Black
people who were already cursed to be the lowest of servants.[32]

If Christian teachings were embedded into the founding of
the United States as this conservative perspective claims, then it
was done so in a way to elevate and prioritize whiteness. After all,
when Thomas Jefferson wrote in the Declaration of Independence
that "all men are created equal, that they are endowed by their
Creator with certain unalienable Rights," he and the other Found-

ing Fathers were explicitly excluding Native Americans and Africans who had been forced into indentured servitude. As Butler
explains, scriptural inference was part of these underlying policies
and was frequently used to justify slavery and to sanctify racial
proscription and violence.[33] This view of who counted as a person
was reflected in who counted as a citizen. The Naturalization Act
of 1790 limited U.S. citizenship to whites only and is bound to a
missionary imperative that other races and ethnic groups are "less
than" if they do not practice Christianity according to cultural
norms. Being "saved" via colonization is predicated on receiving
a white version of Christ.[34] Promoting the idea that religion should
drive government intervention encourages conservatives to weave
Christian racism into their beliefs about capitalism, God, and the
nation.[35]

THE UNITED STATES AS A REPUBLIC

The voting restriction laws passed in the wake of the 2020 election
were clearly meant to suppress the Black vote. In a leaked video,
The Heritage Foundation boasted about its ability to draft and
pass model legislation suppressing voter access in states like
Georgia and Iowa.[36] Some might be surprised that a party that so
values the sanctity of the Constitution would fervently support
laws designed to disenfranchise voters. Yet for conservatives,
closely reading the Constitution supports their understanding of
the United States as a *republic,* not a democracy.

This argument is not possible without an originalist reading
of the Constitution and fervent support of the electoral college.
In the *5000 Year Leap,* the twelfth of twenty-eight principles that
Skousen outlines is that the United States was designed to function as a republic. He explains that a democracy requires full
participation of the masses, whereas a republic is designed for
only some to vote and ensures that the government of the United
States will not be elected by the unwieldy wishes of a majority. To
support this argument Skousen relies on the "Madisonian model"
discussed in Federalist 10, a document described by conservative
groups as holding "quasi-constitutional status."[37] As James

Madison writes, it is essential that such a republic "be derived from the great body of society, not from an inconsiderable proportion, or a favored class of it."[38] By outlining the importance of staying true to "the Republic" designed by the Founding Fathers, Skousen goes on to describe how democracy in its truest form is akin to socialism.

My respondents echoed this idea. During one interview, a college sophomore named Lee explained how he was frequently frustrated with the "Bernie crowd" who wanted to abolish the electoral college. When I asked why he felt this way, he pointed me to a PragerU video titled "Do You Understand the Electoral College?" First posted online in 2015, the video currently has over five million views on YouTube. Using scriptural inference to dissect the Constitution, lawyer Tara Ross describes why it is important to elect the president using the "538 electors" rather than via a "pure democracy." She argues that the electoral college protects against the tyranny of the majority, encourages coalition building, and discourages voter fraud. In her detailed account of coalition building, she emphasizes how the electoral college defends the interests of rural states like Montana, Iowa, and West Virginia that would otherwise be "forgotten" in a popular vote—evoking the feelings of neglect documented in academic studies.[39] Scriptural inference creates an opportunity for conservatives to celebrate the idea that in 2016 Trump won the electoral vote but not the popular vote. Preserving the electoral vote, according to conservatives, is what prevents our country from being overtaken by socialists and allows conservative values, preserved in rural areas, to be heard and not overtaken by the interests of those living in large cities.

In keeping with the scriptural inference approach, this interpretation does not include the historical context of those provisions. The Founding Fathers purposefully excluded indigenous people, Black people, women, and poorer white men from their vision of who should control the future of power in the newly colonized nation.

Conservatives' style of media literacy, in this case scriptural inference, backfired on U.S. House Speaker Nancy Pelosi (D-CA) when she recited the Pledge of Allegiance on December 18, 2019, during the proceedings on two articles of impeachment against President Trump. Behind Pelosi was a sign saying "To the *Republic* for which it stands" with a picture of a waving American flag. Shortly thereafter "Pledge of Allegiance" began trending on Twitter. Using scriptural inference, conservatives attacked Pelosi's understanding of the Constitution, furthering the idea that Trump's impeachment was being driven by the popular vote, akin to "mob rule." Conservative media capitalized on the moment, pushing out a series of stories around Pelosi's (mis)use of the Pledge and using search engine optimization to ensure that the top stories regarding Pelosi's use of the Pledge were from primarily conservative outlets like the *New York Post, Washington Examiner, Wall Street Journal,* and *The Daily Wire.*

SUPPORTING PRESIDENT TRUMP

When I discuss the five f's and how people who support Trump are driven by protecting these values, interlocutors will often highlight what they see as a glaring contradiction. How can those who seek truth in the Bible support someone who vehemently opposes so much of what it stands for?

One might think that those who make meaning via a literalist translation of scripture would break with Trump after he bragged about grabbing women "by the p***y" with *Access Hollywood* host Billy Bush, or after it was revealed that he paid adult film actress Stormy Daniels $130,000 during the 2016 election cycle so she would not disclose that she had slept with him after the birth of his youngest son.[40] But as other scholars point out, this perspective fails to account for the way conservatives engage with the Bible. His candidacy was not an outlier; it was the culmination of centuries-long patriarchal and racist practices.[41]

Those whom I interviewed, and the information system I was immersed in, often drew on the Bible to *support* Trump's racist positions or sexist behavior. For example, Trump's promise to "build the wall" continues to resonate with his base. The phrase serves as a code for Christian Nationalism that involves a reference to biblical verses and signifies that religious insiders are privileged in the United States.[42] The literal wall not only aligns with law and order; it also evokes a reference to protecting Christian interests.

Bush used similar signals to garner support for invading Iraq. Drawing on the language of a "crusade" and juxtaposing America (good) against Iraq and Al-Qaeda (evil), he could both speak disparagingly of Islam while deepening national embraces of American exceptionalism.[43] These dog whistles are also built into the names of Christian organizations. Take WallBuilders, a conservative multimedia organization run by evangelical Christian activist and author David Barton. The name of the organization is a reference to barriers erected to protect Jerusalem and restore stability and safety to the city, a narrative from the Old Testament book of Nehemiah. While the organization is not particularly large, it was frequently mentioned in many interviews. Conservative voters pointed me to the website so I could see for myself how Christianity played a central role in the creation of the United States. The WallBuilders' website characterizes the organization as "a national profamily organization that presents America's forgotten history and heroes, with an emphasis on our moral, religious, and constitutional heritage." References to "rebuilding the walls" are meant to evoke citizens' desires to "rebuild the nation's foundations," which Barton argues is linked to a faith in God.[44]

Even though Trump routinely participates in what many would deem un-Christian behavior (including dishonesty, disloyalty, greed, fraud, multiple extramarital affairs, multiple divorces), conservatives use scriptural inference and biblical references to facilitate forgiveness for President Trump's indiscretions. Prominent televangelist Billy Graham, for example, frequently reminded his followers that God worked through many sinners, reminding conservative voters that Abraham lied, that Moses disobeyed God, and that David committed adultery and had a man killed.[45] Several called on passages from the Bible, specifically the story of King David, to reaffirm their support for Trump as a flawed leader still "chosen by God" to serve as president.

In October 2018, Dennis Prager wrote a *National Review* op-ed titled "In Defense of Pro-Trump Christians" in which he took issue with the argument that religious conservatives who support Trump are hypocritical. To support his argument, he drew on the story of King David. Prager asked if God was flawed in "voting for" King David, an adulterer and murderer, and maintaining him as king.[46]

During an event to help gain more conservative support for Trump, Ben Carson, a former brain surgeon and Trump's secretary of Housing and Urban Development, explained how elections are like a chess match where "God is the great grandmaster." If conservatives wanted to reshape the Supreme Court, they would need to look past what they disliked about Trump and remind themselves that sometimes God "uses a pawn" to win the match.[47]

In a television interview in August 2017, then U.S. Secretary of Energy Rick Perry made a more explicit connection:

> I tell people from time to time . . . you know the good Lord used King David and the best I can tell, King David wasn't perfect either. But he was the chosen man of God. Let's go make America great again.[48]

Time and again, conservative thought leaders draw from the Bible to signal that all voters have access to and understand this sacred text. This strategy ultimately uses the Bible to recommend that believers overlook Trump's shortcomings in favor of the greater good: advancing the conservative agenda. In other words, while Trump's own moral compass might be broken, lifting passages from the Bible keeps him in office and protects the five f's.

MEDIA DISTRUST

For the past ten decades, conservative media creators have worked to change the meaning of objectivity from unbiased coverage to equal coverage.[49] As I describe in Step Two, this shift helped conservative leadership to land interviews on mainstream media outlets desperate to seem objective, and to build their own lopsided media network devoted to exclusive coverage of conservative news and cultural information.

Different age groups accessed this media network in distinct ways. In my study, respondents who had been out of college for some time and were affiliated with the women's group or similar organizations started their news day early at 6:00 am with *Fox & Friends*. This traditional weekday morning news show and network pillar first premiered in 1998 and currently features anchors Steve Doocy, Ainsley Earhardt, and Brian Kilmeade. Trump was an avid watcher and fan of the show, so much so that he often called in to discuss matters of the day live on air with the hosts.

Respondents in their early twenties reported watching less television news than their elders did. They stayed up-to-date by setting their smartphones to ping them with Fox News alerts, and they reported listening to Ben Shapiro's podcast, the *Ben Shapiro Show*, for their preferred commentary and analysis.

Everyone I interviewed also consulted more "mainstream," or what they referred to as "liberal," news sources like the *New York Times*, CNN, MSNBC, or *Pod Save America*. For example, an older gentleman I interviewed had a collection of newspaper clippings from the *Wall Street Journal*, the *Washington Post*, and the local paper. College-aged respondents had apps from outlets like CNN on their phones.

Regardless of age, my conservative respondents relied on scriptural inference methods to compare conflicting data or interpretations across sources. As they dug into the texts, inconsistencies would emerge, thereby bolstering their belief that the mainstream media was fake. In particular, they came to believe that mainstream media (1) focused on issues that did not deserve media attention, such as hit pieces against President Trump or stories contrived to direct public attention toward unimportant issues; and (2) got their facts wrong. By directly accessing original transcripts of Trump's speeches and comparing "his words" with mainstream media coverage, respondents would cite inconsistencies in coverage and use this to classify mainstream media as "fake."

DISTRACTION AND HIT PIECES

Olivia, a junior in college and a former leader in the college Republican group I observed, was the first to tell me that "fake news" included trivial news subjects. Talking as we crossed the quad together, Olivia recalled a recent conversation she had just had with her father.

"My dad likes to say this, and even though I'll make fun of him for saying it, I think it is a little bit true. He says there's two types of fake news, right? There's news that's false. These facts are made up or it's not fact checked or whatever, it's false news."

I nodded as our shoes crunched over the fallen leaves. The election was getting closer and the college Republicans were stepping up their efforts to get out "good" information to the voters. Olivia continued:

> But [my dad] also thinks there's a version of fake news where news media will amplify what he considers to be non-news, at the expense of real news. His token claim for this is the transgender bathroom issues. He's like, "How's it possible that our entire nation for weeks and months is consumed by this thing, which affects a very small percentage of the population?"

In other words, my conservative respondents characterized the alleged promotion of stories that countered the five f's as fake news.

On the flip side, they also classified the alleged withholding of stories that supported the five f's as fake news. Sean, a college junior, elaborated on this in relation to firearms:

> Just recently there was just a shooting, a prevented shooting in a Tennessee area church. What stopped the shooting was one of the people in the congregation had a firearm and shot the guy before anyone could get hurt, beside the shooter. That news story was overlooked and was really only brought up by Fox News and it was a true story. Basically, I see that as if that does get into the news like CNN that will give more reason to promote gun control than gun and safety because it was the gun that protected a lot of other people.

These reactions by Olivia and Sean show how framing is tied to perceptions about credibility. Because mainstream media channels seem to focus on topics deemed un-conservative, such as transgender rights, and so fail to devote sufficient attention to issues supported by the five f's, conservatives believe that they lack credibility.

Sean also used "the little Harambe incident" to explain what he saw as a link between the twenty-four-hour news cycle and manufacturing fake news to keep up:

> I mean, the fact that the gorilla died is not fake news, but the fact that they're focusing more on that animal than the child, yeah, I consider fake. So I wouldn't say if the event that happened is true, it's not fake. But how they're presenting it, just because it's emotion-driven, then yeah, it's fake, that's how I see it within terminology.

Emotional appeals also applied to what my respondents described as an "unnecessary focus" on Trump's actions. One college student described his frustration with CNN coverage, which he said is constantly creating stories just to make Trump look bad.

> I remember them [CNN] though, like this past summer and stuff them reporting on, it sounded like satire. The story was about Trump, about how he had two scoops of ice cream and anybody else had one.[50]

To combat what they described as misinformation traps, conservative respondents avoided engaging in topics that they deemed unnecessary or irrelevant. Strategies included changing the channel, turning off their device, or "scrolling past" postings on their social media they decided were not newsworthy.

Respondents felt that reporters covered "sensational" stories to elicit emotional reactions from audiences, and repeatedly described a desire for "just the facts" in their reporting instead. It was this quest for "facts" and "truth" that led the college students in my focus groups to PragerU content.

"I love Prager!" exclaimed one of the young women in the group. "[Their videos] are short and I can watch them between my classes." Another student in the group elaborated on why PragerU's content responds to the desires of conservatives:

> I think Prager does a really good job of taking very emo-
> tionally charged issues and breaking them down and
> simplifying them in terms of, "Okay, so this is what hap-
> pened, and then this happened, which made this." It kind
> of makes the issues more black and white, and so more
> objective, which is always good in my mind.

In a separate interview, another college student expressed a
similar desire for what he felt was fact-based versus emotion-based
journalism:

> I love sources that will give you a timeline, that'll just say,
> "Here are the facts, here's the timeline of it, here are the
> transcripts," and that's it, and don't try to put in some
> analysis at the end. Those are harder, fewer to come by,
> but I actually really like that because you're not having
> all this extra language around it. It's like, "Here is exactly
> what happened, you make the call."

A desire for "just the facts" and allowing audiences to make
their own sense of what happened again evokes the Protestant
traditions of close reading and scriptural inference, according to
which no intermediary or higher authority is necessary for an
ordinary person to understand divine truth.

INCONSISTENT OR INACCURATE COVERAGE

In addition to classifying "sensational" news as fake, conservatives
draw on the practice of scriptural inference to compare inconsistencies in media coverage. By consulting a variety of sources, and
then determining the differences between how various outlets
covered the story, this method of analysis reinforces conservatives'
distrust in mainstream media.

A pioneer of online citizen engagement, Eli Pariser, drew a
connection to this process back in 2011: "as masses of news readers went online and began to hear from multiple sources, the
differences in coverage were drawn out and amplified."[51] Rather
than relying on the potentially corrupt interpretations of an elite
political punditry, my respondents describe a process whereby

they go directly to the transcripts to see what Trump said and determine their *own* interpretation of his words. With just a few clicks, they can access, analyze, and evaluate a variety of media sources and then compare what they read to, say, Trump's speeches or the original text of the Constitution.

Hunter, a young man in the college Republican group, explained:

> Well, first off, I would look at the news to see, okay, what has Trump been doing so far? I would compare sources like CNN and Fox News and see, okay, Fox News is saying this. CNN is saying this. Two totally different things. I had to go on the internet a lot and I had to go through reliable sources.

The way conservatives were able to detect media bias (what they described as fake news) was by going back to speeches given by Trump and other Republican politicians and comparing what they said in the speech to the media coverage. Relying on scriptural inference, they concluded that media outlets like CNN had "twisted his [Trump's] words" or "amplified" part of what he had to say while hiding other parts of his speech. This is what Olivia and her dad referred to as the other kind of fake news:

> Either news media or social media outlets will amplify Trump or his opinion at the expense of real news. It's taking something like that and using it to fit the anti-Trump narrative . . . to me, that's not news.

Consider how this process played out when Trump characterized members of the notorious MS-13 gang as "animals." Mainstream media coverage focused on his use of a racial epithet, claiming that he used the phrase to refer to undocumented immigrants. As an example of this coverage, see the *USA Today* headline from May 16, 2019: "Trump ramps up rhetoric on undocumented immigrants: 'These aren't people. These are animals.' "[52]

Because the mainstream media covered the context of Trump's rhetoric instead of simply offering a literal translation of his words, Trump, and his conservative supporters, were able to double down on his comments instead of taking ownership for his racism. That is, because Trump did not say "immigrants are animals" but rather referred to members of MS-13 as animals, conservative audiences were guided by conservative pundits and politicians to discredit the entire message. Conservative media organizations that understand how their audiences validate truth added to the effect by publishing their own stories that drew on scriptural inference. Using "the words" of Trump, Tucker Carlson claimed that mainstream media was "defending MS-13."[53] The effect was to bury the context surrounding Trump's comments in the minutia of his "actual" words. It also served as a mechanism whereby conservative outlets could continue to insert a racial epithet into mainstream media coverage, thus confirming the power of MS-13 as a dog whistle. Repeated reference reaffirms nonwhites as a threat while alleging white victimization and emphasizing racial divisions.[54]

A similar failure to engage with conservative media practices led to a mainstream journalistic misfire regarding new voting laws enacted in Georgia following the 2020 U.S. presidential election. Signed into law in May 2021, the Georgia legislation passed significant restrictions including (but not limited to) strict new identification requirements for absentee ballots; less time to request absentee ballots; expanded early voting for small rural towns but not for more populous metropolitan areas; and making it illegal for election officials to mail out absentee ballot applications to all voters.

Yet most news coverage about the proposed bill focused on prohibitions against providing food and water to voters waiting in lines. On March 25, 2021, Reuters ran an article with the headline "Georgia bans giving water to voters in line under sweeping restrictions."[55] On March 26, 2021, CNN ran a headline: "It's now illegal in Georgia to give food and water to voters in line."[56] An NBC Charlotte affiliate story on March 31, 2021, read, "Yes, it's illegal to give water, food to Georgia voters in line for polls."[57] And on April 9, 2021, the *Washington Post* published an article titled "New limits on food and water at Georgia's polls could hinder Black and low-income voters, advocates say."[58]

While the laws are clearly aimed at reducing the already pre-
carious voting rights of Black Americans, the mainstream media's
coverage of food and water meant that conservative groups could
easily rebuke the coverage by going directly to the text. The provi-
sion denying the dissemination of water applies only to those
persons distributing or displaying campaign material.[59] The bill
does not prohibit poll officers from distributing non-promotional
materials and it allows polling locations to make "available self-
service water from an unattended receptacle to an elector waiting
in line to vote."[60] Water distribution was a tenuous concern compared to the larger impact these restrictions could have on voter
turnout. As noted earlier, The Heritage Foundation was central
to the drafting of this and other states' laws and openly boasted
that these laws would *restrict access to voting.* But this news was
buried by the media attention on food and water. On April 16,
2021, The Heritage Foundation released its own story, encouraging fellow conservatives to "fact check" the "egregious lies" being
perpetuated in the media about the bill.[61] Once again, the right-
wing information ecosystem drew on scriptural inference to
"prove" that the law did not actually deny anyone the right to
stay hydrated. In doing so it reaffirmed larger conservative
arguments—that the Left is hysterical and the mainstream media
cannot be trusted—while making the voting legislation seem
harmless.

During our interview, Hannah, a lawyer in her thirties, scrolled
through the news alerts on her phone to show me the news
sources she relies on, which included *The Daily Wire,* PragerU,
Conservative Tribune, and Breitbart. As she swiped past news
deemed fake, she described how scriptural inference guides her
news consumption habits. She told me that she can only trust
news sources that are true to the words, intentions, and leadership
of Trump.

When I asked her to expound on the concern she expressed
about mainstream or liberal news outlets "twisting [Trump's]
words," Hannah described how the press had covered Trump's
remarks after the white supremacist rally in Charlottesville, Virginia:

All the left-wing media, all the mainstream media, all of a sudden jumped on that and said, "Oh, he said there were fine white supremacists." No, he didn't. He never said that. Those words never came from his mouth. He never uttered those words. And so, it was a thing where again it's I can't take mainstream media seriously when they do that. Because I hear what is being said, they take a snippet and completely twist it.

Active college Republican Emily echoed Hannah's statements, also referring to the way the mainstream media covered President Trump's response to the Unite the Right rally:

That's kind of like a fake news deal to me. Like, the whole thing is just not . . . He never talked to that person or we have the whole recording of the speech and he never said that. That's fake news.

Much like they had with MS-13 and voting rights, conservatives were able to absolve the underlying racism by failing to engage with subtext. By referring only to his exact words (that is, "very fine people on both sides" not "neo-Nazis were fine people"), Trump's supporters could quickly dismiss the problematic nature of Trump's use of "both sides." Trump's words were not the only words studied by the conservative voters I interviewed. I spoke at length with Juliette, a former journalist and a wealthy donor to area Republicans, about what she described as a decline in journalistic integrity. These days, Juliette told me, she almost exclusively follows leading conservative thinkers like Newt Gingrich, Sean Hannity, Laura Ingraham, and Ben Carson on Facebook. The news she used to read, she reasons, was "blatant . . . fake news." Juliette described how "they" would report that an interviewee said something even if they did not.

[Take] Newt Gingrich. He was interviewed somewhere, I think it was on CNN, and he did not say what they said. They just made it up, and I think the lack of integrity is rampant.

Chrissy, a middle-aged woman with a daughter who had just started her first year at a highly competitive university, said:

> I can't just take any source that I can go to and just read and take it for what it's worth. I take bits and pieces of it to further explore, but I have to explore every bit of information out in several different ways.

In a separate interview, Phoebe, a recent college graduate who still attends college Republican events from time to time, described how she skims CNN, Fox News, and MSNBC to "see what topics are trending," but then does her "own studying and research elsewhere."

William, a college senior, also does his "own research," especially when it comes to breaking news. This was particularly important for him during the Russia investigation. In an effort to combat what he called "an avalanche of information," William would search for "calmer sources." He would "stop," he told me, making a gesture with his right hand like he was clicking a mouse, and:

> [open a] new tab. Then I go over to a little more of a drier source that is just giving you a timeline. NPR is a good place but nobody's sharing stuff from NPR on Facebook. Everybody's posting BuzzFeed stuff and CNN stuff and clips of Tucker Carlson going off on, that's what people are going to share, so that's what you tend to see on Facebook . . . Then I evaluate the facts.

Hannah also described a need to fact-check the news when she sees suspicious content on her social media news feed:

> I could be flipping on my Facebook, I'll see a story and I'll say, "Okay. Let me find out more about this . . ." If I end up seeing that it's on both CNN and Fox, then I'll go and see how they go and tell the story. Usually, if it's something that Trump has done or said I have already seen him say it or heard him say it because he's on the news constantly saying stuff. So, when it comes to him having a certain stance . . . and again, if I end up seeing

that it's one way or the other. I'll go to him; I'll go and see what he's tweeting or what he's said on Facebook.

Interestingly, this process of "lateral reading" is like the way fact-checkers approach evaluating credible web sources.[62] This strategy allows fact-checkers to quickly discern who is behind the information and the strengths and weaknesses of the source.[63] Rather than engaging in vertical reading (staying on a single website), fact-checkers model lateral reading as a way to check what other websites are saying about a given subject and try to identify possible sources of bias.[64]

This process of doing their own research in the form of seeking out the original words was particularly important given the upcoming election. As one new member of the college Republicans I observed said:

> That [was] how I became a Republican, because I was doing my research on Trump, and as soon as Trump was showing me the light as to what being a Republican [is] all about, that's what got me into it, because it was him that brought me to it.

For those in my study, "doing your own research" often entailed querying a search engine, primarily Google. Conservative voters trusted Google to locate facts that they believed the mainstream media had twisted, neglected, or buried. But as we will see in Step Four, this online "search for alternative facts" is complicated by biases coded into the very keywords used. Since few really understand how search engines work, lateral reading is complicated by the information seeker's intention.

What my research reveals is that conservatism is both a worldview and a media practice—a way of looking for and understanding information. And conservatives like to use the techniques that they have learned through Bible study in assessing and interpreting news and cultural information. Studying the Bible is something that individual Protestants do, but scriptural inference is a way of looking at information that is not bound to the word of God. As my data demonstrate, conservatives regularly transfer the practice to other documents deemed sacred, such as the Constitution or a transcript of one of Trump's speeches. Conservative thought leaders know and exploit this use of scriptural inference to buttress their ideas.

While the empirical evidence indicates that "trickle-down economics"—a belief that cutting taxes stimulates business investment—does not work, "trickle-down media practices" seem to benefit propagandists.[65] In other words, it is easier to spread propaganda if you understand how your target audience seeks out and uses information about the world. It allows conservative elites to discredit the mainstream media as fake news, because their audiences approach doing their own research as a duty, and are compelled to "unpack" major events on their own, rather than rely on the interpretation of elites like academics or journalists.

Such findings complicate existing strategies and the cultural emphasis on media literacy as a way of combating "information disorder."[66] Based on my research, conservatives do not lack media literacy. Instead, conservative pundits and politicians exploit unique media practices to spread propaganda. At one college Republicans meeting, a Christian News Broadcast station representative spoke at length about how users should be fact-checking what they read, especially in an era of fake news. Pausing in front of his young audience, the twenty-something writer and producer for the network emphasized the importance of being vigilant on social media sites.

"If you are sharing information on Facebook that has been manipulated," he warned, "then you are part of the problem."

He went on to explain how searching for the truth ties into conservative ideology, evoking the importance of finding "just the facts" that sounded like what others in my study had described. "If you are sharing this stuff, you're not a conservative," he cautioned. "You don't have to manipulate facts if you have the truth."

STEP FOUR

UNDERSTAND HOW INFORMATION FLOWS

It is both appealing and naïve to think of search engines as a consequence-free way to find new and different knowledge. Google, DuckDuckGo, Bing, Yahoo!, and other search engines are all designed to "best match" customers' needs, but they are not neutral arbiters of truth. Algorithms are programmed to connect information seekers with relevant predictions based on previous decisions.

The inner workings of search engines are proprietary, so researchers cannot definitively know how these corporations index the internet to help users access returns. But the search process itself is not magic. Search engines rely on a series of algorithms that dictate who gets what information. An algorithm may sound complicated, but it can be simply understood as a set of instructions given to a computer. Since algorithms are computer programs, they do not read like humans do. In order for datasets to be machine readable, they must be tagged and categorized. This information about the data is called "metadata." A webpage's metadata or meta tags provide a description of the page's content. Search algorithms rely on metadata to transform inputs (users' geolocation, click-through data, browser history, and keywords) into outputs such as driving directions, YouTube videos, news, or lists of local restaurants.[1]

Several scholars have considered the way that algorithms force users into filter bubbles.[2] This rich and important work, however, often neglects the role that search queries play in the algorithmic process.

IN GOOGLE WE TRUST

On June 13, 2017, the State of Virginia held a tightly contested gubernatorial Republican primary. The general election would take place a few months later, in November. I drove around towns in the Blue Ridge Mountains that summery day, chatting up voters as they exited the polls. I started by asking them a simple question: *Where do you go for news that you trust?*

Voters' knee-jerk response was often laughter. Not unlike the conservatives I would observe over the following months, most people told me there were few sources they really "trusted." How did they learn about the candidate they just voted for, then? A few people mentioned that Facebook had reminded them to vote and provided a link to help them find out where their polling station was. To learn about the candidates, the overwhelming answer was simple: "I googled it."[3]

After hearing this same response multiple times, I decided to dig a little deeper. "What do you mean, 'you googled it'?" Most often, people stared back at me in silence or confusion as if they had no idea how to explain something so obvious. One elderly woman spoke slowly to me while pretending to type on an air keyboard, as if concerned about my mental state.

"Well, I took the names of the candidates and put them into Google." She smiled brightly at me.

"But then what?" I pressed.

Silence.

The simple act of googling something is such a common methodology for answering a diverse array of questions that the company name has become nearly synonymous with searching for information in the twenty-first century. The term and practice are so embedded in American popular culture that questioning it, as I did with voters at the polls, causes confusion.

What did I mean, *then what?*

Regardless of party affiliation, it was clear from my interviews that voters' primary method for finding political information was via Google. Yet although they relied on Google, they did not understand how it worked. Repeatedly people told me that the place they went for news they could trust was Google. These answers implied that Google was considered a neutral arbiter of trusted information.

Moreover, few seemed to understand how much keywords drive returns. Given the clear role that Google played in informing the voters I spoke with, I decided to explore how different political language might shape the kind of information returned. To remove any local data or previous search history that might influence my browsing experience, I opened a new "incognito" (private) window and typed each of the candidates' names on the ballot.

On the Democratic ticket, then–lieutenant governor Ralph Northam was running against the more progressive candidate Tom Perriello. When I searched for each of the Democratic primary candidate's names, Google's top return was each candidate's official website and related news coverage. On the Republican ticket, Ed Gillespie was running against Corey Stewart and Frank Wagner. Google's search returns for Stewart and Wagner were similar to those for Northam and Perriello—official websites and news stories. But then something odd happened: when I searched for Ed Gillespie, the first return was Corey Stewart's website, not Gillespie's.

In a tightly contested election where Gillespie beat Stewart by fewer than five thousand votes, Google's algorithms decided the most relevant link for an "Ed Gillespie" search the official campaign website of his top competitor. Somehow, Stewart (the most conservative candidate on the ticket) had influenced the algorithm—Google considered his website, not Gillespie's, to be the most authoritative result.

SURVEILLANCE CAPITALISM AND FILTER BUBBLES

Many researchers study how large media corporations exploit users and their data to predict and drive all kinds of decisions, from purchases to voting.[4] For years these academics have argued that large tech companies are economically and ideologically problematic because they limit what we see, what we buy, and whom we interact with. Despite Big Tech's assurances that search results are ranked by popularity, trustworthiness, and credibility, this research also demonstrates that algorithmic ordering is inextricably driven by profit and connected to gender, race, and class biases.[5]

Facebook and other platforms are ultimately products, and their designers have programmed them to keep us engaged with them as long and as often as possible.[6] Not unlike casinos, Google (and its subsidiary YouTube), Facebook (and its subsidiary Instagram), Twitter, and other participatory media platforms design their user interfaces and experiences to feel addictive.[7] This deliberate social architecture enables corporations to elicit, extract, commodify, and profit from our personal data.

Services like Google are free for a reason. Information seekers are both users and raw materials, in the sense that their behavioral data are harvested to improve the speed, relevancy, and accuracy of the site.[8] Despite research revealing the problem with content customization practices, the CEOs of tech giants like Facebook, Twitter, and Google repeatedly sit before Senate and House judiciary committees denying any wrongdoing. Moreover, users continue to think of platforms like Google as a trusted and reliable source. Those I interviewed repeatedly describe Google as a neutral way to get "unbiased" information.

Yet users' faith in information communication technology counters a number of studies that have documented the way that datasets, algorithms, search engines, statistical models, and artificial intelligence (AI) are predisposed with human biases.[9] Take the way that algorithms affect news consumption. Tools for sorting news, like real simple syndication (RSS), tags, filters, aggregate summaries, or email notifications, have been around for some time.[10] Some theorists worry that tech companies go too far with customization, filtering out news and information that might challenge our point of view.[11] These scholars are concerned that such practices lead us into echo chambers—spaces where people engage only with concepts and people they already agree with. One worrisome outcome of this filtering could be an uninformed, polarized society.[12] This position is only reinforced by the findings of sociologist Robert Putnam, who in the early 2000s argued that active news consumption, the process by which a user would read a newspaper in its entirety, is positively correlated with civic engagement, while customized news content has a negative impact on civic engagement.[13]

Yet it is equally important to recognize that niche publications provide a voice to underrepresented voices that have historically been marginalized from mainstream media coverage. As a study of the Black press demonstrates, customized news based on group interests can be key to exhorting social change.[14] Prior to the advent of the Black press in 1827, for instance, no Black perspectives existed in mainstream news coverage. In these early days, someone who wanted to break ranks and write a dissenting view had to pay the editor or print a rebuttal as an advertisement. Change didn't come easy—it took serious, tireless, danger-defying journalism by members of the Black press to inform the public about the scope and depth of their unjust treatment, and to inspire reforms.

Indeed, personalized news advanced anti-slavery, anti-segregation, and anti-miscegenation legislation, and worked toward better educational, economic, and health outcomes for Black people. If anything, the Black press demonstrated that mainstream coverage is inherently filtered. If it were not for the bravery of journalists like Ida B. Wells, there would have been no historical coverage of the grievances against Black citizens, including but not limited to the military barring Black men from most branches of service and promotion; the Red Cross refusing to accept "n***o blood"; and rampant anti-Black domestic terrorism, mob violence, and lynching.[15] *Jet* magazine, a weekly publication by and for the Black community, published the searing open-casket funeral images of Emmett Till. The mainstream news followed the Black press's lead only after the images had already begun to wreak havoc on the hearts and minds of Black Americans. Till's mother's determination to expose the daily brutality that Black Americans face forced white residents, who were otherwise watching supposedly comprehensive news coverage, to witness the systematic racial violence happening in their country. Niche publications devoted to specialized interests can break the insular coverage of mass media.

Amplifying stories of importance based on a user's individual history, then, is not necessarily problematic, nor is customization indicative of an internet-driven news environment. But user-driven selection is different from when platforms customize the internet experience for users. The digital information that people willingly surrender when they post a status update, seek out information about a product, or self-select their news filters informs algorithms.[16] But there are other unconscious ways that people engage with online content that fuel the digital ecosystem.

After all, search engines like Google collect data on much more than just the keywords that people enter. The company also engages in a practice called datamining: culling and storing how queries are phrased, grammar errors, which links were most useful, and the geographic location of the information seeker.[17] In an effort to predict and drive consumer information, large tech companies have begun engaging in surveillance capitalism—tracking, and then selling, records of everything that seekers search and consume.[18] This practice seems more troubling when one considers its connection to news and information access. According to a September 2019 Pew Research Center report, the percentage of Americans who prefer to get their news online is growing: one in five adults in 2019 reported getting their news on social media.[19]

Studies such as these, however, fail to capture the complexity of this statistic, since many people likely use social media as an intermediary when they engage with traditional news sources. That is, many of my respondents said they used Facebook or Twitter to get the news, but that it was a two-step process. First, they would follow or "friend" trusted news sources or elected officials, or pay attention to the news articles or video clips their friends shared. Then they would engage directly with that source. For example, they would click on and read the article from the *Wall Street Journal* shared by their neighbor or watch the Tucker Carlson clip shared by Fox News. Facebook wasn't the *source;* it was the platform where they found the source. To ignore this two-step process is to miss capturing where and from whom these people are actually getting their information. Such a misunderstanding of how people engage with news media reminds me of the conversations I had with voters after exiting the polls in Virginia. They conceived of Google as a neutral creator of the news, but in fact, Google aggregates information from other places, taking the news from other sources and putting it all in one place to keep users engaged with their platform.

DOING THEIR OWN (RE)SEARCH

On a sunny day in a public park, I worked hurriedly with five other volunteers from the Republican women's group to set up the annual BBQ fundraiser. Winding my way through the sprawling, wooded park, I passed a large public pool, tennis courts, and covered porches numbered for convenience. For an hour we worked to cover the wooden picnic tables with red, white, and blue tablecloths, taping the corners on the ends to keep the wind from ruining the decorations, then covering the tape with large, glittery stars. Just as we were finishing up, people began arriving.

Interns from a local state university set up a table to check people in and sell raffle tickets. Sitting among a group of attendees in their thirties, I listened as they talked about the weather, the upcoming election, and what camps their kids would attend that summer. After "the prayer and the Pledge," a small number of political officials stood to say a few remarks. The first was a tall, slender, white man, a longtime Republican incumbent up for reelection. As he addressed the crowd, he talked about the uphill battle conservatives had before them:

> A lot of Democrats will be coming out to vote because they are not too happy with our President. This does not deter me, and it shouldn't deter you. You know what is going on, that the President is doing good work—you do your own research! Keep up the hard work because the press is not our friend. If there is something important to you, you have to learn about it for yourself![20]

When I asked respondents what information they were looking up for themselves, many referenced the controversy around NFL players kneeling during the national anthem. Specifically, interviewees discussed the September 24, 2017, Pittsburg Steelers versus Chicago Bears NFL game in which Alejandro Villanueva, a Steelers offensive tackle, stood alone on the field during the anthem with his hand over his heart while the rest of the Steelers stayed inside the tunnel in protest. This case was of significance to my respondents because Villanueva was a veteran who had deployed to Afghanistan three times, in 2011, 2012, and 2013.[21]

That Villanueva's team had not supported his right to stand for the anthem incensed Sarah, a new grandmother in her midfifties. She had been flying back from a vacation during the game but had seen stories about what had happened on social media. "Now I heard one story about the Pittsburgh Steelers," she told me. "You know, the one where that guy that went out—that one who had done three tours in Afghanistan. He put his hand over his heart, but the rest stayed in the tunnel. Well, I've heard from a lot of people that was disrespectful, blah, blah, blah. [The players] weren't allowed to go. But I've also heard that Tomlin [the Pittsburgh Steelers head coach] did not want them to go out there and kneel. He wouldn't give 'em a chance to kneel, . . . just to go out after the national anthem. So, I don't know which is true, and which is not. My son actually texted me last night and was the one that told me he researched it, and found out that Tomlin made them stay in, because he didn't want them to be kneeling."

For Sarah, and other conservatives in this study, "doing their own research" was an extension of the scriptural inference method of looking for truth in sacred texts. Instead of relying on news coverage about the event, Sarah sought out sources of information she trusted that allowed her to reach conclusions aligned with her own conservative values. "Doing their own research" was frequently connected to the idea that mainstream media was burying issues related to the five f's of conservatism and that it was up to them to "fact-check" the news and find "the truth" for themselves.

GOOGLING FOR TRUTH

Americans generally trust Google more than traditional news outlets.[22] It should be no surprise then that conservatives in the groups I observed, as well as the people I spoke with as they left the polls, all characterized Google as central to how they learned about political candidates and made voting decisions.

Michael, a man in his late forties who participates in a city-wide Republican group that often co-hosts events with the women's group I observed, described how Google is a vital way to "get off social media" and get perspective from good, reputable sources of information. "One of the things I may Google, is take a person, and then maybe Google 'em just to get a history of where they came from and their background, maybe what their experiences were," he told me.

Understanding where someone is coming from and whether he could relate to that person informs Michael's voting decisions. He feels like he cannot trust journalists or his social media newsfeed unless he has done his own research. This process indicates two levels of trust. The first is trust in the information returned—users must be able to discern if the websites returned contain credible information. But the process of search also implies a confident belief that the search engine will return the most useful and accurate information in response to queries.

Many I interviewed believed that top returns were more legitimate and held more value than returns lower down the page, or on later pages. Yet a page's rank has less to do with credibility and more to do with what information scientists refer to as relevance.[23] The three elements that make up search algorithms are "linguistic," or the keywords/query of the user; "popularity," that is, how connected the webpage is to other websites; and "user behavior," or which websites people most frequently click on.[24] Formally known as "page rank," this process originated in a belief that structuring search returns around websites that other users and websites found credible would mimic an academic citation system, and make it so the most desired links would rank highest.[25]

Research indicates, however, that the order in which search results appear is not as simple or neutral as it seems.[26] Search engines crawl the web for URLs, videos, and other content to create a map of available content, but these machine learning systems are designed with financial interests in mind.[27] Data indicate that Google regularly tinkers with the information it provides and that identical searches made by two different people can yield different results, or the same results in a different order.[28] It is also clear that different search engines order information in different ways.[29]

Using sophisticated analyses of seventeen keywords over a three-month period, a team of investigators at the *Wall Street Journal* found that Google's results are different from those of comparable search engines.[30] Combining this quantitative data analysis with qualitative interviews, the reporters argued that Google regularly manipulates its search results and page rankings to favor larger firms at the expense of smaller ones. While Google repeatedly claims that its algorithms are objective and essentially autonomous, this *Wall Street Journal* investigation argued otherwise, reporting that Google hires thousands of low-paid contractors to convey what the multinational tech giant considers the "correct" ranking of results.

Google has been in business since 1998, and at the beginning its purpose was simple: to send users to other documents for information. It stood out from other search engines because of its streamlined design that featured only the Google name and a small window for typing in search terms. But as the internet developed, and search became monetized in various ways, Google's mission became more complicated. In particular, since 2012, Google has been steadily trying to keep users on the platform for as long as possible.[31] Rather than directing people to Wikipedia, it began inserting a "knowledge graph" into the first page of search results. The year after this change, English-language Wikipedia had 21 percent fewer page views.[32] A more recent investigation of more than fifteen thousand recent popular queries found that Google devoted 41 percent of the first page of search results to its own products (Google Flights, Google Translate, Google Maps).[33]

Psychologists and internet researchers have found that the order of results influences how credible or trustworthy people think the information is.[34] My respondents echoed these findings. Silas, the communications officer for the college group I observed, summed it up best:

> There's a lot of influence on the first couple of results that show up when you type the words. Because oftentimes, for me, and I know it's the same with a lot of other people, the first information we see is what I'll remember and I'll keep with, and I'll assume it's true. And oftentimes, specifically when you type in a certain phrase, sometimes a special bio [knowledge graph] will come up and sometimes that's the only source that I'll look at, or other people too. So, Google has a lot of influence on the role of information.

In addition to putting more value in the top returns, few seem to realize that returns are rooted in the search engine's monetary interests. In fact, those in my study repeatedly described the search engine as the only way to receive unbiased news. Many respondents turned to Google for "facts" when they felt confused by what they read online or wary of news they did not trust. Bethany, a sophomore member of the college group I observed, told me that she "started researching more than I had to because I was really into it." Like my other respondents, her enthusiasm for learning started with a search engine. "I would go on Google and I would just type in questions that I had," she told me.

Many respondents began googling because they were suspicious of something they saw on social media. I witnessed this firsthand while hanging out with Sam during the slow shift at his part-time job at a regional store that specializes in Confederate memorabilia. In addition to the emblematic flag bearing the blue X with white stars, flags of the other Confederate states hang from the ceiling. Along the walls, shelves of books professing "the truth" about the Civil War, biographies of Confederate soldiers, and copies of the Bible were available for sale.

The store also specialized in mugs, lawn signs, and T-shirts with slogans that read "Heritage not Hate," and "If this shirt offends you, you need a history lesson" on the front, with the Confederate flag on the back. As we scrolled through his social media feed, the smell of kettle corn from the shop next door drifted in through the open window. Although he "tries to keep an open mind," Sam also likes to arm himself with "facts" so that he can interject when people post content that he disagrees with.

"If I'm interested, I'll research further," he explained. "There's not really a black and white, clear-cut, way of me doing things. If I'm interested in it, I'll research it more. I'll discuss it with my friends. I'll be proven wrong, or I'll be proven right."

"What do you mean when you say you research something?" I asked.

"Well, Google," Sam replied. "What does Google have to say about it? I'll click on the first three, four, five articles that appear. Look at what so and so said about this, okay, let's go to that, see what that says. Go to the next one down. I do try to consider where it's coming from, too."

Jared, a college junior and active member of the Young Republicans group, characterized his own research process similarly. During our interview, Jared expressed frustration by what he saw as an increase in subjective reporting, so I asked him how he distinguished between objective and subjective news, between stories worthy and unworthy of his trust. He shared that the only way to sift through news bias is by using "critical reason, thinking, and discourse." When I asked him to specify what he meant by critical reason, Jared described how the first step is to use a search engine rather than newspaper as mediator.

I'd google search it, number one. Number two, look for the same general theme, the news has a theme, usually. You'll see if the news has a theme in that or there's another article that talks about it, you can begin to see oh, is this true, is this a liberal bias, and I can just overlook the bias and get the essential information out. Or is this completely false, like Pizzagate, and I can't really find anything else from it except from like *Info Wars* and from sketchy long-listed sites that do not cite the source.

The idea that "the news has a theme" and a reliance on Google to find the truth was also expressed by Juliette, a wealthy donor to conservative causes and an active member of the women's Republican group:

> I'll do Google some. I'll look it up, and I'll find if it's more than one place, it usually has some validity involved. And it may not be totally brought out yet, or totally exposed yet, but the truth is there.

Time and again, respondents told me that they turned to Google to do their own research, validate sources, or search for truth. They trusted the search engine to return accurate information, but they also trusted themselves to formulate an unbiased query.

Yet few researchers have considered the way search is influenced by "deep stories," narratives that feel true about a highly salient issue like immigration, abortion, or guns. As Hochschild explains, a "deep story" might frame immigrants as "line cutters." Likewise, deep stories impact *ideological dialects*—immigrants might be referred to as "illegal aliens" or "undocumented workers" depending on the narrative. Exploring the social dimension of search provides important insights into how ideological dialects influence keywords, and how this can lead to the reinforcement and siloing of existing beliefs.[35]

"SEEK, AND YOU WILL FIND"

It was a hot summer day, at a trendy farm-to-table restaurant, as I sat down with a member of the women's group I was observing. Trish had chosen that location for our long lunch because she likes to support local businesses and farms. When I asked her why that was important, Trish told me that she "eats and votes with [her] dollars." It's important for her to know that the companies and brands she patronizes with her business share her values. In 2017 she stopped going to Starbucks when they announced an initiative to hire ten thousand refugees. She felt that the American company should prioritize veterans over immigrants.

Trish also expressed frustration with Target when she heard that they had stopped participating in Toys for Tots. Rather than partner with the well-known program run by the Marines, Target had, in Trish's view, championed interests that did not align with the five f's. For example, according to Trish, Target was "the first ones in line to support the transgender bathrooms."

I had not heard that Target was no longer supporting Toys for Tots, so I asked her for more. "Is that true?" I asked. "How do you know if something is true when you hear claims like that?"

"I will go and google it, see what I can find out there," Trish told me. "I'd google 'Toys for Tots' or 'support of U.S. military.'"

For Trish, either phrase would return accurate, reliable, and relevant information about Target's policies. Yet "Toys for Tots" and "support of U.S. military" are very specific queries, and each one would mean something very different to search algorithms coded for relevance. How Trish conceptualizes what she's looking for and how she frames her query will influence the information returned. "Toys for Tots" would likely return general information on the U.S. Marines initiative that gives presents to children in need at Christmastime. By contrast, "support for U.S. military" would not necessarily provide Trish with any information pertaining to Toys for Tots, much less Target's official corporate policies.

To get a better understanding of how Trish and other conservatives might do their own research on Target's Toys for Tots program or its attitude toward the U.S. military, I used Google in private mode to ask a series of search queries based on Trish's central concerns: "Does Target support the military?" Interestingly, Google returns seemed to address the issue that Trish raised in our interview. One of the top returns was the official Target website, asserting that the organization "supports veterans and military members as they serve our nation." The second return was the fact-check site Snopes debunking the "rumors about Target."

Clicking on the hyperlink quickly refutes Trish's allegation as false.[36] But the text immediately visible underneath the Snopes link appeared to *support* Trish's accusation. Under the Snopes URL read "TRUE: TARGET STORES DO NOT SUPPORT VETERANS!!" The way that Google presented the information meant that a user could walk away from their query thinking that the false claim was instead true. If someone like Trish only scanned the returns and did not click for more information, she might have believed that her inaccurate claims regarding Target's position on Toys for Tots were supported by "doing her own research."

Next in the list of search returns was a link to a Facebook post from an individual claiming that "Target DOES NOT Support our Troops." When I clicked on that link, I was redirected to a nine-year-old post on the Target Facebook page where a disgruntled customer voiced a nearly identical claim to the one Trish had mentioned over lunch. While others on the page refute the claim, it again requires seekers to click through to see the truth. For users accustomed to deep readings of texts, the rank ordering of information matters. In this case, Google's algorithm effectively created a hierarchical structure that indicated to those participating in scriptural inference that Snopes is as valid as unsubstantiated claims on Facebook. Further, if one fails to click on hyperlinks for more information and just scans the list of search results, inaccurate beliefs are easily confirmable.

A great deal of research has already explored how context influences information seeking.[37] Just because content exists online doesn't mean that it is easy to find, and many users lack the skills necessary to effectively navigate online content.[38] As sociologist and internet scholars Eszter Hargittai and Heather Young note, search terms play an important role in what information is returned.[39] More important, they find that people's prior knowledge of a subject influences both the keywords they use as well as their ability to successfully find an answer to their question.

How information is ordered is not particularly concerning if the question being asked is an innocuous one like "What is the capital of Colorado?" and there is only one right answer, Denver. But when seekers turn to search engines like Google for deeper questions with convoluted answers, it gets more complicated. As mentioned earlier, when Google first started, it acted as an intermediary, directing users to documents where information could be found. But over time, it has replaced its simple list of hyperlinked websites with its knowledge graph and/or suggestions for like-minded queries. This design shift conflates the explorative search processes—searches that embody learning and investigating—with queries focused on fact retrieval or verification.[40] Further, as Google has worked to "oversimplify complex phenomena" and to prioritize profits over societal engagement with complicated ideas, the tech giant has transformed itself from an exploratory platform into one designed around verification, a space where users can easily confirm unsubstantiated claims.[41]

But even if Google does return content contradictory to one's beliefs, it is unclear whether conservative audiences will accept the veracity of that information. Earlier in the book, I explained how conservatives turn to Google to fact-check mainstream media. Yet Kayla, a conservative college junior, told me that she questions if the returns are valid or have been manipulated if they produce information contradictory to what she expects.

> I'll click that and then read it and if it's still like, "that seems plausible," then whatever hinge point or fact that might change my opinion, I'll go Google that. I'll look into that and then Google that phrase. Then see if there are any people on the opposite end of the spectrum saying, "Oh, often people say this," but really, they're twisting the facts. To see if there's some way that I'm being deceived.

Moreover, most of my respondents were skeptical of fact-checking sites like Snopes and PolitiFact. They believed that liberals ran most of these sites and were therefore biased in how they allegedly validated truth claims. Trish summed up these suspicions:

> I hear a rumor that Snopes leans toward the liberal side anyway. So again, what can you trust? I don't know what you can trust anymore.

These findings suggest that confirmation bias and distorted notions of objectivity are easily supported when they rely on search engines to "do their own research." If their searches did not return a contradictory perspective, that seemed to be evidence that one did not exist, but if the searches failed to yield conservative positions, they were suspect. Respondents indicated that they would keep searching for the facts until they found content that confirmed what they were searching for. Any search returns that were discordant with their own views were deemed media manipulation.

Sarah admitted that her Google searches rarely revealed alternate points of view, but she did not consider how this might be linked to her search practices or Google's desire to best match her query. Instead she used her search returns to validate her claims, as though Google's failing to return an alternative perspective meant that one did not exist. In her words,

> I'll google the keyword, key phrase, a name, event, whatever, to try to see if there's anything out there. Sometimes all's I get is from the same things I read on Twitter.

Search engines are not designed to guide seekers through existential crises or challenge existing beliefs. Instead they return the results that, according to an algorithm, best match the user's inputs. One of the most important of these inputs is the keyword.

THE POWER OF INPUTS

The world of search consists of crawling (the search engine reads new webpages and updates existing ones), indexing (the search engine copies the crawled pages into a cataloged database), and ranking (the search engine serves up the results in a certain order based on the user's query).[42] Crawling and indexing create a map of the web that links pages to keywords to URLs. If it is not indexed, a page is unrecognizable to mainstream search engines. Unindexed sites are accessible only via the "dark web."[43] And without ranking, users' searches would yield more irrelevant information than targeted answers. Search engines like Google also designed the algorithms so that adult content is not returned unless a person is specifically searching for sexually explicit results.[44]

In order to protect the intellectual property of the search engine company, the exact programmatic way that search engines index and rank information is not fully known. We do know,

however, that ranking is performed using a combination of lin-
guistics (the words that appear on the webpage), popularity (the
number of other websites that link back to the site), and user
selection (the number of unique clicks a page receives). If someone enters a search term and clicks on the first link served up
without returning to the search page and clicking on the next, it
sends a signal that the information procured was relevant. By
contrast, if a user starts again with a similar search using different
phrases or doesn't click on any of the links offered, it sends a
signal that the information procured wasn't relevant. While the
system's approach to relevance is binary—information retrieved
is either relevant or not—more recent studies have pointed out
that "relevance is subjective, idiosyncratic, hard to predict and
unstable."[45] To take just one example, search results are not consistent for Google users across different countries.[46]

Part of that inconsistency is connected to how one sees the
world. Preexisting knowledge affects the kinds of questions a
seeker asks, when they ask them, and the information they might
consider relevant.[47] Social interactionists argue that interpersonal
exchanges shape group norms and constrain individual action—
that reality emerges out of interactions with others and becomes
rooted in a set of shared experiences.[48] But few sociologists have
considered how culture interacts with search engines, and how
returns from internet searches shape how twenty-first-century
reality is constituted.[49]

Every interaction between people and search engines yields
more data for tech companies to refine and modify their algorithms.[50] In the past, searches might have been conducted in the
library—a time set aside to "look something up." Today, however,
high-speed internet connectivity, mobile devices, and the internet
of things (often connected through voice services like Alexa) have
led search to become a part of everyday tasks.

A central part of search is related to what sociologist Erving
Goffman referred to as "frames," or the way people make sense
of the world around them.[51] One good example of framing is an
approach used by Karl Marx to shed light on the labor that is
involved in the making of material objects. Marx used the concept

of reification, or commodity fetishism, to unearth this labor, and further, to explain the inherent inequality of production.[52]

Eviatar Zerubavel, a renowned sociologist specializing in the sociology of everyday life, applied the same concept of reification to consider how what we consider to be "objective truths" are also created through a process of labor.[53] Specifically, Zerubavel explains how mechanisms used to create frames (religion, science, reason, universalism, and eternalism) allow humans to consider everyday norms as conventional or inevitable without recognizing the inequality behind those norms.[54] Zerubavel argues that the process of creating an objective reality is ultimately a socially constructed process. In addition to socialization, a person's relationship to power structures shape what Sandra Harding, an American philosopher of feminist theory and epistemology, refers to as one's standpoint.[55]

While these theorists were not postulating about search engines, keywords also define reality, shape belief systems, and influence truth. Take, for example, very basic claims about the color of the sky. Growing up in the United States, I learned at a very early age that the sky is blue. The notion of a blue sky, however, is context specific. As researchers have found, the ability to detect blue is largely determined by one's surrounding social structure and whether a community has a concept of blue.[56] Through content analysis of the Hebrew Bible and Homer's *Iliad*, these researchers found that since few blue things exist in nature, communities did not start to "see" the color blue until it was produced synthetically. In this way, the age-old saying about the sky being blue is not a scientific or universal truth; it is a socially constructed reality.

Algorithmic relevance is also predicated on a socially constructed reality. Search "the sky is blue" and returns include scientific websites that explain how the color of the sky is created by sunlight interacting with gas molecules.[57] Google image returns are nothing but a sea of blue-sky pictures.

Search "the sky is not blue," and returns include YouTube videos titled "The Sky IS NOT BLUE" or a public radio station explaining that the color of the sky is correlated with pollution levels and not a uniform color.[58] Search for something entirely different, like "the sky is red," and search engines will confirm that reality with a news story about how wildfires change the color of the sky to red or black, or a hyperlink for information about the meaning of the phrase "red sky at night, sailor's delight; red sky at morning, sailors take warning." Googling "the sky is green" returns links to sites where weather forecasters warn that the sky often turns green or yellow before a tornado.

These examples illustrate that users' worldviews and life circumstances are correlated with the kind of information that search engines deem relevant. Search engines are not built to challenge people's existing opinions; instead they are primarily advertising companies, tracking and selling users' behavior to other companies.[59] Part of the way that search engines become co-constructed is by creating profiles of people's online activity based on search history, browser history, email logs, social media profiles, and geolocation.[60] Understanding how preexisting beliefs influence keywords and how the syntax of search queries influences returns is essential for understanding the *sociological dimensions of search*—or how users interact with search technologies.[61]

Safiya Noble's *Algorithms of Oppression* describes the problematic nature of Google being deliberately opaque about its algorithms to protect its commercial interests and argues that data organization fortifies discriminatory beliefs.[62] Specifically, Noble considers how Google's algorithms are trained to match our ideological convictions, not challenge our mind or even inform us. Noble's research points to the manifesto of Dylann Roof, who allegedly searched the phrase "black on white crime" when doing his own research on the death of Trayvon Martin. While Roof might have thought that using this phrase for searching the internet was an objective way to "verify the facts" of that case, that search query exists inside an ideological vacuum. That is, by googling "black on white crime," Roof was able to easily connect to what sociologist Jessie Daniels refers to as cloaked websites, or sites that feign legitimacy to disguise their racism.[63] According to Roof's manifesto, the first website he saw was the Council of Conservative Citizens, which has been identified by the Southern Poverty Law Center as a hate group.[64] In this way, the search engine provided a gateway for Roof to shape his reality through the lens of white supremacy.

Noble also noted that the phrase "black on white crime" is a query coded in racist sentiment, for which the Council of Conservative Citizens was the most relevant result. Part of the blame for this top search return falls on Google, which tries to convince us that its results are ranked by popularity, trustworthiness, and credibility without acknowledging that its returns are heavily influenced by those willing to pay and take advantage of search engine optimization.[65] But part of the blame is also on Roof, who sought to defend the erroneous idea that Black people regularly commit crimes against white people.

The problem of how worldviews shape returns and expose viewers to extremism was recently discussed in a report from the Center for Technology and Society.[66] Researchers found that people who reported high levels of racial resentment were more likely to interact with hate speech produced by extremist and alternative channels. These findings indicate that YouTube plays an important role in exposing people to potentially harmful content, even though there is no clear evidence that YouTube algorithmically exposes people with neutral or mixed views to radical content. Rabbit holes of extremism are out there, but the path seems to start with a person's preexisting beliefs.

Politically coded language shapes search-engine feedback loops. For example, conservatives are more likely to speak about "freedoms" or "liberty," whereas progressives are more inclined to focus on "equality."[67] When these words are combined with other topical terms in search phrases, the information returned from Google becomes increasingly tailored to political interests. For example, "religious freedom" and "religious equality" return different perspectives. Returns for "religious freedom" link back to conservative Christian organizations, while returns for "religious equality" are more likely to connect seekers with organizations like the Equality and Human Rights Commission—a statutory body established by the Equality Act of 2006. These parallel experiences with internet search effectively keep information seekers in silos of their own making, thereby influencing how groups understand current events and their memories of the past.

An example of how this media practice plays out in real life is the conservative perspective on the separation of church and state versus the traditional understanding of it as "a wall of separation between the two." When I sat down with Tom to discuss this topic, he challenged me to "find the language of the law of the separation of church and state in the Constitution," arguing that the words were not there. After our interview, I hopped on Google myself, thinking about how Tom's invocation of "the words" holds historical significance, but also shaped his query. Would the phrase "wall of separation" return different information than the query "separation of church and state"?

Interestingly, when I conducted this search, both queries returned the same hyperlink (mtsu.edu), but "separation of church and state" also had a knowledge graph confirming that the phrase is a concept used for defining political distance in the relationship between religious organizations and the state. The query "wall of separation," by contrast, returned information that confirms Tom's argument—that it was from Jefferson's letter to the Baptists of Danbury and was about protecting the church from the state, not the other way around.

The controversy surrounding NFL players who took a knee during the national anthem is another case in point. During my fieldwork, President Trump got involved, tweeting on September 24, 2017, that the NFL ratings were "WAY DOWN," insinuating that the anthem protest was impacting ratings. In my 2018 Data & Society report, I note that audiences fact-checking Trump's claim with Google could find support for contradictory positions.[68] If one supported Trump's position and searched "NFL ratings down," Google returned a series of headlines, blog posts, and tweets confirming Trump's claims that the anthem protests had hurt ratings. But googling "NFL ratings up" returned entirely different results.

This phenomenon is not exclusive to the United States. For example, in a comparative study of returns procured by Google and Yandex, a Russian-owned search engine company, researchers showed how the search phrases "annexation of Crimea" and "incorporation of Crimea" produced sharply contrasting results. Since Russian officials and elites believe that Crimea was not "annexed" by the Russian Federation, the results for the query "incorporation of Crimea" feature more links to pro-regime, state-media websites, while the query "annexation of Crimea" yielded results dominated by independent media and nongovernmental websites of predominately Ukrainian and Belarusian origin.[69]

In short, queries are not created in a vacuum. Our everyday experiences and cultural histories influence which keywords we use for our internet searches, and in turn shape the kinds of information these searches offer.

SEARCH AND SCRIPTURAL INFERENCE

The practice of using Google to find more information on a topic of interest is by no means exclusive to conservatives in the United States, but how these results are interpreted is connected in profound ways to the hermeneutical method of close reading I term scriptural inference, as well as to ideological dialects.

Hannah details the connection between a reliance on Google and the practice of scriptural inference.

> I punch it in [to Google] and I'll see different articles and then I'll see also the tweets. I'll end up seeing all of the different media sites that have covered the story and then what happens is that they'll have the bar there with all the Twitter accounts that have mentioned this particular issue.

Since Google returns everything from news to YouTube videos to tweets, it can be easy to conflate opinions and punditry with investigative journalism, even though this is something my respondents insist they do not or would not do. Google's return structure creates an environment in which it seems like everyone is talking about the same thing with the same level of legitimacy, authenticity, credibility, ethics, and expertise.

The relationship between ideological dialects and keywords is how respondents like Sean can feel like the information that Google procured for him was "a consensus of what everybody else is trying to say about it." I asked him to elaborate on what he meant by "consensus," questioning if he thought Google presented him with all sides of an issue.

> I have no comment on that. I believe basically it works as a fact checker. I check a couple of those sites and see which ones; what similarities are they sharing together. I more click on the top ones because I know how Google works. It takes stuff that's really new and relevant and tries to put it on the top thing.

Search engines facilitate conservatives' ability to find original texts on which to practice scriptural inference. Keywords animate this process but are driven by ideological dialects. Moreover, although scriptural inference encourages conservatives to analyze original sources, the way that search engines return information is changing, blurring difference between searching for content and searching for documents.[70] Consider the example of Mount Everest; query its height, and your search returns will be in two forms:

- Indirect—links or references to a source where the answer can be found. For example, a link to the Mount Everest Wikipedia page; or
- Direct—the answer itself. For example, "The height of Mt. Everest is 29,002 ft."

Whereas Google started as only an intermediary, always directing users to third-party sites to seek out more information, today it provides direct, supposedly factual answers to user queries. Distorting the distinction between searching for content and searching for documentation further complicates the role of scriptural inference as a media practice. A politic unaware of the confirmation bias in their search returns is problematic, to be sure. But if Google itself seeks to answer user queries, and by extension to moderate narratives of truth and history, the tech giant will further complicate how information seeking, fact-checking, and scriptural inference are intertwined.

Another change by Google is relevant for the practice of scriptural inference: summarized search returns. In the Target and Toys for Tots case, for example, the link summaries told a different story than the full texts. This means that instead of simply giving information seekers a way to "dig in" to original texts, Google is itself offering content that can be analyzed as though it is the same as the original document.

In both of these situations, conservatives wary of the mainstream media who are on a quest for just the facts are now using as their arbiter of objectivity a multinational corporation that is spoon-feeding them—and the entire world—the answers they want to hear.

Since most of Google's revenue comes from selling information about its users to third-party businesses, it, like other search engine companies, has a financial interest in matching users with content it thinks they want to see. While this process of tailoring returns to users' needs and desires is a good business model, the algorithmic process that drives it can end up altering the ways that different groups understand current and historical events. In other words, search-engine companies like Google ultimately help to shape what we understand as truth. And as we will see, conservative users' trust in Google as a "calmer," "unbiased" source, one that they can use to "fact-check" claims made by the mainstream media, is particularly worrisome considering that search engine optimization allows individuals and companies to game the relevance, and thus the ranking, of their websites.[71]

STEP FIVE

SET THE TRAPS

So we know that keywords play an important role in fortifying filter bubbles, that ideological dialects influence search queries, and that these phrases shape the kind of information returned. We have also seen that conservative politicians and pundits play a central role in crafting these dialects, and that these wordsmithing tools come in handy as people increasingly turn to search engines to access news and information. But how do conservative elites manipulate the power of search?

THE POWER OF KEYWORDS

To make their content searchable, webpage owners reverse-engineer how algorithms intext information, then use metadata to optimize their content as relevant. Search engine optimization (SEO) is about influencing the rank of results. For decades, marketers relied on SEO techniques to maximize the likelihood that prominent search engines will point users to content that highlights their cause or company. In this way, they have encoded corporate interests into modern media operations.[1]

Information that fails to conform to dominant search engine rules can end up functionally invisible to the average user.[2] Google's pay-per-click campaigns are modeled around optimizing keywords for their search engines, and the tech giant offers an entire suite of paid Google Ad services for businesses. Its Keyword Planner provides clients with historical data on a search term, forecasts how those terms might perform for their ad goal, and helps them select the "right terms" to drive traffic to their site or store.

Web owners can even "buy keywords" so that seekers are automatically routed to the highest bidder. For example, Amazon once had an arrangement with Yahoo! that if a seeker submitted a search with the term "book" in it, an author's name, or a book title in the Amazon database, they would see the appropriate Amazon URL in their search result screen.[3] But because large companies are paying to manipulate metadata and redirect web traffic, information seekers are less likely to find sites operated by small businesses, nonprofits, or less media-savvy politicians with limited funds.

The practice of relevance spamming or tricking algorithms to return technically irrelevant content is more ethically complicated.[4] This kind of "ranking warfare" is a more nefarious form of SEO in which corporate actors or political operatives strategically manipulate webpage heuristics to include keywords unrelated to their content, or to encourage seekers to click on certain webpages to improve their rank.[5] These sorts of manipulations may explain why I received Corey Stewart's official campaign website when I searched for the name of his opponent, Ed Gillespie (see Step Four). Stewart's campaign probably used Gillespie's name in a font color invisible to readers but readable to the search engine algorithms that matched results to the keyword "Ed Gillespie."

Conservative elites engage in the same tactics. They leverage a niche understanding of SEO strategies and methodologies to maximize the exposure of conservative brands, causes, and content. Much like Marshall McLuhan writes in his influential 1964 book *Understanding Media,* conservative pundits and politicians understand that messaging is effective only if it leverages the intimacy of the technology at hand.[6] As I described in Step Two, prominent personalities within the right-wing information ecosystem understand the media technology du jour, and use that medium to cross-promote their ideas and serve as guests on one another's shows. Conservative thought leaders also signal-boost specific keywords and phrases in their ideological dialect to ensure that their message dominates users' search results. Digital marketers call this process "seeding"—distributing content across the web to increase brand awareness and turn viewers into customers.[7]

One way to better understand how content creators engage in ranking warfare is to analyze how they tag their content. Tagging content with metadata like keywords allows search algorithms to index websites in prescribed ways and helps determine relevance.

These tactics are typically invisible and inaccessible to users, but I used a script written by data scientist Leon Yin to analyze the metadata of videos uploaded to YouTube across eighteen different channels. This sample included ten conservative channels—Blessed2Teach, *The Daily Wire*, Fox News, Glenn Beck, *The Joe Rogan Experience*, Jordan Peterson, PragerU, Steven Crowder, The Red Elephants, and *The Rubin Report;* and eight progressive channels—*The Daily Kos, Democracy Now!,* HBomberguy, *The Majority Report,* MSNBC, Shaun, TBTV, and The Young Turks. These channels were selected because they have high levels of engagement; that is, large numbers of subscribers and many video views. Lin collected the data using the YouTube Data API created in Python Client and exported the metadata into a CSV file for my analysis. Lin collected all publicly listed videos for all given channels and pulled the data on June 10, 2019. The scrape consisted of video metadata (over 200,000 tags) for content uploaded from January 1, 2016, to June 10, 2019.

Analysis of this YouTube metadata sample demonstrates that the right-wing information ecosystem more actively engages in strategic tagging, using keywords outside of conservative ideological dialects to reach broader audiences. For example, conservative vlogger Steven Crowder is more likely to tag content on his channel with "liberal" or "left" than with "conservative" or "right." PragerU's channel tags more of its videos with "transgender" than with the more conservative phrase "free market."

The *Majority Report* (a progressive channel) tagged nearly half of its 8000+ videos with "feminism," but it was an outlier. The other progressive channels used the keyword on 1 percent or less of its content and produced far less videos in general. By comparison, PragerU tagged more than 8 percent of their videos with the keyword "feminism," followed by *The Rubin Report* (4.6 percent), Steven Crowder (4 percent), and *The Daily Wire* (2 percent). When *The Majority Report* is removed as an outlier, it means that during that time period, conservative content was about twice as likely to be tagged with the phrase "feminism" than progressive content (327 conservative videos vs. 145 progressive videos).

Of all the channels analyzed, Jordan Peterson's channel (conservative) was the most likely to tag content with "social justice." More than 17 percent of his videos are tagged with the keyword, and nearly a fourth are tagged with "social justice warrior/s." Sometimes the tags being used had nothing to do with the content of the video. For example, *The Daily Wire* uses the term "social justice" to tag a video where Ben Shapiro, Andrew Klavan, Michael Knowles, and Matt Walsh "take turns shutting down third wave *feminism* . . . one by one" (emphasis added). PragerU uses the keyword "feminism" for a video whose description reads "The Left is obsessed with *race* [emphasis added]. It gives them purpose. And it is harming society creating more problems, which also gives them . . . more purpose. Stop it." Looking at it proportionally, throughout the progressive stations, only 102 videos were tagged with the phrase "social justice" whereas 196 conservative videos were tagged with the phrase during the same period. So not only are conservative channels using progressive tags more frequently than progressive stations; they are also creating more content associated with that metadata.

These findings indicate that progressive channels are more likely to tag their content with keywords that best match progressive dialects. Data suggest that these channels' use of keywords is meant to facilitate informative search queries about topics they consider of interest to their viewers. By contrast, conservative channels deploy tags that help lead existing conservative audiences to their content, but they also use keywords to try to game search heuristics. This strategy is meant to make conservative content more widely read and accessible to those who do not necessarily speak their ideological dialect. A similar engagement strategy was recently documented by data reporter Corin Faife at *The Markup*. Using data from their Citizen Browser project, they found that *The Daily Wire* (a conservative outlet) better utilizes interest targeting and more frequently made use of "lookalike audiences" to try to improve the reach of their content.

Alongside advertising, strategic metadata also increases the likelihood that conservative videos will rank first when people search for keywords embedded in progressive subjects like social justice or feminism. Studying metadata in this way helps to explain why the top return for the phrase "social justice" on YouTube is frequently part of the right-wing information ecosystem. As I have routinely demonstrated with my research, PragerU, The Heritage Foundation, or Jordan Peterson are often considered the most relevant sources of information on progressive causes for this very reason.[8]

GAMING THE SYSTEM WITH UNIQUE TERMS

In addition to tagging their videos with phrases that are not part of conservative dialects, the right-wing information ecosystem also creates keywords associated with a specific topic or issue. John Rendon, a strategist for former president George W. Bush, argued that "the key to changing public opinion is finding different ways to say the same thing."[9] Using a similar technique as that used by legendary conservative rhetorician Frank Luntz, Rendon identified synonymous words and phrases that resonated better with the public in order to "gradually nudge a debate" in the direction that George W. Bush wanted.

Rendon also described how using linguistic manipulation could compromise the integrity of search inquiries:

> It begins with getting inside the algorithm. If you could find a way to load your content up so that only your content gets pulled by the stalking algorithm, then you'd have

a better chance of shaping belief sets. If one looked in the right places, they would be able to observe the algorithm shifting sentiment over time.[10]

Microsoft programmer Michael Golebiewski and internet scholar danah boyd coined the phrase *data void* to conceptualize this phenomenon. A data void exists when search queries have few results associated with them. These "voids" are ideal candidates for ideological manipulators because they don't require the programmer to bury much existing or potentially disconfirming content. In these situations, the "most relevant" information for a query connected to a data void is easy to replace with problematic content, which the authors define as low-quality, conspiratorial, extremist, hate-orientated, terroristic, graphic, or illicit material.

How media manipulators exploit data voids relates to the co-optation of existing phrases. One example is *crisis actor*. The term originally referred to people who played victims in simulated disaster-management and first-responder training exercises. Conspiracy theorists interested in protecting gun rights took over this term, painting the victims and families of victims of mass shootings across the United States as "crisis actors" and therefore as unreliable narrators. As mainstream journalists began learning about the term, largely from social media trolling of parents who had lost children in the mass shooting at Sandy Hook Elementary School in Connecticut, they unwittingly generated more attention and traffic. The more that news outlets used the term, and the more that users queried the phrase, the higher the conspiratorial content rose in the search rankings.[11]

A similar tactic was used to spread misinformation about the White Helmets, a volunteer humanitarian response group helping Syrian residents affected by rebel conflict starting in 2014.[12] After the White Helmets' efforts brought international attention to human suffering in Syria, they became the target of an online disinformation campaign to delegitimize them. This was primarily done by flooding Twitter and YouTube with false information, but the disinformation effort bled into search engine returns. At the time, a search for "White Helmets" returned overwhelmingly critical content meant to vilify the group and justify violence against them.[13]

Tagging content to best match a set of keywords already in circulation engages producers in difficult head-to-head competition against a critical mass of existing information. By contrast, *keyword curation* allows media manipulators to circumvent this competition, creating new concepts and phrases that can be used to divert attention away from media coverage that would otherwise damage their interests. These keywords gradually come to embody more than just the initial term and frequently refer back to the larger themes identified in Step Two (that the Left is dangerous and the media is biased). And because they understand how to very precisely tag the flood of information that ensues, future searches will return only the designated, and deliberately curated, results.

NELLIE OHR AND THE COLLUSION DELUSION

A quick political litmus test I used leading up to the 2020 presidential election was to ask people if they knew who Nellie Ohr was. Based on their response, I could accurately guess for whom they were voting. I will provide context for the readers who voted for Biden.

Nellie Ohr is an American woman in her mid-fifties who is married to Bruce Ohr, a Department of Justice (DOJ) official and a former independent contractor for FusionGPS. FusionGPS is a research and strategic intelligence firm based in Washington, DC, that offers "expertise in media, politics, regulation, national security, and global markets."[14] After Trump's electoral win, the Democratic National Committee hired FusionGPS to independently investigate if Trump's campaign interfered in the election. At the same time, FusionGPS subcontracted Christopher Steele's firm to compile the now notorious dossier. Since Nellie Ohr and Christopher Steele knew each other, and the Steele dossier was leaked, the right-wing information ecosystem created a keyword around Nellie Ohr to symbolize government distrust and try to absolve President Trump from any wrongdoing.

To be effective at spreading disinformation, keywords cannot exist in isolation. They must refer to a rational, verifiable, set of ideas.[15] It is true that Nellie Ohr worked at FusionGPS. The connection between Nellie Ohr and Steele was first made public when Representative Devin Nunes (R-CA) released a public memo questioning the legitimacy and legality of DOJ and Federal Bureau of Investigation (FBI) interactions with the Foreign Intelligence Surveillance Court. In the memo, it notes that before and after Steele was terminated as a source, he maintained contact with the DOJ via Bruce Ohr. The memo also notes that "Ohr's wife" was employed by FusionGPS to assist in the cultivation of opposition research on Trump.[16]

By late March 2017, when Attorney General William Barr asserted that the DOJ had not found any evidence to support claims of collusion between Russia and the Trump campaign, the web was already loaded with mostly legitimate content on FusionGPS, making returns associated with that keyword harder to manipulate. Before the right-wing information ecosystem could encourage audiences to dig in and "do their own research," they needed a data void to spread the rumor that the inquiry was part of a liberal coup seeking to remove Trump from office. Another key phrase created around the same time was "collusion delusion," a term coined by media mogul Roger Stone in May 2018 during a Fox News interview.

Conservative political strategists are not the only ones engaging in keyword curation. Progressive content producers can also take advantage of the mechanics of mediated information flow. For example, Tarleton Gillespie, a principal researcher at Microsoft Research, demonstrates how sex columnist and podcast host Dan Savage used similar processes to make his content "algorithmically recognizable."[17] In response to the inflammatory homophobic rhetoric of then–U.S. senator Rick Santorum (R-SC) during his 2004 campaign for the Republican presidential nomination, Savage successfully manipulated search returns to promote an explicit (and incorrect) definition of the former senator's last name.

Savage leveraged his media network and financial capital to pull off the stunt. His connections in podcasting, radio, and print allowed him to popularize a new definition of "santorum," one designed specifically to offend Santorum's anti-gay supporters. Savage tagged the splash page (santorum.com) with a series of keywords that would draw the attention of search engines' indexing function. He then encouraged his followers to Google "santorum" and click on his URL in order to promote his version of santorum in the rankings, a practice also known as "Google bombing."[18] The campaign worked; Savage and his followers unseated higher-ranked sites, including the senator's official website. Savage's search-engine optimization tactics were effective, and his new slang term spread like wildfire. Many years later googling "santorum" still returns evidence of Savage's efforts.

KEYWORD APPROPRIATION

The "santorum" example demonstrates that data-void exploitation is not exclusively the purview of conservative media manipulators, but this example should not imply equivalent scale and scope. For while keyword curation may appear equitable, and anyone technically possesses the ability to leverage keywords, language exists within a larger power structure. Discourse determines what speech patterns and dialects are acceptable, who has a right to speak, and whose words matter.[19] Keywords can empower groups if they resonate with target audiences, but keyword curation is predicated on the ability to hire communication and marketing strategists to perform this skilled labor. The entire operation, then, requires financial capital and a network to seed the concepts. In addition, for keywords to resonate, for discourse to "stick," actors need authority. They need power.

Power and language are deeply entangled. Groups already in power can suppress the language of subordinate groups seeking justice. For this reason, internet scholars must unpack how keywords are constituted and contested in order to understand how societal power affects the virality of keywords.

Social scientists have long studied the role and power of language through the lens of reappropriation.[20] Reappropriation refers to how a group reclaims a term, idea, or object that had been previously leveraged against it. For example, the LGBTQ+ community reappropriated the formerly pejorative term "queer" to signify pride.[21] Media manipulators, however, often appropriate concepts from groups seeking to enhance civil rights to try to dilute the meaning of phrases meant to empower. As my data demonstrate, conservative elites have repurposed contentious phrases like "Black Lives Matter," "sanctuary cities," "cancel culture," and "critical race theory" while incorrectly amplifying aspects of their ideologies. By appropriating keywords associated with progressive social movements, conservative pundits and politicians undermine the discourse of subordinate groups so that their key concepts hold less rhetorical weight. In doing so, conservative elites maintain and solidify existing power dynamics, exploiting anti-Black fears to mobilize their constituents.

Propagandists disempower subversive keywords by redirecting focus away from original ideas toward apolitical concepts. This rhetorical process, called "keyword appropriation," effectively co-opts keywords that challenge the existing power structure, neutralizing radical ideas to mean something they are not. Ultimately, keyword appropriation is a silencing tactic meant to maintain the ideological balance of power in favor of the privileged—those who, by definition, are already well-positioned to effectively mute or neutralize subversive expression. This process happens so often that our cultural lexicon is a proverbial linguistic graveyard of examples. As one scholar noted in a conference I attended, "This is how whiteness works."[22] Two examples unfolded while I was researching for this book: *Black Lives Matter* and *sanctuary cities*.

BLACK LIVES MATTER

After George Zimmerman was acquitted of murder, civil rights activist Alicia Garza took to Facebook to express her grief for the loss of Trayvon Martin, the young Black boy who was walking home after trying to buy a pack of Skittles when Zimmerman shot and killed him:

We don't deserve to be killed with impunity. We need to love ourselves and fight for a world where black lives matter. Black people, I love you. I love us. We matter. Our lives matter.

Moments later, fellow community organizers Opal Tometi and Patrisse Cullors sprang into action. Tometi created a website and Cullors launched the hashtag #BlackLivesMatter.[23]

Social media, especially Black Twitter, is central to the global and intersectional #BlackLivesMatter public awareness strategy. But almost as soon as #BlackLivesMatter gained trend-type traction in the United States and abroad, conservative media manipulators responded with the vehicle for their own keyword appropriation efforts: #AllLivesMatter. An analysis of Google Trends bears this out; #AllLivesMatter appeared as a searchable subject four months after #BlackLivesMatter did.

For those who are unfamiliar with Google Trends, it is an unbiased sample of the billions of queries that the search engine handles each day. The results can be viewed at any time, by anyone, at trends.google.com. Trends normalize search data to make comparisons easier. Each data point is divided by the number of total searches based on geographic location and time. The resulting numbers are then scaled on a range of zero (the minimum search interest for the time and location selected) to 100 (the maximum search interest), based on a topic's proportion to all searches on all topics. It is a powerful tool for understanding how people are reacting to specific moments. "Spikes" in a Google Trend graph document a dramatic increase around a specific keyword compared to usual search volume.

Understanding how and when the #AllLivesMatter hashtag surfaced accounts for its cultural significance. Like other forms of keyword appropriation, #AllLivesMatter claims inclusivity, but if the phrase were designed to foster equality it would have circulated before #BlackLivesMatter did, or at least simultaneously. Instead, it surfaced as a response, a tactic designed to strip the aspirational goals of #BlackLivesMatter and try to make it seem confrontational and exclusionary.

Since conservative elites coined #AllLivesMatter, they have worked to undermine #BlackLivesMatter even further with yet another keyword appropriation effort: #BlueLivesMatter. According to its now defunct website, the #BlueLivesMatter Organization seeks to "honor and recognize the actions of law enforcement, strengthen public support, and provide much-needed resources to law enforcement officials and their families."[24] The keyword also signals to one of the five f's—the armed forces. By blatantly appropriating the #BlackLivesMatter name, #BlueLivesMatter reframes key cases surrounding the success of the #BlackLives-Matter movement. For example, #BlueLivesMatter described the shooting death of Michael Brown and the subsequent response this way:

> On August 9[,] 2014, Ferguson PD Officer Darren Wilson was doing his job as he stopped Michael Brown, who had just committed a robbery of a local convenience store. Brown attacked Officer Wilson in an aggravated assault. Officer Wilson was forced to defend his life by shooting Brown. In the months that followed, agitators spread outright lies and distortions of the truth about Officer Wilson and all police officers. The media catered to movements such as Black Lives Matter, who's [sic] goal was the vilification of law enforcement. Criminals who rioted and victimized innocent citizens were further given legitimacy by the media as "protestors."[25]

Pro-police organizations co-opted the #BlackLivesMatter movement idea of lives that matter in order to reverse the message. Rather than emphasize the imperative to serve and protect Black bodies or shed light on the fact that Black Americans are more likely than any other group to be killed by the police, #AllLivesMatter and #BlueLivesMatter were launched after the rise of #BlackLivesMatter as a way to return dialogical authority to those already in power.[26] By portraying white people and police as *victims* in the fight for racial equity, these variations on the original hashtag help to absolve these groups from their responsibility in maintaining laws that discriminate.

The power of keyword appropriation is both far-reaching and consequential. In 2016, Louisiana passed a Blue Lives Matter law that automatically considers any attack against a law enforcement officer a hate crime. This effectively forces Louisiana state law to recognize police officers as a protected class, a designation previously reserved for groups that had experienced identity-based discrimination and needed an extra layer of legal protection from hateful and unequal wrongdoing. Louisiana's "Blue Lives Matter" law claims that police officers need additional protection, even though killing a police officer is already a capital felony, a federal crime punishable by death or life in prison without parole.

SANCTUARY CITIES

The term *sanctuary city* has existed in the public lexicon since the mid-1980s. A sanctuary city is "a city or police department that has passed a resolution or ordinance expressly forbidding a city or law enforcement officials from inquiring into individuals' immigration status."[27] Advocates for undocumented immigrants deliberately designed sanctuary cities to foster more open and trusting relationships between law enforcement and immigrant communities. These advocates wanted all citizens, regardless of the immigration status of themselves, relatives, coworkers, classmates, and neighbors, to feel safe calling 911 without fear of deportation. City officials who seek sanctuary status argue that it makes communities safer because it allows more community members to call for help in an emergency, report a crime, or cooperate in an investigation. Researchers have largely determined that sanctuary policies have no effect on crime rates, positive or negative.[28]

Despite the multi-decade history of sanctuary city policies, the keyword was not relevant in media ecosystems until it became a plank in the 2016 Republican Party platform. According to Google Trends data, people didn't start searching for the phrase "sanctuary city" until six months before the 2016 U.S. presidential race. Following Trump's 2016 election, the phrase was queried more frequently. After taking office, Trump threatened to cut federal funding for all sanctuary cities. The number of bills for or against sanctuary policies introduced into state legislatures shot up from 11 in 2016 to about 150 in 2017.

Conservative elites implied a relationship between sanctuary cities and crime, despite no evidence that any such relationship existed.[29] To make their point, Republicans rallied around the story (and data-void-turned-keyphrase) of Kathryn Steinle, a thirty-two-year-old San Francisco woman shot and killed by an "illegal immigrant." By amplifying the phrase "sanctuary city," conservatives shifted public discourse away from human rights toward law and order. Sanctuary cities were created to protect immigrants, refugees, and asylees as keystone leaders in a global community, but conservative elites co-opted the keyword to portray undocumented immigrants as criminals, as people from whom "Americans" need protection.

Conservatives also appropriated what a "sanctuary" is and who it is meant for, shifting the focus away from immigrants and toward those who embody the five f's. There are now "Second Amendment sanctuaries" meant to protect gun owners and "sanctuary cities for the unborn" created by pro-life activists. Co-opting phrases and ideas that already hold cultural significance is different from creating a keyword in isolation. To take over and overwrite mottos that historically disenfranchised people created to elevate their own narratives is to engage in a type of data exploitation.

STRATEGIC SIGNALING

Research on disinformation shows how media influencers use shared practices and routines to spread propaganda.[30] In order to draw attention to a specific idea, person, or phrase, conservative pundits and politicians use a technique called *strategic signaling* to boost the influence of their keywords, helping make them more visible above the sea of information available online. One way that conservative politicians do this is to amplify unsubstantiated claims from conspiracy theorists and tie them back to bits of credible information in order to bolster their legitimacy.

Take again the example of Nellie Ohr, a keyword curated by conservative groups to assert that the federal investigation into Trump's alleged collusion with Russia to win the 2016 election was a hoax. This signal was repeatedly used to divert negative attention from Trump. Based on Google Trends data, conservative propagandists used Nellie Ohr's name to fill a data void. The phrase was so infrequently searched that it had a score of zero prior to December 2017.

The first step in this keyword curation endeavor was to seed the internet, generating multiple digital-first stories about the connection between Nellie Ohr, FusionGPS, and Christopher Steele across multiple platforms. It all began with QAnon, an anonymous, far-right social movement that claims to have insider information on the government. It was one of the first organizations to post suspicions about Nellie Ohr's role in the conservative-nicknamed collusion delusion in their regular updates on Reddit and Twitter. In December 2017, QAnon circulated an unverified allegation that Nellie Ohr had applied for a ham radio license a month after FusionGPS hired Christopher Steele.

On its own, Nellie's name would have fizzled out on search engines without sustained focus. To keep people searching the name Nellie Ohr, and to ensure that those searches kept returning the same conservative narrative, the right-wing information ecosystem kept repeating Nellie Ohr's name in its headlines, TV copy, and content. Much like other forms of propaganda, this included simply copying and pasting content from other websites.[31] This practice signaled to the search engines that this content was a relevant match for anyone searching for her name. By hyperlinking stories together, it also boosted the number of "inbound links" to the websites spreading misinformation about Ohr. This networking effect signals legitimacy to search algorithms.

It was not until stories about Nellie Ohr surfaced on *The Daily Caller* and *The Federalist* that people started to search for the phrase "Nellie Ohr." According to Google Trends, interest in her first peaked in February 2018, the same month that various outlets in the right-wing information ecosystem wrote about her supposed connection to Steele. *The Daily Caller* released an investigation insinuating that FusionGPS was trying to buy access to the DOJ by paying an "official's wife" (that is, Nellie Ohr). The National Legal and Policy Center, a conservative nonprofit focused on reducing the size of government, cross-posted this article to their website.

A few weeks later, on March 2, 2018, *The Federalist* expanded on its Ohr fixation by publishing another article—this one on her ability to speak Russian, her doctoral studies in Russian history, and her decision to obtain a technical-level amateur radio license in May of 2016. The story claimed that Ohr's ability to operate a ham radio is significant because it allowed her to collect information against Trump "under the radar," and cited as evidence the "Nunes Memo," a memorandum that Congressman Devin Nunes had released on January 18, 2018.

This feedback loop tying together network news, search engines, and politicians was also fully activated for the phrase "collusion delusion," which conservatives used to undermine the idea that Trump had teamed with Russia to win the 2016 U.S. presidential election. To signal-boost the phrase, Fox tweeted "collusion delusion" the same day that Roger Stone was interviewed. It was an effective SEO tactic. There were so many searches for the term that Google started to autocomplete searches for the phrase "Russia collusion" with the term "delusion."[32] For over a year, returns for the manufactured keywords were almost exclusively conservative content supporting the perspective that the allegations against Trump were unsubstantiated. The phrase was a conservative silo of information until March 2019, when Trump announced that the "collusion delusion" was over and publications like the *New York Times* began reporting on the phrase.

Strategic signaling is not just web-based, however. Algorithmic signals ensure that search engines match queries, but if conservative elites want their audiences to search for specific keywords, they must repeat those keywords throughout the ecosystem. When politicians publicly interrogate American citizens on the premise of conspiracy theories, for example, or when cable TV hosts interview guests to discuss such theories, they publicly signal their legitimacy. That is, simply elevating keywords meant to capture conspiracies promotes enhanced public discourse and intrigue. It becomes what people are talking about and encourages them to seek out more information on the subject.

In this way, strategic signaling is a two-part process. One part takes place behind the veils of the Google algorithm using search engine optimization. The other part takes place offline, relying on traditional media outlets like radio and newspapers, as well as a network of like-minded public officials, to boost the credibility of the misinformation and suggest the public "do their own research" on certain keywords and phrases.

THE SOUND OF SILENCE

The independent press enshrined in the Constitution's First Amendment is considered by many to play an essential role in checking and balancing the power of an executive presidency, a bicameral Congress, and a tiered judicial system. Many journalists, including editors and producers, take this commitment to public service seriously and manage their coverage in different ways to reduce social harm.

Nonetheless, stories inevitably fall through the cracks at the local, national, and global levels. Sometimes political or commercial agendas dictate exclusion or censorship, and sometimes this oversight is unintentional. Even if no ill-will is meant, decisions about which stories to print and to air are made by people who live and work in cultural systems that have long silenced the experiences of historically marginalized groups. And silence can cause harm because mainstream media narratives and images actively construct public ideas about information, credibility, and values.

Media coverage of any given topic cues audiences as to who the heroes, villains, and victims are, and therefore whom to empathize with or demonize. During the Civil War, for example, colonial newspapers refused to publish news, columns, or letters that supported abolition or the rights of enslaved people.[33] It was not until the Civil Rights Movement began to gain momentum that mainstream journalists began covering rallies and marches.[34]

Media silence also serves those with economic power.[35] During the Great Depression, for example, newspapers largely ignored the socioeconomic effects on the average person in the United States to run headlines that promoted economic confidence and a national rebound. The deliberate use of strategic silence to repress historically marginalized voices remains a serious issue. Systemic anti-Black racism and white supremacy still govern legal decisions, schooling, and many other aspects of everyday life for Black Americans, but the mainstream press rarely covers these experiences or phenomena. When white girls and women go missing or are exploited, the news coverage is much greater than when the same tragedies befall girls and women of color.[36] Failure to document the loss of poor, nonwhite, and precariously employed non-men only reifies their deaths as natural, inevitable, and inconsequential to society.

Nonetheless, strategic silence can also serve as a public good. Known in newsrooms as quarantines or embargoes, editors and producers purposefully avoid engaging with certain topics to avoid fanning the flames of hate speech or conspiracy theories.[37] To avoid attracting more attention to the KKK, for instance, mainstream media stopped covering the media stunts of the white nationalist hate group.[38] Scholars, journalists, and media experts use a similar approach when deciding how to cover suicide.[39] In an effort to discourage copycat suicides, the World Health Organization has released a set of guidelines that include avoiding sensationalistic language, explicit description of the method used in the attempt, details about the physical site, and front-page or repeat coverage.

The other end of the silence spectrum is strategic amplification or signal-boosting.[40] While far-right media have unquestionably brought visibility to neo-Nazi propaganda, mainstream journalists, too, ultimately have given bigotry a larger platform because they felt obligated to cover "both sides" of the issue. For this reason, researchers of this phenomenon have been urging journalists to pay closer attention to the coverage they grant extremist groups. As we have seen, extremists often engage in coordinated media manipulation attacks, and journalists should be wary not to fall into rhetorical booby traps.

One such trap is the antiquated notion of "balanced" news coverage.[41] As discussed in Step Two, conservatives' reframing of the meaning of "objective" to "equal coverage for both sides" was one of their earliest successful strategies for shaping media coverage. In efforts to appear fair and objective, journalists at mainstream media outlets inadvertently set false equivalencies when they give the same respect and airtime to, for example, hate group leaders as they do to their victims. This is not a hypothetical or distant memory; this happened in 2017, when journalists thought there was ethical value to sharing "both sides" of the Unite the Right rally in Charlottesville, Virginia. Audiences bore witness as the mainstream news media balanced the views of white supremacists in ways that made them seem equal to those of leaders of faith communities, and when they presented neo-Nazi talking points as valid counter-arguments to calls for equality and justice.[42] Mainstream coverage also created an illusion of the "alt-right," conflating disparate personalities, groups, and motivations in a single term, while failing to engage with the much more powerful keyword "neo-Nazi."[43]

Coverage of what happened in Charlottesville in August 2017 also perpetuated the idea of racism or a racist as an isolated, horrifying single person or event, rather than explaining how these people and events are symptomatic of endemic oppression and worthy of in-depth investigative reporting. The coverage thus elevated and normalized white supremacy in mainstream media discourse. But the damage didn't end there. When media ecosystems elevate problematic content without proper context, the likelihood that search engines will return misinformation, conspiracy theories, and other low-quality content skyrockets. For example, Hillary Clinton's reference to the alt-right inadvertently drew attention to movement leaders like Richard Spencer, which, in turn, allowed him to promote white nationalist values to mainstream media audiences.[44]

At the same time, journalist caution can also leave the door open for misleading content to spread unchecked. For example, when right-wing politicians and pundits, Trump included, began circulating the name of the alleged whistleblower involved in the Trump-Ukraine scandal, mainstream media refused to publish the person's name. This well-intended effort to follow the law and maintain journalistic integrity left open the opportunity for the right-wing information ecosystem to game the data void: even today, internet searches for the alleged whistleblower's name send users to misleading information.

WHO IS THE WHISTLEBLOWER?

Type "who is" into Google's home page and autocomplete can give you an idea of which sociopolitical issues, music, and public figures are trending. Trends are a way of thinking about what is on the top of people's minds at that moment. The most consistent of these queries is about wealth (who is the richest person in the world?), but the top suggestions usually tap into the zeitgeist more directly (who is playing in the Super Bowl, who is Miss Universe, who is the pope, who is the Mandalorian, who is Hamas?).

Studying the nuanced shifts in Google's autocomplete suggestions can provide context, even texture, to what's going on in the world. These automated suggestions can also provide a window into misinformation campaigns, which draw on the power of ideological dialects to game search engine optimization.

At the close of 2019 and into early 2020, Google's, Bing's, and DuckDuckGo's top autocomplete suggestion for "who is" was "the whistleblower." This question was top of public mind when Donald Trump Jr., first tweeted out a protected civil servant's identity on November 6, 2019, and it continued to remain relevant through January 2020, as Trump's first impeachment hearings were getting under way. That "the whistleblower" was a top autocomplete suggestion, and for a sustained period, signaled to search engines that the alleged identity of "the whistleblower" was the most relevant search at the time for people starting with the query "who is." So many people were querying to find out the alleged whistleblower's identity that search engines ranked it above queries about the Super Bowl and the new Star Wars movie.

In addition to autocompleting "who is" with "the whistleblower," Google, Bing, and DuckDuckGo all autocompleted the alleged whistleblower's full name after just a few keystrokes. This means that during a five-month period, the name of a person who may have had absolutely nothing to do with the legal whistleblowing process or any media leaks came to symbolize key villains in the right-wing information ecosystem (that is, the Dangerous Left and the Dishonest Media mythologies detailed in Step Two). Because ethical standards prevented other media ecosystems from ever mentioning this person's name, the name itself transformed into a highly effective keyword that led conservative information seekers to misleading websites and problematic content.

Keyword curation efforts around the whistleblower's name began in October 2019, when RealClearInvestigations reported the identity of a government worker who allegedly fit the rough description of the whistleblower. The report went on to accuse the suspected whistleblower as vendetta-driven, claiming that he or she was an opponent of Trump's foreign policy and a believer in the "Putin fired Comey" narrative. The piece also accused House Democrats of blocking their Republican peers from asking questions about the alleged whistleblower, and of intending to redact the alleged whistleblower's identity from all deposition transcripts. Using the RealClearInvestigations' piece as evidence, conservative politicians and pundits started to repeat the identity of the whistleblower and create keywords around that name while simultaneously increasing the number of inbound links to the original RealClearInvestigations article.

Identifying the whistleblower plays well within familiar conservative narratives. It frames the Left as emotionally driven (the whistleblower only came forward because they disagreed with Trump's policy decisions) and the media as biased (only conservative outlets will report the name). Shortly following the RealClearInvestigations publication, *The Daily Caller* published two stories supporting the release of the alleged whistleblower's name. Both of these pieces insinuated that knowing the name was important for understanding how political bias had motivated that person.

Trump Jr. spread the conspiracy further, when he tweeted the alleged whistleblower's name in order to disseminate it beyond the right-wing information ecosystem. Engaging in the unethical practice of revealing private information over the internet is referred to as doxing. The article he tweeted repeatedly used the alleged whistleblower's full name throughout the body of the article and even featured the name in the headline. According to the Whistleblower Protection Act of 2012, disclosing the name of a federal employee who speaks out against government fraud, waste, or abuse is prohibited. While it is unclear if this law applies to journalists, mainstream reporters did not publish any stories around this person's supposed identity, and Trump Jr.'s government role at the time means that his tweet may have indeed violated the act.

The following day, Candace Owens tweeted a photograph of the alleged whistleblower with a hashtag of the person's name and the following text:

> Please do not retweet this photo of the scam-whistleblower. [They] [do] not want [their] name or picture to go viral so please, whatever you do, do not hit the retweet button. Thank you in advance.

Within fifty seconds, it had been retweeted 633 times, a flurry of Twitter handles associated with the person's identity began cropping up, and the hashtag of the alleged whistleblower's full name began to trend.

After the U.S. House of Representatives impeached then-president Trump for the first time in January 2020, Trump stood trial before the U.S. Senate for abuse of power and obstruction of Congress. During this trial, the alleged whistleblower's name-as-keyword began to circulate again.

In late January, Senator Rand Paul (R-KY) read the alleged whistleblower's full name on the Senate floor, then exhorted presiding judge Chief Justice Roberts to repeat the name aloud. (Roberts declined.) Senator Paul next took to Twitter and the airwaves to defend his comment. During later interviews with the press core, he claimed that his question was not about "the whistleblower," but then proceeded to read his original question to the press using the alleged whistleblower's full name. By persistently focusing on the identity of the alleged whistleblower, the right-wing information ecosystem successfully created a steady, merciless drumbeat of distracting information designed to downplay the allegations of Trump's misconduct being investigated by Congress.

Herein lies the tension between strategic signaling and strategic silence. Mainstream journalists refused to publish the whistleblower's identity in order to protect citizen privacy, preserve public safety, and prevent incendiary content. By choosing not to print the unsubstantiated claim, mainstream media upheld their journalistic standards. Yet in doing so, the right-wing information ecosystem was able to manipulate the wide-open data void. This practice of exploiting professional cautiousness is a common practice of propagandists.[45] Since little to no information about the whistleblower existed before the disinformation campaign began, that person's name is now a keyword that will send internet searchers to specifically curated content on Breitbart, *The Daily Caller,* the *Washington Examiner,* and *The Federalist.* My own search using this name as a keyword brought up a trove of conservative opinions and conspiratorial speculations. Google Image searches returned photographs of the alleged whistleblower shaking hands with top Democratic officials. Clicking on those photographs led to personally identifiable information about the alleged whistleblower alongside unsubstantiated claims implicating them in the alleged conspiracy to take down Trump.

None of this was accidental. My analysis of YouTube metadata revealed that *The Michael Knowles Show,* produced by *The Daily Wire,* tagged its content with the alleged whistleblower's name (see episodes 442 and 451). By contrast, no progressive websites included the alleged whistleblower's name in their metadata during that timeframe.

SCRIPTURAL INFERENCE TO DENY CULPABILITY

Although the right-wing information ecosystem created a keyword out of the alleged name of a person who may have had nothing to do with the allegations that led to Trump's first impeachment, they tried to claim that the Left was the reason behind the violation of the

Whistleblower Act. To support this argument, key figures inside the right-wing information ecosystem used *scriptural inference* (a deep reading of texts deemed sacred) to deflect any blame associated with doxing a potentially innocent and certainly defenseless ordinary person. The argument wielded by conservatives was that Representative Adam Schiff (D-CA), in a hurry to unlawfully impeach the president, did not adequately redact the memos he shared with the public. That it was *his* fault the alleged name was released.

On November 6, 2019, the *Washington Examiner* published a story alleging that the name of the whistleblower had been raised by a Republican investigator when he questioned the former American ambassador to Ukraine, William B. Taylor Jr. On the November 7, 2019, episode of his radio show, Rush Limbaugh read a few sentences of the transcript of a closed-door session of the House Permanent Select Committee on Intelligence. The transcript was of Chairman and Representative Schiff questioning Dr. Fiona Hill in her capacity as the former senior director for European and Russian Affairs on the National Security Council (NSC) and as a former deputy assistant to Trump. Limbaugh claimed that the alleged whistleblower's name surfaced during the testimony and called out Representative Schiff: if the chairman had really wanted to keep this person's identity private, Limbaugh said, he should have been smarter about redaction.[46]

The next day, the *Washington Examiner* claimed that the alleged whistleblower's name had been redacted from the testimony of Alexander Vindman, the former Director for European Affairs for the National Security Council (NSC) and a retired, decorated Army Lieutenant Colonel, but not from the testimony of former Ambassador Taylor. On November 10, 2019, *The Federalist* used the same practice, publishing a line-by-line copy of the transcript of the House Permanent Select Committee on Intelligence questioning of William Taylor, "proving" that since the name of the supposed whistleblower was redacted in some documents but not others, the accusations by the right-wing information system were accurate and releasing the name was justified. A closer examination of the transcripts, however, reveals that only conservative representatives use the name in their line of questioning. Using scriptural inference as a tool, the right-wing information ecosystem used official transcripts to support their own allegations and deny any role in doxing an American citizen.

Conservatism as a media practice involves distrusting others' interpretations of media narratives and instead studying the words of original texts to understand the world. The problem is that conservative content creators are circumventing search practices to control the messages that are returned to those searching for information. By leveraging the power of data voids, for example, conservative elites can steer their audiences toward media coverage designed to best match their political interests. Keyword curation and strategic signaling, too, take advantage of how search engine algorithms work to ensure that curated conservative content will dominate search returns.

These multifarious rhetorical strategies to control the public narrative and public access to information advance conservative narratives on two key fronts: (1) they enable conservative media manipulators to galvanize voters' beliefs and behaviors, and (2) they divert public attention from news coverage that damages conservative interests. Together these tactics, which are designed to mislead, not only contribute to an increasingly bifurcated and partisan media environment; they also elevate sources that misinform the public.

STEP SIX

MAKE OLD IDEAS SEEM NEW

L everaging keywords for search engine optimization, or even
for messaging more generally, is not inherently nefarious.
Corporations continually create and adapt keywords to differen-
tiate their products and services. The right-wing information
ecosystem, however, relies on the interconnectedness of the internet, and techniques such as *keyword curation* and *strategic
signaling*, to methodically and habitually amplify extremist concepts that in the past have justified human rights atrocities. This
strategy is extremely effective because it leverages the original
architecture of the world wide web—connecting websites within
the conservative information network via hyperlinks.[1]

YouTube is a video-sharing platform that has become a powerful cultural force, with over a quarter of Americans now getting
their news there.[2] While this may lead to a more informed public,
it also increases the reach of YouTube personalities spouting dangerous rhetoric. White supremacists, for example, have built on
YouTube what researchers refer to as an "alternative influence
network" that exposes mainstream audiences to extreme ideology.[3]
When extremists appear as guests, they introduce or reinforce extremist ideas and keywords, which conservative mainstream pundits
then promote. This cross-promotion extends the reach of white-
supremacist thinkers, validates their logic, and introduces "information pollution" into the mainstream conservative environment.[4]

Much of the content rebranded by twenty-first-century extremists as new is rooted in decades-old propaganda efforts. By posting their content on YouTube, media influencers can breathe new life into defunct concepts, while quickly and seamlessly connecting conservative voters to extremist content.[5] In this way, the public is reintroduced to harmful concepts used throughout history to justify the denigration of human beings—including but hardly limited to anti-Black racism, anti-Semitism, xenophobia, sexism, and homophobia—and this destructive messaging comes to them in their personal spaces, on laptops, smartphones, and other devices. Leveraging mainstream outlets to normalize extremist ideas is also not a new strategy. The messages put out by white supremacist publishing houses, independent newspapers, and local radio programs have been picked up by mainstream media, which have normalized their extremist rhetoric and blended it seamlessly into modern American (white) culture, rebranding it as patriotic, law-abiding, and "pure Americanism."[6]

Blurring the boundaries of mainstream conservatism by normalizing extremist ideas has serious consequences for the public's understanding of civil rights and racial equity. It normalizes mass-criminalization efforts and widespread incarceration of Black persons and minimizes threats to overthrow the government of the United States.[7] My data demonstrate that the white supremacist ideas amplified by the right-wing information ecosystem were repeated by the people I studied, fostering the practice of "othering" by extremist groups.

In my analysis, I draw on a sociological definition of extremism that includes messages or symbols that promote xenophobia through the valorization of violence, whiteness, Nazi ideology, and colonial history.[8] My analysis specifically focuses on two white supremacist tropes:

1. Race realism: a rebranding of eugenics, a long-debunked theory that the Caucasian man is biologically superior to all nonwhite humans. This myth, which was used to justify slavery, discriminatory housing policies, and unequal drug enforcement, is still in circulation today.[9]

2. White shift (also known as white decline or white genocide): the use of demographic data to argue that whiteness and Christianity are declining and in need of protection.

The normalization of extremist rhetoric is a grave worry given the persistent, lethal threat that white supremacists pose to the United States. According to the FBI, this group is responsible for more fatalities than any other domestic terrorist organization.[10]

WHITE SUPREMACY IN THE UNITED STATES

White supremacism in the United States is primarily an anti-Black racial project, but it is also linked to religious, ethnic, and sexual discrimination.[11] There is no denying that the wealth and freedom afforded by the colonization of the Americas was made possible because enslaved workers harvested cotton, the most valuable export of the early United States. The Smithsonian Institution, many prestigious universities, the White House, the Capitol—all institutions and buildings that represent symbols of freedom in the United States—were built with slave labor.

As slavery became less acceptable over time, white supremacists recast the Civil War as a defense of traditions and genetic superiority.[12] They framed Southerners as victims under attack when the federal government deployed troops to the South because of resistance to integration.[13]

Since the founding of the United States, politicians, intellectuals, lawmakers, and wealthy Americans have used race realism and white decline to create policies that protect Western ideals and religion.[14] The fear that whiteness can be spoiled or overtaken serves as the cornerstone of oppression. Race realism and white decline have been both legally codified, in legislation like anti-miscegenation laws, and socially codified, like in the one-drop rule.[15] The current white supremacist project is to repurpose this content and make antiquated ideas seem trendy and innovative.

"BUT I'M NOT A RACIST!"

Classifying white supremacy only through the lens of extremism can be dangerous. Doing so undermines the ways that white supremacy is embedded in our social and informational systems, making it easier for those who benefit from the status quo to feel comfortable continuing to be part of the problem and stalling efforts to make reparations. If Americans conceive of white supremacy as only an individual or pathological problem, we won't feel responsible for our role in systemic racism and may not work together to abolish it.[16]

Clearly not everyone who identifies as a conservative is "a racist." And progressives are also culpable in the perpetuation of white supremacy. Self-identified liberal whites may reject racism, but they still benefit from white privilege. What my data demonstrate, however, is that the right-wing information ecosystem recycles white supremacist ideology by relying on new personalities and different-sounding talking points, and that these techniques effectively bring extremism to mainstream American media markets. Such rhetorical distancing reintroduces the public to harmful ideas, legitimizes and normalizes extremist concepts, yet absolves conservative pundits and politicians of responsibility.

This revelation will no doubt be met with hostility. Many conservative elites fundamentally deny that their collaboration, cooperation, or coordination with extremist thinkers serves as an endorsement of white supremacist ideals. They often justify hosting a white supremacist on their show as simply being open to different ideas or engaging in free speech. Careful content analysis, however, reveals that conservative hosts and guests regularly use coded language to allude to white supremacist ideas about racial superiority and racial fear. And ethnographic analysis shows just how widespread the appeal and adoption of these techniques are.

More important, the themes I document through content analysis and ethnography align with extremist rhetorical strategies.[17] White supremacists frame nonwhite, non-Christian "others" through a lens of perceived subjugation. "Others" are a threat to their own existence. They are perceived as culturally and genetically inferior and are often the focus of blame during periods of distress. For example, during economic turmoil, extremist groups might use language that faults "others" for "stealing" jobs, "flooding" the country, or "overrunning" an economy. These "others" are also perceived as a cultural threat, capable of eroding white supremacists' sense of national identity or religious customs. Extremist groups often use the language of an "awakening" or "renewal" to foster a sense of belonging among those who now realize that "others" are to blame for their economic, social, or cultural loss.[18]

Why conservative elites *choose* to affiliate themselves with extremists is not answerable with my dataset. My analysis only details that conservative pundits and politicians do indeed amplify and normalize extremist rhetoric or symbols that reflect an idealized community based on racial, ethnic, linguistic, or religious criteria.[19] In doing so, the right-wing information ecosystem recycles old themes of race realism and white decline in ways that perpetuate the white racial mindset.[20] In order to counteract this extremist propaganda, we need to understand how what Whitney Phillips and Ryan Milner call "polluted information" spreads, as well as its short- and long-term effects.[21]

OH, WHAT A TANGLED WEB YOUTUBE WEAVES

In 2019, Kevin Roose, internet reporter for the *New York Times,* wrote an interactive account of how a liberal college dropout got sucked into a vortex of far-right politics on YouTube.[22] Roose's account of radicalization focused on the content consumed by one user, but I found a similar pattern in the media I was immersed in for this project. Through systematic content analysis, this chapter documents how reactionary YouTubers espouse outdated claims via the right-wing information ecosystem as though they are new ideas. My findings are meant to hold accountable those media producers who knowingly amplify the message of white supremacists and to educate those media producers who may be unwittingly letting extremists gain visibility and attention through their media platforms.[23]

EUGENICS

In the early 2000s, Stanford University geneticists offered the most advanced scientific proof to date that the groups Americans refer to as "races" do not have distinct genetic identities.[24] By looking at the distribution of thousands of alleles across seven geographic regions, they found that most gene variants are shared over multiple regions: fewer than 8 percent of the alleles were specific to one region and fewer than 1 percent of people from within that region were genetically distinct from one another. One year later, Craig Venter successfully mapped the human genome, finding that 99.9 percent of human genetic makeup is identical across individuals.[25] For comparison, fruit flies have ten times more genetic diversity than humans.[26]

In other words, race is not a genetic phenomenon.

This finding fits with what sociologists have long argued: that racial markers are not inherent or endogenous but are, instead, socially constructed stereotypes meant to justify inequalities.[27] The creation of racial categories is about grouping people and bestowing power and privilege based on perceived characteristics. Think about it this way: if race were genetic, racial categories would not change over time, and neither would individuals' feelings about racial identity.[28] Yet such shifts in our thinking about race have long been a part of the American experience.

Despite this wealth of research by geneticists and sociologists, myths about IQ and genetic superiority continue to circulate as "proof" that genetic differences between racial groups are natural and inevitable. These myths rationalize racial inequities and play into the white-supremacist narrative, which claims that white people deserve more privileges because nonwhite people are intellectually inferior.

One of the most outspoken of these figures is Stefan Molyneux, a self-described libertarian classified by the Southern Poverty Law Center as a white supremacist extremist. In 2005, Molyneux started his own podcast, *Freedomain Radio*. His show streamed on his self-titled YouTube channel, which had over 900,000 followers, until it was banned by the company in January 2020.[29]

Despite YouTube's decision to ban the incendiary figure, Molyneux can maintain his influence by appearing on other shows in the alternative influence network.[30] As a guest on *The Rubin Report*, for example, Molyneux exposed audiences to radical, and radicalized, thinking. In that episode (still available on YouTube as of June 2021), Molyneux used the Bell Curve as "evidence" of a hierarchical ranking of intelligence by race, and claimed that the brains of Black and white men are "different sizes." (The term comes from the 1994 book *The Bell Curve*, which controversially and inaccurately promotes racial reasons for variations in intelligence across the U.S. population.)[31] He has made similar claims during appearances on *The Joe Rogan Experience*, in two episodes that are still available on Spotify.[32]

The Bell Curve and its concepts are rooted in psychometrics, an alleged subfield of social science that differentiates and hierarchically ranks people according to how they perform on a timed test of academic problems (that is, an IQ test). Since the book was published, a plethora of established psychologists, sociologists, and evolutionary biologists have spoken out against the validity and reliability of the IQ test for measuring intelligence because the exam demands specialized test skills with little real-life relevance and because it fails to account for test-takers' contexts.[33] Claiming race realism as scientific truth only validates racist and debunked claims that the minds of Black people are inferior and the minds of Jewish people are superior.

Trying to "sort" racial groups by genetic inferiority or superiority is part of the same disinformation campaign eugenicists and politicians have long used to maintain segregation, ensure wealth gaps, illegally detain immigrants, and restrict human rights.[34] Starting in the early twentieth century, IQ testing was used in the United States as part of a program to sterilize "genetically inferior" Black people without their consent.[35] The U.S. Supreme Court upheld these eugenics procedures in the 1927 case *Buck v. Bell*, when it struck down the case of Carrie Buck, a Black woman fighting for her right to reproduce. In its remarks, the Court elevated eugenic prejudices to constitutional status, proclaiming, "It is better for all the world, if instead of waiting to

A historical marker in the city of Charlottesville, Virginia, honoring the memory of Carrie Buck

execute degenerate offspring for crime, or to let them starve for their imbecility, society can prevent those who are manifestly unfit from continuing their kind . . . Three generations of imbeciles are enough."[36] After striking down her case, the State of Virginia mandated the sterilization of over eight thousand additional Black women before parts of the original law were repealed in 1974. Since the law was never officially overturned, parents and guardians have used the same precedent to sterilize individuals living with developmental disabilities without their consent.[37] Eugenics policies such as these were the inspiration for Nazi laws and were publicly endorsed by the American Eugenics Society in 1933.[38]

Molyneux is not the only one to promote the eugenic mindset as an explanation for racial disparities. In 2017, clinical psychologist and tenured University of Toronto professor Jordan Peterson appeared on Molyneux's podcast for an episode entitled "An Antidote to Chaos" to argue that racial disparities are natural and just. Despite Molyneux being banned, clips from this episode continue to circulate widely on YouTube under other channels: see, for example, "IQ and Race: Jordan Peterson and Stefan Molyneux" posted by Aerial View or "The IQ Problem: Jordan Peterson & Stefan Molyneux" posted by Geordi Corgione. In the episode, Molyneux and Peterson discussed the "ugly truths" of science, claiming that IQ and cognitive performance are fully biological and racially predisposed, despite overwhelming genetic evidence that these ideas of racial superiority are false.[39]

Personalities like Peterson use the same script to support anti-Semitic conspiracy theories. In the same segment, Peterson explained to Molyneux the IQ point advantage that Ashkenazi Jews allegedly have over "the rest of the Caucasian population," which in his view explains their "radical overrepresentation in positions of authority and influence and productivity." While Peterson claims that this overrepresentation is not a "bad thing," his statement that there "is a real reason for it that no one wants to contend with" gives weight to white supremacist conspiracy theories that Jewish people dominate the media system, the political system, and the economic system.

As Eric K. Ward, a civil rights strategist and former Ford Foundation program officer writes, "Anti-Semitism forms the theoretical core of white nationalism." Ward explains how the success of the Civil Rights Movement was inconceivable to white supremacists who believed that Black Americans were genetically inferior. In Ward's words, white supremacists promote the idea that "a diabolical evil must control television, banking, entertainment, education, and even Washington, D.C.[,] . . . brainwashing white people, rendering them racially unconscious." White supremacists selected Jews as the evil racialized "other" driving white dispossession.[40]

This same logic is in place today. As noted throughout this book, conservative elites often claim that George Soros, a Hungarian-born billionaire of Jewish descent who has donated a significant amount of his wealth to the Open Society Foundation, is the mastermind behind civil rights protests like Black Lives Matter.

Peterson also claims that IQ differences are the reason that "40% of Google's workforce is East Asian." Akin to the argument espoused by former Google employee James Damore, who was fired for circulating a memo that attributed gender and racial disparities in tech to biological differences, and that wielded eugenics arguments as "fact." Tying inherent, genetic superiority to employment outcomes helped Damore find a sympathetic ear on Peterson's and Molyneux's shows. Since Google fired Damore for it, it also supported the argument that Big Tech, a supposed arm of the mainstream media, is biased and silences conservatism.

Damore also starred in PragerU's Five Minute Video "What Happens When Google Disagrees with You?," in which he claims that he was fired for saying men and women are different and that famous evolutionary psychologists have verified his genetics-based claims. At the end of the video, Damore pivots, arguing that Google's decision to fire him based on "facts" made sense because the organization "already manipulates its products to fit a certain viewpoint." To support this argument, Damore points to Google's decision to classify some PragerU videos as not suitable for children.

The conservative fringes were not the only ones to validate Damore's use of the Bell Curve as "real science." The *Wall Street Journal* published an opinion piece by Damore in which he argued that he had been fired for raising questions about how cultural taboos cloud thoughts about gender diversity in the tech sector.

A few weeks later, Tucker Carlson hosted Damore on his show, claiming that Damore's arguments were rooted in science, when much of what Damore espoused was in fact an essentialist and outdated understanding of IQ difference. Google did not fire Damore because of his claim that men and women are biologically different; Google fired Damore because he attempted to draw on scientific claims used to normalize eugenics.

When Fox News hosted Damore, he used the same arguments he had made on Molyneux's podcast—legitimizing the Bell Curve as "fact-based evidence." But although, as he claims, IQ scores use scientific metrics, these measures only hold scientific meaning within the paradigm of psychometrics. When Molyneux asserts that "if there is no such thing as a valid IQ test, then there is no such thing as social science at all," he is spreading disinformation. Psychometrics does not *embody* all social scientific research; instead the Bell Curve has been widely *refuted* by biologists, geneticists, sociologists, psychologists, and philosophers.

WHITE AND WESTERN DECLINE

The Bell Curve also claims that "dumber" (which the authors define as nonwhite) people have more children than smarter people do, a phenomenon that white supremacists refer to as "dysgenesis."[41] Molyneux and other guests on Freedom Radio readily promote this argument, to sow fear that Christianity and whiteness are declining.

For example, Molyneux interviewed Candace Owens while she was the communications director and spokesperson for Turning Point USA, a conservative organization. At the beginning of the interview, Molyneux and Owens mostly engaged in what sociologists Karell and Freedman refer to as radicalism of reversion, a moralizing frame built on intimacy and immediacy.[42] To create this frame, Molyneux and Owens promote the idea that they live on a higher moral plane than everyone else, and that villainized "others" bring down society and erode morality.

On the episode, Owens describes how conservatives are "better people" than liberals. She claims that this is because conservatives believe in Christian principles and read the Bible, while leftists' principles of equality come at the cost of civilization. To back these claims, Owens draws on demographic data:

> MOLYNEUX: It's kinda weird so you can get this kind of equality but it comes at the cost of your entire civilization because if you're going to aim for this kind of equality, birth-rates drop and when birth-rates drop, quite interestingly you kinda run out of people very quickly and then you have to, you feel like you have to bring in all these people from the third world, but it's like oh, ok, we've got more equality but we're kinda out of people and that's it for us and our civilization.
>
> OWENS: That's true, I mean that's what's going on in Europe right now, the birth rate at 1.3 and they're not going to make a comeback. France will be a Muslim majority country by 2040, probably sooner, 2040 is putting it nicely. I looked at all the stats, and it's terrifying. You know the birth rate in France is 8.1 for Muslims and 1.3 for French people. They've got more mosques than churches in the south of France. They are completely giving up their culture. And listen, that is also because of the pro-liberation of the welfare state over there as well. And all of these ideas, this cultural Marxism that has seeped via our universities into our minds and our brains. Not me.

What is particularly interesting here is that Candace Owens is a Black woman. Her use of white supremacist logic—Muslims "overrunning" France is "terrifying"—demonstrates how conservatives make special efforts to reach out to Christian Blacks along denominational lines, obscuring the racism embedded in the logic. In reality, however, this "color-blind" gospel is about making Black and other ethnic groups conform to whiteness and accept white Christian leadership as the religious and social norm.[43]

When Molyneux interviewed Dennis Prager, the two pundits also found common ground in their belief that Western and Christian civilization is superior. Their conversation further explored the correlation between their moral superiority and a perceived cultural decline that they link to changing religious demographics. Prager claimed that the only winners right now are "fundamentalist Islamist" terrorists. Prager's evidence that "they [Islamist terrorists] are winning in Europe" was that "there are far more mosques being built than churches," and that "mosques are being built at the same rate churches are being closed." Since new mosque construction is on the rise in Europe and new church construction is not, Prager is "not optimistic" about the survival of "Western civilization."[44] Prager's use of the phrase "civilized" harkens back to a colonial mindset, where only the white male was fully human compared to the "uncivilized" nonwhite figure.[45]

Often demographic "data" are used out of context to "prove" that Western civilization and whiteness are in jeopardy. As Adam Serwer, a political writer for the *Atlantic* and fellow at the Shorenstein Center on Media, Politics, and Public Policy at Harvard demonstrates in his most recent work, the false doctrine of race suicide originated in the early twentieth-century United States. This allegedly data-driven crisis was propelled by the 1916 book by Madison Grant called *The Passing of the Great Race*, which "went on to become Adolf Hitler's 'Bible.' " New editions of Grant's works include introductions by white nationalist Richard Spencer and are available for sale on Walmart.com for less than fourteen dollars and Target.com for around sixteen dollars.[46] Similar ideas were also propagated by French author Renaud Camus in his 2012 book *The Great Replacement,* an alarmist novel claiming that white (that is, native) Europeans are being reverse-colonized by Black and brown immigrants.[47] This focus on birthrates and fears of replacement were heard during my ethnographic observations at the Unite the Right rally and were central to the manifesto released by the New Zealand terrorist who killed fifty people in a mosque in 2019.[48]

But the fears of a global white decline articulated on Molyneux's show and repeated on *The Joe Rogan Experience* or *The Rubin Report* have not stayed confined to YouTube. Concepts like white decline, white genocide, or cultural displacement have reverberated throughout the right-wing information ecosystem, finding their way into the mouths of Fox News pundits and Republican politicians. On a late summer evening in 2018, Laura Ingraham opened *The Ingraham Angle* with a focus on "The Left's Effort to Remake America." In her opening monologue, Ingraham claimed that "the America we know and love doesn't seem to exist anymore" in some parts of the country.

> Massive demographic changes have been foisted upon the American people and they are changes that none of us ever voted for and most of us don't like. From Virginia to California[,] we see stark examples of how radically in some ways the country has changed. Now much of this is related to both illegal and in some cases legal immigration which, of course, progressives love.

As Ingraham spoke, video of dark-skinned men scaling fences played behind her on a loop. Ingraham explained that a rise in both legal and illegal immigration is exactly what "socialists like [Alexandria] Ocasio-Cortez want" and that over time, this influx of "others" (whom Ingraham frames as murderers and rapists) will "remake and reshape America . . . eventually diluting and overwhelming your vote." Much like Grant, Prager, Owens, or Molyneux, Ingraham claims that immigrants will be the decline of "our society" since "they aren't too big on Adam Smith and the Federalist Papers."

Former KKK grand wizard David Duke wrote in a now-deleted tweet that Ingraham's monologue was one of the most important and truthful in the history of the mainstream media. The next day, Ingraham opened *The Ingraham Angle* with a new claim: that her views had been distorted by people including "all white nationalists and especially one racist freak whose name I will not even mention."[49] Ingraham claimed that her comments "had nothing to do with race or ethnicity" but rather reflected on how border security was once a shared goal between Republicans and Democrats.

Ingraham distanced herself from white nationalists in general and David Duke in theory, but she did not walk back any of her comments from the previous evening. In so doing, she further legitimized fears by reemphasizing her original claim that an influx of illegal immigrants will make America unsafe.[50] By not apologizing for her comments, and asserting that her ideas were dissimilar to those held by "freaks" like David Duke, she strategically positions the fear that immigrants will reshape America and dilute votes as somehow different than white supremacy. Yet her assertions in her August 8, 2018, opening monologue were not all that dissimilar to the chants of "You will not replace us!" that I heard during my fieldwork in Charlottesville a year earlier.

Similar statements have been made by Iowa Republican Congressman Steve King, first elected to the House in 2003. King has publicly stated that he does not see anything wrong with claiming white superiority when "Western civilization" is better. In a tweet posted on March 12, 2017, Representative King wrote that "we can't restore our civilization with somebody else's babies."[51]

In the lead-up to the 2020 election, Madison Cawthorn, the young Republican congressman who won the seat for North Carolina's 11th district, evoked the same racialized narrative to disparage immigration. During an interview on *The Charlie Kirk Show* on July 19, 2020, Cawthorn argued that the United States should stop all immigration processes during COVID-19. His rationale for this position was first and foremost that "we'll lose our national identity."

WHITE SUPREMACIST SYMBOLS AND KEYWORDS

A central aspect of belonging is rooted in symbolic significance, a concept Emile Durkheim developed in the early 1900s to explain how religious groups formed a collective consciousness.[52] Durkheim contended that sacred objects follow a binary logic: something can be either good or bad, rational or irrational. But the sacred is defined by what it is not—profane.

Durkheim also theorized that objects hold less power if someone in the group bestows its symbolic significance. If the community gives a symbol meaning, it seems biased or less authoritative. Recent scholarship on extremist symbolism, however, suggests otherwise.[53] Studies show that extremist symbology is often sui generis (Latin for "of its own" meaning). Moreover, members forge belonging through these meaning-making processes. In other words, extremist groups create symbols, determine their real or secret meanings as part of an initiation process, then use these symbols together.

For the faith communities that Durkheim observed, symbols' meanings remained static. But extremist groups deliberately design ambiguous and evolving symbols and ways of talking about them.[54] In other words, the meanings of successful symbols are context dependent. They could mean something else to someone outside of the group and the ambiguity of coded iconography allows extremist group members to "get the joke." This strategy maximizes exposure while maintaining plausible deniability and avoiding legal consequences.[55]

Symbolic ambiguity is critical to extremists' efforts to infiltrate mainstream culture. If extremist symbology is too explicit, it becomes vulnerable to censorship. Ambiguous symbology, however, allows extremism to spread more widely because the content seems innocuous to mainstream media and law enforcement. When the mainstream media covers memetic extremism or uses extremist keywords, this becomes part of the joke for extremists.[56]

Conservative elites engage in similar ambiguity when they interview white supremacists, promote their books/shows/podcasts, and repeat their keywords. They may not explicitly agree with what they say, but they also fail to counter extremists' claims, amplifying and normalizing race realism, white decline, and extremist symbols. The use of ambiguous symbols also makes it more difficult to scrub platforms of hate speech. While de-platforming or demonetizing content can effectively curtail the spread of extremism, ideas and references end up sprinkled across channels and platforms, making effective censorship an impossible game of whack-a-mole.

For example, when Damore appeared on *The Rubin Report* on September 7, 2017, to critique liberal intolerance and reassert that his views were based on scientific evidence, host Dave Rubin opted to read aloud an audience question littered with neo-Nazi language and references. Rubin smiled and suppressed a laugh when he posed the listener's question to Damore: would he "join the people of Kekistan to create an algorithmic weapon to surpass Metal Gear?"

"I guess I would," Damore responded, laughing with Rubin.

The reference to Metal Gear, the titular superweapon of the long-running video game, appeals to extremist gamers.[57] "Kekistan" is a dog whistle reference to a fictional country that 4chan/pol users made up to symbolize the origin of "s**tposters." Certain white nationalists also discuss an ironic belief in a "Kek deity," and I encountered multiple "Kekistan" flags during my ethnographic observations of the 2017 Unite the Right rally in Charlottesville, Virginia.

Yes, these two adult men—alleged thought leaders, experts, and professionals in their niches—giggled about mainstreaming extremism. Rubin signaled approval of white supremacy when he read the extremist listener's question aloud. He used the listener's words, not his own, to showcase extremist language, cultural references, and ideas, and he laughed the whole thing off to neutralize the extreme nature of the listener's question. This deliberate process, which might otherwise appear to be a pair of pundits making fun of a fringe listener, ultimately serves to normalize white supremacist content on their programs.

Jordan Peterson used the same dismissive stance to spread hate symbols after he was pictured with a Pepe the Frog flag and a supporter wearing a Make America Great Again (MAGA) hat. In his rationale, Peterson said that he thought Kek was "silly" but finds the mythos surrounding Pepe fascinating. By saying this, Peterson shrugged off any personal culpability, dismissed the symbol as pejorative, while also winking to the crowd, letting them know that he is indeed "in" on the joke with them. "It's satire," Peterson has said. "A lot of these things are weird jokes."[58]

Candace Owens takes a different approach, making frequent and flippant use of the extremist keyword phrase "red pill." In addition to branding herself as Red Pill Black, Owens repeatedly claims that any association between red-pilling and white supremacist logic is leftist propaganda. When Candace Owens appeared on Fox's *Watters' World,* the network relied on Owens's interpretation of the term to promote the content on Facebook. In a post by Fox News on September 24, 2017, the network writes, "On 'Watters' World,' Candace Owens talked about 'taking the red pill' and leaving liberalism for conservatism." Four years later (September 24, 2021) the post had over 29,000 likes and 1,400 comments, and it has been shared more than 4,000 times.[59] Alongside the post is a link to another story published by Fox News on September 13, 2017, titled "Liberals sick of the alt-left are taking 'the red pill.' " In the opinion piece, the author repeatedly links back to Owens's YouTube videos that claim that she "took the red pill" herself, and that this embrace of true conservatism "awakened" her to what was really wrong with liberals.[60]

Let's be clear: white supremacist media outlets (such as The Right Stuff and *Radix Journal*) devote entire sections of their websites to red-pilling. Extremists use the metaphor to describe being reborn into racist and anti-feminist thought. And users of the extremist thread 4chan/pol/ frequently argue that being truly red-pilled requires embracing other, even more fundamentalist beliefs, including:

- that feminism is just one symptom of a much bigger problem: of men losing wealth and power, and
- that white males have been subjected to a broader campaign of diminishment and soon there will be nothing left for them.

When Owens or Rubin openly and frequently suggest that liberals disillusioned by the Left take the red pill, they are signaling to white supremacist logic. Regardless of whether these media personalities do or do not know what red-pilling is, or are intentionally promoting an inaccurate message, these rhetorical tactics suggest that audiences do their own research on the subject.

Using keywords in this way also has the power to shape search engine results (Step Five). If one were interested in learning more about red-pilling after seeing Owens on *Watters' World* or reading Ames's opinion piece on Fox News, the returns confirm a distorted reality. Search "what is the red pill" and the top return is a Google Dictionary entry reference to "a process by which a person's perspective is dramatically transformed." But a more simplistic search—"the red pill"—brings up an infographic on the documentary *The Red Pill*. Produced by American director Cassie Jaye, the film advances a sympathetic depiction of men's rights activists.

The film is also mentioned in Ames's "educational" op-ed of why conservatives take "the red pill," as an accurate portrayal of the men's rights movement that was trolled by radical feminists and "largely ignored by most of the mainstream media."

The guest appearances are not innocuous, and neither are the channels that actively engage in white supremacist rhetoric. While conservative influencers like Candace Owens, Joe Rogan, Dave Rubin, and Fox News may appear to distance themselves from extremism, their cross-promotion with extremist guests and embedded content forges algorithmic connections. When Dennis Prager is a guest on Stefan Molyneux's show or Fox News hyperlinks to Laci Green's content, it connects Molyneux and Green to the broader PragerU/Fox News network, enabling white supremacist data pollution to impact YouTube's algorithms and therefore the platform's "Up Next" feature. These connections also influence the recommendation algorithms that give suggestions on what viewers should watch next. Such connections are the building blocks of the web's interconnected ecosystem of information.[61]

One can easily see the impact this has on platform recommendation systems. Before Molyneux was de-platformed in June 2020, YouTube created a list of "featured channels" to the right of Molyneux's content. The top three featured channels were well-known political extremists and conspiracy theorists like Paul Joseph Watson, Mike Cernovich, and Lauren Southern. Directly below them were personalities like Candace Owens, Jordan Peterson, and Steven Crowder. Owens, Peterson, and Crowder have all created PragerU videos and made appearances on Fox News, spreading the reach of Molyneux's ideas even further. By connecting with a wide range of hosts from extreme to mainstream, Molyneux's content can link across platforms—with smaller sound bites shared on social media and in hashtags. As a result, white supremacist logic like race realism and white decline, coupled with keywords like red-pilling, have become commonplace in supposedly moderate or mainstream programming.

Like the dirty waters of a river churning after a storm, lessons about IQ hierarchy, and the myth of white genocide, contaminate less-extremist views, like the importance of the electoral college or why meritocracy matters.[62] Mixing and remixing as short clips and memes, these ideas spread across the country's smartphones, tablets, and laptops. In this way, white supremacist talking points of the past become future rhetorical strategies, arming conservatives with the rationale necessary to vote conspiracy theorists into office.[63]

FREEDOM UNDER FIRE: ETHNOGRAPHY IN ACTION

Many of those in my study articulated a belief in white victimhood, or the fear that America is headed in the "wrong" direction. They were thus in favor of anti-immigration and anti-refugee policies that they believed protected the United States from perceived threats.

Juliette, a prominent figure in the Republican women's group whose family donates large sums of money to politicians and university sports teams, claims that she's not necessarily for or against hot-button issues like abortion:

> I believe in freedoms, and I believe in the Constitution, and I believe in family, and I believe in marriage. All of those things that are threatened severely in society right now. We are right on the precipice of just ruining ourselves. I think we're in trouble.

Other respondents described their ideals as being "threatened" or their freedoms as "under attack." Michael, a contractor in his mid-fifties, expressed a concern that he or his wife could not be openly conservative without fear of reprisal.

> Well, she'll tell me, and she tells me to shut up, don't say anything. So, I feel restrained. She might fear for her employment.

When I asked Michael, Juliette, and others who articulated a need to hide their conservatism why they felt fearful, they described tensions around the 2016 presidential election. Nearly everyone I spoke with described how their discomfort with public perceptions prevented them from putting a Trump campaign sign in their yard.

When I asked Trish, an active member of the women's Republican group, if Democrats had the same fears of reprisal, she interrupted, her hand out, shaking her head. "I'm sorry, I just didn't
see any news that was showing how the other side had their signs
stolen, or lit on fire, or the different forms of vandalism that were
occurring," she said. "I didn't see anything coming out about that."

Given the consistency with which people described a "silencing of conservatism," I asked them to specify why they felt that
conservatism was under attack. Among the responses, two central
issues emerged: the removal of Confederate monuments and the
rise of immigration.

THE REMOVAL OF CONFEDERATE MONUMENTS

After Dylann Roof opened fire on July 10, 2015, at a predominantly
Black church in Charleston, South Carolina, killing nine members
of the congregation, many government buildings in the state
decided to retire the Confederate flags they had been flying from
official state flagpoles until that day.[64] Cities nationwide, too, in
addition to taking down Confederate flags, raised serious questions about statues and other monuments celebrating Confederate
leaders in their communities.

Historians note that states and other private organizations,
notably the Daughters of the Confederacy, commissioned the
majority of Confederate monuments long after the secessionists'
defeat, during the Jim Crow and Civil Rights eras, in order to
demarcate legally segregated, white-only spaces.[65] Confederate
statuary was meant to celebrate white supremacy, commemorate
its late military leaders, and underline its continued power in the
Jim Crow South (though some memorials appear north of the
Mason-Dixon line as well).[66] The symbol was frequently part of
anti-integration messaging and Confederate flags were regularly
flown at rallies associated with upholding segregation.[67]

Many conservatives, however, argue that removing Confederate statues is a liberal effort to "erase" a cherished part of Southern
heritage. Preserving Confederate statues was central to Republican
Corey Stewart's platform in the 2017 Virginia governor's race, and

after the more moderate Ed Gillespie narrowly beat Stewart in the primary, he, too, started to include Confederate statue preservation in his stump speeches.

Gillespie first addressed the issue at an annual barbeque hosted by one of the state's congressional representatives. Hundreds of people made their way down winding back roads to a large exposition center. Country music played, constituents mingled over sweet tea, and volunteers set up long tables loaded with Southern classics like coleslaw, baked beans, pulled pork, and potato salad. After "the prayer and the Pledge," politicians addressed their constituents. One after the other, they reiterated their support for Trump and indicated a need for the state to elect a new governor, one who would work with Trump toward conservative goals.

When it was Gillespie's turn, he assured the audience that he would work with Trump to ensure that Virginia would continue to be "the northernmost southern state," not "the southernmost northern state." Rhetorically positioning Virginia as part of the South enabled Gillespie to support Confederate statues under the narrative guise of historical preservation.

> Virginia has always been at the forefront of history. Now we've not always been on the right side of it, but we need to learn from this and teach from it, we need to keep up our monuments! Now, my opponent wants to take them down!

At this point, a woman at the end of my table audibly gasped. Other attendees started shouting "No!" Gillespie smiled and shook his head. "I'm not gonna let that happen," he assured fearful conservatives. "We will keep them up."

Gillespie's casual, cultural reassurance asserted his commitment to keeping Confederate statues intact, but also invoked "us versus them" language framing conservatism as under attack, a common extremist theme.[68] It also alludes to cultural displacement and white decline.

The idea that Confederate statues are critical reminders of history and a way to ensure that "mistakes aren't repeated" became a central talking point for my respondents after the city of Charlottesville voted to remove statues of Generals Robert E. Lee and

Thomas "Stonewall" Jackson from two public squares. Michael, for example, was clearly frustrated when we discussed the city council decision—"a total bunch of crap" verdict, according to him. Michael echoed Gillespie's stump speech when he warned me:

> Those who don't read history are doomed to repeat it. I feel like those, you can call them memorials or monuments, are there to remind you of the sacrifices that were made on both sides. I get tired of the argument that they're there to memorialize the generals who supported slavery. It's not what all the Civil War was about. It was the states felt like there was too much federal control over their politics.

Michael's states' rights claim is another important one to note. It furthers the Lost Cause narrative that the Confederates' goals were just and heroic because they were fighting for self-governance, as opposed to oppressive and exploitive because they were fighting to maintain and expand slavery. As historians have noted, concepts like these were created by segregationists looking to circumvent the Civil Rights Act.[69]

Conservative op-eds, stump speeches, and social media posts repeatedly claimed that removing Confederate monuments would not only erase history, but also waste taxpayer money, to the tune of an estimated $3 million. Some speculated that removing the statues from Monument Avenue in Richmond, the state capital, would hurt tourism and therefore business and tax revenues. Others expressed the slippery slope concern that once the state had removed the Confederate statues, pressure to remove other statues and memorials would follow, and things would get out of hand.

A college student was the first to broach this topic with me. "It's a very slippery slope to be going down," she told me, if "we just remove a statue just because it disagrees with something that someone values." Like Gillespie, this respondent used the hyperbolic "we" to both indicate a collective concern and situate "others" as people against conservatism more broadly. Moreover, she failed to contextualize what supporters "value" in keeping up the marker.

The slippery slope narrative showed up in my interviews, in focus group conversations, and during my ethnographic observations. Respondents repeatedly expressed concern about "what would be next" if the Confederate monuments were re-moved. In one interview, a woman (incorrectly) informed me that "they were going to rename Monticello and stop giving tours because Jefferson was a slaveholder." During a casual conversation before a rally, a group of women worried about Mount Rushmore, because some of the presidents carved into the mountainside had enslaved people.

Some conservatives interpreted the public focus on Confeder-ate statuary as a liberal-manufactured "smear tactic" to focus voter attention on the fact that "our founding fathers and every-body was a slave owner." Though conservatives prefer to focus on the aspects of their Confederate heritage that are associated with the preservation of political freedom, the ultimate conservative ideal, that narrative fails to account for the fact that freedom is relative. As Cain Hope Felder explains:

> Political freedom from Europe meant dominance over native Americans, who were partially exterminated, de-prived of their ancient lands, and confined to Indian reservations or offered halting opportunities to assimilate into the American mainstream. A similar pattern is evi-dent in the history of Central and South America, where the descendants of the Spanish and Portuguese presented equivalent options to the indigenous aboriginal peoples. Freedom in the Americas has also meant the enslavement, socioeconomic deprivation, incarceration of and/or "equal opportunities" for Blacks.[70]

Conservatives, my respondents included, recognize this on some level when they refer to "our" freedom. "Us" or "our" means white, Christian persons born in the United States after 1776.

IMMIGRATION AND ASSIMILATION

At the same rally during which Gillespie promised to protect Con-federate statues if elected governor of Virginia, he also promised, to thunderous applause, to support Trump's line on immigration:

Now, we are all immigrants. Our country is a country of immigrants. But we are also a nation of laws. We must defend our country and protect our borders! We cannot support sanctuary cities. If someone commits a crime and is here illegally, we need to work with law enforcement. I will sign a bill that banishes the idea of sanctuary cities. We will also crack down on gang violence and MS-13!

Focusing on an international criminal gang as representative of why immigration is problematic exemplifies how conservative propagandists rhetorically tie concepts of safety to both whiteness and Christianity.

This gang name "MS-13" is also a dog whistle, signaling that politicians like Gillespie or Trump are "in the know" about the "problems" of immigration and reinforcing racist tropes that Latinos are criminals.[71] Gillespie's use of MS-13 and my respondents' ideological alignment with Trump's anti-immigration rhetoric reflects a "deep story" that immigrants are dangerous.[72] Trump himself underlined this explicitly when he said on June 16, 2015: "When Mexico sends its people, they're not sending their best . . . They're bringing drugs. They're bringing crime. They're rapists."[73]

The use of MS-13 creates an image of a criminal immigrant without having to tell the whole story.[74] Despite Fox News coverage portraying MS-13 as starting in El Salvador and migrating to the United States, it has been documented that Mara Salvatrucha-13 began as a gang in Los Angeles and "migrated back" after members were deported to Central America as part of Bill Clinton's crime policies.[75] This racist rhetoric that immigrants are criminals helped Trump increase spending on border security, including billions of dollars for a fence between Mexico and the United States. Trump's administration also enabled Immigration and Customs Enforcement (ICE) to partner with local law enforcement all over the country. Unsurprisingly, these partnerships are often associated with arrest, detainment, and exportation practices characterized by racial profiling and violations of constitutional rights.[76]

In addition to a fear of immigrants—illegal and otherwise—and their perceived gang connections, my respondents also reported support for the "Muslim ban" because they felt it would crack down on ISIS entering the country. During my interview with a college student couple, both respondents expressed support for Trump's decision. The boyfriend answered first:

> I feel like we need to watch who we bring into the country. It's great that we want to be more open to people that are suffering from hardships like war, famine, natural disasters such as people from Islamic countries and people from Spanish countries [*sic*], it's great that we want to be open to them, but we need to make sure that these people that we're bringing in, some of them, they can't be very nice people, what if they're terrorists from drug cartels or even from groups such as ISIS? We don't want that.

The girlfriend was quick to agree.

> We have to be careful because if you look at everything that's happened over the year, with terrorists coming in and out of America, I think that's something we have to be more close and careful about than ever.

Islamophobia also framed how conservatives interpreted the sight of a woman or girl wearing a hijab. Their fear was about more than just ISIS; my respondents interpreted hijabs as a signal that Muslims were not willing to "assimilate" into American culture.

In hushed tones, one woman told me about an anti-assimilationist sighting in her neighborhood—a family who all wore "you know"—she swirled her finger around her head. In a separate interview another woman praised Melania Trump for not "conforming" to Saudi Arabian cultural norms: she had refused to wear "a head scarf" on a state trip. Respondents regularly shared information on Facebook from ACT! For America, a U.S.-based organization combating what it describes as "the threat of radical Islam" to the safety of Americans and to democracy.

"When I say these stories out loud," a third woman confided to me, "they label me as Islamophobic. Well, I'm not Islamophobic or whatever you want to call it because phobia is an irrational fear."

The assimilation imperative goes hand-in-hand with calls to limit immigration over fears of white decline. Respondents in my study were concerned about letting in "too many immigrants" that might be a threat to "their" country's way of life. Despite studies that indicate most immigrants tend to assimilate to the dominant culture to avoid ostracization, conservatives frame immigrants who do not assimilate as a threat to "American" culture.[77]

At an anti-immigration rally I attended, speakers voiced concerns that the city was "spending too much" on "too many immigrants," putting "too much pressure" on public facilities. Similar to arguments surrounding integration, public was code for white—when public facilities were "overrun" with too many nonwhite residents it became a cause for concern.[78] When I asked one respondent if the immigration debate was all about resources, they shook their head.

> It's also about protecting the city from being overrun to the degree that we lose our culture and we cease becoming who we are.

They gestured to a nearby ethnic restaurant storefront and continued:

> I'm fine with the culture assimilating to a degree, a variety of peoples, but primarily those peoples who are going to be able to assimilate into our culture and not change our culture to something that it wasn't. Every civilization has the right to protect its borders, to protect its culture. Angela Merkel had just opened up the borders in Germany and just millions of people who do not assimilate into that culture are overrunning that culture.

Others in my study also explicitly categorized racialized differences between themselves and "others." According to many of these respondents, racialized others need to change to be more American. Praising assimilation is wrapped up with the idea of whiteness being under attack. Immigrants who did not assimilate contributed to white decline. Focusing on the removal of the Confederate statues also served as a literal focus on what they perceived to be white diminishment. Likewise, policies outlined at the rallies I attended focused on welfare and immigration reforms laced with racial overtones. While these policies were often framed around economic concerns, such as a drain on public resources, the underlying fear was of cultural displacement.

The belief that the United States "has always" been white and Christian completely erases the Native experience. This is just one example of what Charles Mills refers to as "white ignorance," because it implies that the Native American culture (which existed prior to colonization) was not real.[79] This ideological frame is predicated on the understanding that whites are superior and other cultures are savage.[80] This shared perspective among my respondents is based on misinformation that the United States is naturally white.

The "prayer and the Pledge" ritual, a cornerstone of conservative belonging, repeatedly reaffirms this whiteness (Step One). Those out of place with reciting a Christian prayer or unfamiliar with norms around the Pledge of Allegiance (hat off, right hand over heart) were immediately recognized as outsiders and became easy to reject.

There is a strong link between disinformation and hate; disinformation can contribute to radicalization by strengthening resentment and rewarding outrage.[81] The scale and scope of extremist disinformation campaigns that originate in the right-wing information ecosystem are particularly problematic in the context of how the internet works. Media manipulators cross-promote extreme and moderate ideas and thinkers, facilitating a mainstreaming process whereby audiences searching for information on Google (or its subsidiary YouTube) are returned information that legitimizes extremist ideas. Specifically, my data reveal two extremist tropes that appear with alarming regularity: that genetic superiority exists, and that whiteness is under attack and in need of protection.

Stale content does not go viral. To make old ideas seem new, the right-wing information ecosystem creates algorithmic connections to profit from more extreme YouTube influencers like Stefan Molyneux or Jordan Peterson. By connecting with extremists who espouse these positions, conservative producers leverage those connections. Extremists generate more clicks and increased traffic for self-described moderate hosts looking to boost their follower count, but that engagement comes at a price. By hosting and amplifying extremist thinkers, they breathe new life into antiquated ideas and provide easy talking points for conservative voters. More important, when conservative moderators like Dennis Prager, Joe Rogan, Candace Owens, or Dave Rubin host an extremist like Stefan Molyneux or go on his show, it allows them to profit from his audience while maintaining plausible deniability. It creates a space where politicians like former president Trump or gubernatorial candidate Ed Gillespie can engage with extremist ideas while pretending that they are not racist.

Stoking fears of displacement and legitimizing debunked science to suggest racial superiority encourages conservatives to come together under a common cause: the idea that their nation is being stolen from them, and if they do not protect what is theirs, they will be next in line to lose their legacy. The real power of this propaganda is the ability to skirt around a formal connection to extremists while simultaneously perpetuating race realism and white shift. Yet conservatives bound by libertarian ideals are wary of groupthink. To work around this dimension of conservatism, this network encourages constituents to "do the research" for themselves, allowing people who value individualism to form a set of collective ideas and actions seemingly on their own accord.

STEP SEVEN

CLOSE THE LOOP

The propaganda feedback loop—a closed-circuit information ecosystem that connects media, politicians, and voters—is powerful because it is self-reinforcing.[1] As mainstream media coverage continues to focus on the interests of coastal communities, the conservative platforms, especially radio, fill the local-journalistic void for residents in the middle.[2] And once right-leaning audiences hear conservative messaging, they are encouraged to do what comes naturally: find out the "truth" for themselves, by searching for keywords and clicking on links that have been strategically placed by the conservative elite. Seeding the internet and then encouraging self-discovery is essential, for propaganda is harder to sell when the target audience prizes individual thought and freedom of expression. When information seekers believe they are being presented with evidence so that they can make their own conclusions, they are primed to agree with the conservative message and vote for Republican candidates.

Examples of the propaganda feedback loop in action are PragerU videos, which routinely use scriptural inference (a close reading technique borrowed from Bible study, described earlier) to drill down into documents, speeches, newspaper articles, and scientific claims. By providing textual evidence out of context, these videos invite conservatives to think critically about the lines of text provided, but not question the broader cultural narrative in which those texts were created and now exist.

PragerU has even used scriptural inference to turn a piece of investigative journalism that critiqued it into positive advertising for the company. On March 3, 2018, BuzzFeed released an in-depth report on PragerU, citing research by myself and others.[3] In the article, Joseph Bernstein describes how the organization's proselytizing rhetoric sways public opinion and blurs the line between conservatism and extremism. Five days later, PragerU posted to Facebook and emailed to subscribers an advertisement urging supporters to donate to the nonprofit organization to help change the minds of young Americans. The advertisement lifted a sentence from the report and used it as an endorsement, quoting the BuzzFeed article, "It took two months for PragerU, one of the biggest, most influential forces in online media, to mold a conservative." While this line was written by BuzzFeed, it was taken out of context, making it seem as though the article was supportive of PragerU's agenda.

In a different PragerU video titled "The Dark Art of Framing," Jeff Myers, president of Summit Ministries, argues that the Left "manipulates words and emotions." Myers accuses the Left and the mainstream media of unfairly skewing information and calls on conservatives to get up to speed on the "big issues" to ensure that they can see through weak arguments and appreciate good ones. The video then offers audiences a how-to guide for practicing scriptural inference in their own lives. The video encourages viewers to "read up," "memorize some bullet points," and push back against leftists who confront them, as opposed to relying on someone else to fight their ideological battles.

Tucker Carlson used the same process to dissect James Damore's infamous internal Google memo (discussed in Step Six). In the opening monologue of his August 14, 2017, show, Carlson highlighted key phrases to legitimize Damore's memo and discredit Google for firing Damore. Carlson stated that Google's employees suffer from "emotional outrage" and are known for silencing right-of-center content creators. Damore's arguments are rooted in essentialist and eugenicist understandings of IQ differences, but Carlson ignored that context, instead highlighting a sentence from Damore's memo stating that there are biological differences between men and women (for more on eugenics and IQ, see Step Six). In the next slide, he used scriptural inference to do a close reading of a sentence from Google's public statement indicating the company's desire to foster a safe space for all employees regardless of opinions.

Comparing and contrasting "the words" of Damore and of Google, Carlson made it seem as though Google's actions were hypocritical and sought to silence conservatism. In so doing, he used a media literacy practice that resonates with his audiences. Like a preacher from the pulpit, Tucker guides his audience through the news, highlighting the texts that his audiences should focus on, allowing them to interpret each text in conjunction with their lived experiences.

In the PragerU video "Facts Don't Care about Your Feelings," Ben Shapiro asserts that patriarchy is not real because "young, single women without kids already earn more than their male counterparts" (Step Two). While this statistic might be true—though no source for it was provided in the video—it hardly proves that patriarchy no longer exists. For example, it has been shown that motherhood is the biggest cause of pay inequality.[4] Ironically, by provoking feelings, memories, emotions, and social ties himself, Shapiro makes it more difficult to assess the "accuracy" of his messaging about the inappropriateness of emotional appeals. Like other conservative pundits, Shapiro claims to present "just the facts" while using tactics that evoke an emotional response tied to ideas of biblical "truth."

On the YouTube channel Blessed2Teach, which has around 21,000 followers as of September 2021, Rick Rene analyzes QAnon "drops" through scriptural inference, infusing Q concepts with biblical excerpts. As I mentioned earlier, QAnon is a right-wing conspiracy group based on the theory that Trump was working with military intelligence to take down high-ranking Democrat pedophiles.[5] The YouTube channel's "About" section includes the following text:

> . . . empowers Christian Patriots with Truth. Qanon Posts, Qanon News, Qanon Related Prophesies. I love to teach because I get "blessed" when teaching as it forces me to

learn more and dive deeper into the content. Therefore, I am "Blessed To Teach" not as I feel I have a special gift, but because God truly blesses me through forcing me to learn more!

Outlets like these serve an important function for Q researchers, who also refer to themselves as "Bakers." Analyzing these drops is part of a larger knowledge-making institution whereby Bakers turn Q's cryptic posts into "Proofs."[6]

From PragerU to Tucker Carlson to QAnon, those inside the right-wing information ecosystem harness the power of the five f's, and use scriptural inference, to present "the facts" and support their position with others inside the network—all while meticulously avoiding scientific evidence that counters their claims. Most important, this media manipulation strategy encourages audiences to "seek out" more information, knowing they have seeded the internet with resources that support only one side of the argument (Step Five). Conservative producers frame their use of scriptural inference as giving audiences facts and letting them decide for themselves, but content analysis reveals that conservative pundits and politicians regularly draw on "the words" of prominent figures in duplicitous ways.

I HAVE A DREAM

On August 28, 1963, during the March on Washington, DC, Dr. Martin Luther King Jr. addressed a crowd on the steps of the Lincoln Memorial. He said that "the Negro" still finds himself "in exile in his own land," and described how the United States had failed Black people. He exhorted the nation's leaders to make real on the promises of democracy, ending his speech with a call to action, so that one day his four little children would live in a nation where they would "not be judged by the color of their skin but by the content of their character."[7]

Over the past few years, conservative pundits and politicians have lifted this sentence to try to advance racial color-blindness. Conservatives' appropriation of the term relies on scriptural inference. The concept of being "color-blind" dates back in the

1896 case *Plessy v. Ferguson* where all but one Justice ultimately sanctioned racial segregation. In the lone dissenting vote, Justice Harlan declared that "Our Constitution is color-blind." In 2007, Justice Thomas referred to Harlan's original words to advocate his opposition to affirmative action.[8] Although asserting that policies or people can be "color-blind" may seem like a call for equality, this mindset fails to acknowledge systems that privilege some over others, such as inheritance, affirmative action, and voter protections—and can lead to the erosion of essential legal protections for minority groups.[9] Moreover, conservatives' use of Harlan's words are misplaced and fail to engage with his full argument. Harlan advocated for colorblindness to limit excessive oppression, but he also believed in white supremacy and perceived Black people as naturally inferior.[10] Asserting that we need to see "beyond color" and look at "character" undermines the collective problem of racism in favor of individualism. Insinuating that those who experience poverty or discrimination are somehow morally corrupt or deficient privileges whiteness as the normative standard.

Take, for example, the PragerU video titled "Where Are You, Martin Luther King?" with 6.5 million views on YouTube as of August 2021. Jason Riley, a Black member of the *Wall Street Journal* editorial board, blames the racial differences in U.S. home ownership, income, and leadership on Black culture. Riley claims that Black people don't value education, family, or employment (the five f's). Drawing on the strategy of scriptural inference, Riley points to King's words, describing what he claims King once told a Black congregation in Saint Louis:

> "We've got to do something about our moral standards. We know that there are many things wrong in the white world," he said, "but there are many things wrong in the black world too. We can't keep on blaming the white man. There are things we must do for ourselves." King tried to instill personal accountability, but activists dismiss King's color-blind standards.

Using King's words out of any wider context, Riley tries to claim that King had advocated for personal responsibility over structural changes. This made King's calls for equality seem to fall in line with today's conservative emphasis on individual accountability.

On May 15, 2021, the conservative cable channel NewsmaxTV aired a segment on President Biden's decision to reverse Trump's executive order banning critical race theory in federally funded organizations, including schools. The host describes this reversal as dangerous because it teaches kids to "judge others based on the color of their skin." A guest on the segment was barrier-breaking Black neurosurgeon and Trump's former secretary of Housing and Urban Development Ben Carson. He claimed that critical race theory is antithetical to what Dr. King preached, because King "wanted people to be judged by the basis of their character, not their color." Carson went on to argue that we should be teaching children that their ability to succeed in life is linked to their character.

For those who are unfamiliar, critical race theory is a lens through which historians, sociologists, philosophers, and lawyers have examined systemic racism. First used in the 1980s by legal scholars Kimberlé Crenshaw, Neil Gotanda, and Stephanie Phillips, critical race theory emphasizes the unique role that legal systems play in upholding racial inequality in the United States.[11] The fundamental misunderstanding about critical race theory, and white supremacy more generally, is that critiquing the system is not the same as condemning individual shortcomings or biases. In other words, critical race theory is not about calling out particular people as racists or making people feel bad about themselves, as conservative commentators insist. It is instead about understanding how laws and policies tend to benefit white, straight, Christian men over people from other groups. While an individual might be prejudiced—that is, while a person may unfairly dislike a group of people because of an unchangeable characteristic like race, ethnicity, or gender—critical race theory is a method of looking at structural racism, emphasizing that it is far more than an individual mindset.

Examining the ways in which social systems benefit some over others is a topic well suited for sociology. By analyzing networks that connect individuals, groups, and institutions, sociologists understand how formal and informal social structures both stabilize group dynamics but also perpetuate racial inequality.[12] To understand how the system is unequal, we must examine the role that chattel slavery played in building the United States into the superpower it is today and expose the ways in which the legal system was created to maintain racial divisions.

Yet the right-wing information ecosystem has repeatedly used King's words to intentionally obfuscate what critical race theory is, framing it as a grave threat to American society. Conservatives now refer to complex legal frameworks meant to examine persistent forms of inequality as "race and sex scapegoating and stereotyping."[13] Citing critical race theory as a "destructive ideology," Trump's executive order claimed that racial sensitivity training is racist, and that such an understanding of systemic racism divides the country. The rhetoric of his executive order was shaped by Christopher Rufo, a conservative documentarian with no legal or graduate-level theoretical training. As part of a concerted effort to stop diversity and inclusion initiatives at federal agencies, Rufo has set up a whistleblower email account and encourages government and industry employees to send documents associated with anti-racist training so he can post them on his website.[14] Since starting his campaign, Rufo's undercover reporting has made appearances throughout the right-wing information ecosystem, including *The Rubin Report, Tucker Carlson Tonight, The Daily Wire*, the *New York Post*, and The Blaze.

After Biden reversed Trump's executive order, states with conservative state legislatures like Arizona, Georgia, North Carolina, South Dakota, and Texas have proposed "banning critical race theory" in the classroom. Meanwhile, Rufo and other conservative commentators have used the term to elevate disinformation about critical race theory in the right-wing information ecosystem.[15] To be sure, what Rufo and others refer to as "critical race theory" does not refer to the complex legal lessons taught in law school. It now is shorthand for any discussion or lesson that recognizes the role racism and slavery played in founding the United States (see Step Five for more on keyword appropriation). A simple search on YouTube reveals the extent to which conservatives' appropriation of the phrase is working. As of June 2021, the top five returns for "critical race theory" on YouTube were videos by conservative producers such as PragerU, The Heritage Foundation, and Christopher Rufo on *The Rubin Report*.

To make disinformation about critical race theory seem legitimate, conservatives use quotations by Dr. Martin Luther King Jr. When I searched for "content of character" on YouTube on May 22, 2021, the top returns were dominated by conservative-leaning content. One video is a segment from Fox News titled "Fox News Tomi Lahren Torches Lori Lightfoot: What Happened to Content of Character?" In the video, several conservative media hosts and political strategists lament the mayor of Chicago's decision to prioritize one-on-one interview requests with nonwhite journalists. Evoking similar arguments as those in President Trump's executive order against critical race theory, Lahren claims that Lightfoot's actions are meant to divide: "How are we going to come together as a nation and have true equality if we look to certain people and we're disgusted by their skin color. I mean what happened to the content of your character, not the color of your skin?"[16]

Another top return is the video "All We Have," by the channel titled Free the People. In it, the host uses the same line from King's speech to argue that "people should be judged on character, not color." During the talk he splices clips from King's speech with violent imagery of burning cities, Black Lives Matter marches, and people waving Antifa flags (more on this later). This channel also hosts a five-part video series titled "The Constitution Line by Line," hosted by Senator Mike Lee (R-UT), where he applies scriptural inference to the Constitution. In another four-part series called the "Culture of Wokeness," the host teaches audiences that concepts like critical race theory are racist and that anti-racist leaders are brainwashing the country. The video "All We Have" warns that King preached for peaceful protests and that civil rights groups today are working in opposition to what King would have wanted.

While King most definitely advocated for peace, it is important to note that in the same "I Have a Dream" speech that conservatives regularly cite, King also warned: "there will be neither rest nor tranquility in America until the Negro is granted his citizenship rights. The whirlwinds of revolt will continue to shake the foundations of our nation until the bright day of justice emerges." At the time of his speech, conservatives did not consider King to be a pacifist. In fact, the FBI monitored King for decades after his involvement with the Montgomery bus boycott, justifying their surveillance as an attempt to stop the spread of communism.[17]

Leveraging King's words for conservative ends is particularly egregious considering that conservatives in the South framed leaders like King as "outside agitators" and used constituents' fears of communism to rationalize physical violence against civil rights groups during the Civil Rights Movement. At the time, the country was confronting centuries of white mythology that Black people in the South were happy with their relegation to second-class status, mistaking their fear and silence as acceptance. Since many whites felt that Black people had inferior intellectual capabilities, they believed the work of civil rights organizing had to be the work of outside influencers, "namely the Communist party."[18]

It is interesting to note that the same tactics are used today to spread disinformation about the 1619 Project, the Black Lives Matter movement, and other efforts to promote anti-racism and to push back on societal structures that disproportionately benefit whites. The 1619 Project was first published in the *New York Times Magazine* in August 2019 to commemorate the four-hundredth anniversary of the arrival of the first enslaved Africans to the English colony of Virginia. While a few historians have noted some inaccuracies, the goal of the project was to recenter American history to recognize that slavery defines the way the nation operates today.

In response, conservatives issued *The President's Advisory 1776 Commission Report,* condemning "critical race theory" and conflating a complex legal framework with the investigative reporting of Nikole Hannah-Jones. Unsurprisingly, the report supports its arguments by referencing King, specifically the excerpt "live in a nation where they will not be judged by the color of their skin but by the content of their character."[19] Its authors claim that "identity politics" harm King's legacy and that civil rights were achieved when legislative reforms protecting voting rights, housing rights, and banning segregation were passed. Research demonstrates that color-blind mythmaking is an essential element for giving credence to dog whistles, but conservatives have actually turned King's words into the dog whistle itself.[20]

As a dog whistle, King's words are used to spread propaganda that current-day civil rights protestors, academics, and other cultural influencers promote anti-Americanism. The report, for example, also includes sections on fascism and communism, framing them as moral battles that the United States has fought continuously since the Cold War. While these segments of the report are not specifically accusatory, they are organizationally relevant. Positioning fascism, communism, and socialism along-side today's civil rights movements that rely on identity politics (Black Lives Matter and others) draws from the same playbook as that of conservative politician George Wallace, who once compared left-wing liberals to communist sympathizers and called the Civil Rights Act of 1964 "a fraud, a shame, and a hoax . . . straight out of the Communist Manifesto."[21]

Today, prominent conservative strategists are using the same analogy to discredit what they refer to as critical race theory. In a tweet on May 24, 2021, Christopher Rufo claimed that teaching Black history and anti-racism is less important than teaching kids about the threat of communism. His statement denies that education does not emphasize racial inequality and instead insinuates that it hides the threat of communism:

> I learned about racism, slavery, segregation, Jim Crow, and the Trail of Tears in my K-12 education. I never learned about the Holodomor, Cultural Revolution, and 100 million dead from global communism. American schools haven't "whitewashed" history; they've "red-washed" it.

Using scriptural inference to dig into the words of Dr. Martin Luther King Jr. is more than just a way to bolster a conservative "color-blind" agenda. Repeatedly pointing to fascism and communism pivots attention away from racial injustice in the United States. Not unlike calls during the Cold War to frame civil rights leaders as "out-of-town agitators," these twenty-first-century propagandists are returning to the staying power of anti-communism, blurring together the supposed Black and red menaces.[22] Center to this strategy is evoking fears of socialism, with conservatives frequently claiming that anti-fascists, colloquially referred to as Antifa, are, in the words of conservative think tank The Library of Economics and Liberty, "doing fascism unknowingly."[23]

Yet a closer look at keywords reveals another important play in closing the propaganda loop. By creating a phrase that captures ideological fears about communism and sows confusion about civil rights protestors, conservative politicians and pundits have created a dog whistle to publicly condemn Black Lives Matter without seeming overtly racist in their intentions.

ANTIFA SAID WHAT?

Antifa (pronounced by conservatives as an-TEE-fuh) is shorthand for anti-fascism.[24] Fascism is a form of far-right authoritarianism characterized by extreme nationalism and the presence of a dictator. The Antifa movement is a loose organization of people and groups who believe in active and aggressive opposition to far-right movements.[25]

I first learned about Antifa when I was studying the Unite the Right Facebook group in the months preceding the August 14, 2017, rally. During that time, Jason Kessler, the event's organizer and a University of Virginia graduate, warned of Antifa violence and claimed that the Charlottesville City Council wanted to move the rally to McIntire Park due to "Antifa threats."[26]

During the rally the keyword "Antifa" gained more traction. Shortly after James Fields ran his car into a crowd of counter-protestors, 8chan posters claimed that a fifty-one-year-old Michigan man had gifted the car that "crashed into 20 people at an Antifa rally in Virginia" to his millennial son, "an anti-Trump leftist," and provided doctored images and registration records to "prove" it. Anticipating questions about why a leftist would drive a car into an Antifa rally, posters falsified screenshots from the alleged driver's social media accounts that furthered the narrative that he was an anti-Trumper from Detroit, and posited that he had heard about the rally, drove to Charlottesville, saw white people protesting, assumed they were Nazis, and proceeded to run over them. Others claimed that he had run a "false flag" operation to cause media hysteria and make Unite the Right protestors look bad.

Using Antifa to describe a Nazi protest was a tactical decision to deflect public attention from the real violence that white supremacists incited at the Unite the Right rally. Meanwhile, white supremacists took to The Daily Stormer message board boasting about the torch rally with posts like "We won."

But while white supremacists used social media to organize the protest and claim "victory" when they marched on Charlottesville, they used the same platforms to position Antifa as out-of-town terrorists. This rhetorical strategy framed the extreme Left as the impetus for violence, strategically distancing white supremacists from terrorist acts and claiming that they were the ones "under attack." The media manipulation effort that started on 8chan and The Daily Stormer quickly spilled over into the rest of the right-wing information ecosystem, in a process that internet scholars refer to as "trading up the chain."[27] First, Infowars published an article entitled "Bombshell Connection between Charlottesville, Soros, and CIA." Its author claimed that Jewish billionaire and favorite white-supremacist target George Soros had paid #BlackLivesMatter and Antifa protestors to attend the Charlottesville rally, incite violence, and try to make President Trump look bad.

Then Red Alert Politics published a story alleging that "crazed protestors" from the "hysterical" Left had screamed over speaker Richard Spencer, "ruining any chance of civil discourse." The author made sure to refer to Spencer as "awful," but still managed to imply that he, a white supremacist leader, could or would want to sit down with a Black person and debate ideas. The nod to civil discourse is also a linguistic tool for framing Native Americans or Black Americans as "savages" or "criminals," a disinformation strategy used by colonizers to try to rationalize dispossession and human exploitation.[28] The article implies that people should have polite chats with leaders who do not recognize their humanity.

Narrowing in on and amplifying the idea of hysterical leftists, conservative pundits focused on what they referred to as a "Free Speech Rally" organized in Boston eight days later. In an article published by Breitbart titled "Watch: Leftist Protestor Calls Black Boston Cop 'Stupid-Ass Black Bitch; You're Supposed to Be on Our Side,'" the author frames the rally as one about individual liberties, failing to acknowledge that the national director of the KKK said Massachusetts members would show up at the rally, alongside "Proud Boy" founder Gavin McInnes and Holocaust denier Augustus Sol Invictus, who were both scheduled to speak. On the day of, Infowars contributor and "Pizzagate" conspirator Joe Biggs was also in attendance.[29] The article goes on to describe the counter-protestors as "members of left-wing groups such as antifa and Black Lives Matter." This framing effectively positions Black protestors as the villains, and the violence of an event designed to "replicate the success" of Charlottesville as the fault of Black Lives Matter/Antifa.

On Facebook, *Conservative Daily* retweeted the article with a headline that is nearly identical to the one featured on Breitbart: "Leftist Protestor Calls Black Boston Cop 'Stupid-A*s Black B***h; You're Supposed to Be on Our Side': A Free Speech Rally was Held in Boston Saturday." Accompanying the post, *Conservative Daily* writes, "Sorry, media, this is not what 'peaceful' looks like." This position reaffirmed the idea that Black people were the villains, not the victims, of a highly organized white supremacist event, and uses scriptural inference to make the media seem biased.

According to conservative media coverage shared by respondents on Facebook, Antifa and Black Lives Matter might as well be the same organization. Pundits, producers, and politicians inside the right-wing information ecosystem galvanized around the idea that counter-protestors from Charlottesville, Virginia, to Boston, Massachusetts, were all emotional actors, incapable of "civilized" dialogue. To be sure, I witnessed some protestors resort to violence and carry weapons on August 12, 2017, but the conservative media fixation on Antifa as violent outliers drove public attention away from the larger issue at hand: hundreds of white supremacists had been able to organize multiple rallies, chant "Jews will not replace us," and repeatedly terrorize a city without being held accountable for their actions.

Herein lies the complexity of Trump's claim that there were "good and bad people on both sides," language reminiscent of Nixon's campaign speeches in the 1960s when he blamed the nation's racial conflict on "extremists of both races." According to Trump, and my respondents, the "good people" were those who wanted to preserve the Confederate statues, because removing them was an attack on white culture (see Step Six). The "good people" narrative effectively pathologized Black Lives Matter and other groups that supported removing the statues. It also absolved rally-goers who wanted to preserve the historical legacy of white supremacy in the United States. The "bad guys" on "both sides" were Antifa and Black Lives Matter, the supposed radical leftist and violent Soros-paid protestors, as well as "actual" white supremacists like the former KKK grand wizard David Duke, all of whom attended the rally. For Trump, and my respondents, counter-protestors broke the law at the Unite the Right rally because they didn't have a permit. They were the "out-of-towners" bribed to make President Trump look bad.

This purposeful misdirection and use of the phrase "outsiders" echoes language used by segregationists to describe civil rights protestors in the 1960s. For the truth is that it was not Antifa "outside agitators" who organized the removal of the Confederate statues in Charlottesville, Virginia. A local Black resident and activist named Zyahna Bryant, a high-schooler at the time, led the petition to remove the statues and rename the parks.[30] In trying to remove the Confederate statues, her supporters forced the town to face a legacy of segregation that white residents had refused to acknowledge. For example, the current downtown landscape had once been a vibrant Black-owned neighborhood until it was bulldozed in the 1960s to make way for white-owned businesses. And the school system is still entrenched in decades of racial inequality.[31] Much like myths from the Jim Crow era, these narratives were at odds with Charlottesville's idealized versions of itself. This dissonance opened the door for a resurgence of the "outsiders" trope, which portrayed Black activists as evil villains who had "duped" local Black people into ruining the "good race relations" in Charlottesville.[32]

In the months that followed, the right-wing information ecosystem continued to focus on Antifa as a threat to conservatism nationwide, featuring videos of alleged Antifa activists attacking conservatives on college campuses. During the month of October while I was conducting this study, a respondent shared a video on Facebook from Fox News that read "It has become socially acceptable at UC Berkeley for conservatives to be physically beaten, chased, and stalked." Accompanying the video, they expressed gratitude for being at a university where they wouldn't be attacked for "thinking differently" and said that they would be "praying for" the students at Berkeley who had their speech censored.[33]

In addition to reading stories on social media claiming that Kessler was part of the Left and that Antifa were the true agitators, conservative respondents in my study began looking for evidence that the entire Unite the Right rally had been staged. Juliette was so convinced that she "started doing her own research" for more information about how the governor and mayor responded to the events:

> I said, "Something's not right. Something is not right," when the governor called the state troopers to stand down.[34] And how come they weren't there to begin with? And how come this, how come that? I think there was more staging going on, and that's not a conspiracy theory. They're pretty much proving that it was staged. I know.

While Juliette was vague about who was behind the "staging" of what happened in Charlottesville, Tom was more explicit:

> One of the strategies is creating chaos. So, Soros and other similar groups fund, it's been proven and documented, that all of a sudden, these people from out of town show up . . . and they don't live there. They've been paid to get on a bus to go and incite riot. There've been videos that show people in a crowd, start hitting somebody

to create a riot. Those kinds of activities, I think, adds to the fakeness of the whole thing.

Tom's assessment that there were people there from "out of town" paid to create chaos was not entirely untrue. From my observations and media analysis, it was clear that hundreds of white supremacists had traveled from all over the country to attend the rally, and that some had financed their trips via crowd-sourced fundraising platforms. My Facebook observations indicated that there were hundreds of white supremacists coordinating ridesharing and pickups to Charlottesville along the way. Except for Kessler, the keynote speakers were also out-of-towners.

Most of the counter-protestors, by contrast, were members of Charlottesville Clergy Collective, a group of Charlottesville interfaith leaders who work together to promote racial unity. They applied for and obtained a permit to gather a few blocks away, at McGuffey Park. At 6:00 am on August 12, 2017, they met with other faith leaders from around the United States trained in nonviolent resistance to organize their peaceful countermarch.[35]

Conservative media manipulators tend to throw together the Left as well as the Black Lives Matter and Antifa movements into a supposedly single, giant, nefarious outsider. My respondents drew on the same language to describe the events of that day. While the college students I spoke with believed that the Unite the Right rally was indeed "real," they questioned the mainstream media's subsequent coverage and agreed with President Trump's assessment that "both sides" could be blamed for the violence:

DELILAH: When I started to think about the fake news it was right after I read Trump had blamed the wrong group of people for it [August 12] . . . honestly, like I could not disagree with that because it's a very slippery slope to remove a statue because it disagrees with something that someone values.
RESEARCHER: Who are these "sides"?
LEE: The white supremacists.
DELILAH: Yes, the white supremacists—horrible group.
LEE: Exactly, but then the other side . . .?
ABRAHAM: The An-tee-fa?
LEE: Yes—that's the organization that was there.

ABRAHAM: It creates a big dilemma. How far does free speech
go? Hate speech is wrong but I also believe in the rule of
law, and there's a process by which you react to things you
disagree with and An-tee-fa's way of going about responding to hate is with violence, they incite violence.

In a separate interview, Devin, another member of the college
group I observed, echoed the sentiments of his peers. Devin argued
that:

the people chanting "Blood and Soil" are almost no different than the identity politics of the Left. White supremacists think being of European descent is what
separates the essence of who you are, more so than your
ideas.

For Devin and many other conservatives whom I interviewed,
the Black Lives Matter movement's emphasis on Blackness is
equivalent to white supremacist groups' focus on racial identity.
Such a literalist interpretation of the phrase "Black Lives Matter"
again fails to see context. The movement does not deny that all
lives matter; instead the point is to expose the political, social, and
economic injustice that Black people face worldwide—arguing
that right now, Black lives do *not* matter in society. To support
Trump's positions that "both sides" were to blame, Devin draws
on logic akin to conservatives' use of Dr. Martin Luther King's
speech that people should be judged by the content of their character (in this case, "ideas") versus the color of their skin (being of
"European descent").

Hannah, an active middle-aged woman heavily involved in
the women's group I observed, tied Antifa back to the conservative
theme that the Left chooses emotion over logic and feelings over
facts (Step Two). She used the torch-lit march to back up her claim
that Antifa caused the violence:

Right now, everything is emotionally based. I mean, just
look at Charlottesville. They [the alt-right] did not call for
rioting in the streets. They had their own little rally on
Friday . . . Did they cause harm and damage Friday night?

No. It wasn't until Saturday, when you have your SJWs [Social Justice Warriors], your Antifa, your left side coming out. So, they hate the alt-right, but the alt-left is also wrong, and that's what we're going against.

As the interview continues, however, Hannah conflates the alt-right's ideals with her own, referring to the alt-right in the collective plural:

We're saying we're not going to have our history erased. They [Antifa] are like "Let's damage property. Let's destruct property. Let's harm others." That is exactly what was happening with Charlottesville, they were trying to shut down free speech.

These sentiments echoed what I heard from Trish, another member of the women's organization I observed:

Black Lives Matter and the Antifa, whatever, they are known to be agitators, just as the white supremacists are known to have a stance that probably doesn't agree with 90 percent of the American people . . . but Black Lives Matter and Antifa, they're known for burning down of these cities, and I'll tell you what, as an American citizen, I'm really sick of this crap.

Taken collectively, statements from various interviews imply a few things. First, they create plausible deniability between the presence and meaning of Confederate statues and white supremacy. These statements allow both conservative media and conservative voters to pander to the idea that Confederate soldiers were noble exemplars of old-fashioned chivalry. In doing so, it frames both Confederates and those who showed up to "protect" Confederate heritage as "good people," and therefore as different from white supremacists. Second, they individualize racists and racism, thereby deflecting attention away from the systemic pervasiveness of racism in the United States. Third, they gloss over the fact that wealthy white donors financed these statues decades *after* the Civil War. The goal of these monuments was to create white-only public spaces in defiance of desegregation laws, and to do so by means of fear and intimidation.[36] Framing counter-protestors as the violent out-of-towners, my respondents mirrored conservative disinformation tactics that date back nearly six decades.

Focusing on "the Left's" role in the demonstrations on August 12, 2017, a number of my respondents shared stories on Facebook from Breitbart and *Zero Hedge* that focused on Kessler's past involvement in Occupy rather than his more recent white-supremacist connections. These posts insinuated that Unite the Right was planned by radical leftists trying to make President Trump look bad, a trope that resurfaced after the attempted insurrection at the Capitol on January 6, 2021. To make this argument, the pieces utilize scriptural inference to draw out a few lines from the Southern Poverty Law Center extremist file for Kessler:

> Rumors abound on white nationalist forums that Kessler's ideological pedigree before 2016 was less than pure. Detractors point to involvement in the Occupy movement around 2011 and past support for President Obama. An individual who knew Kessler during his involvement with Occupy alleged Kessler had shown up at then-Lee Park with "his own tent and literature," and noted Kessler was eventually voted out of the group for advocating violence against police using bricks and Molotov cocktails.[37]

Using scriptural inference to claim that Kessler was part of the Left served two functions. First it sought to confuse readers about the intention behind the August 12, 2017, rally. Second, it frames members of the Left as the instigators of violence. By taking words from the Southern Poverty Law Center article out of context, the post effectively promotes the PragerU version of the alt-right: that leftists are more aligned with white supremacist ideals than the alt-right, and because they are "Godless" and believe in "identity politics," they are much more dangerous than neo-Nazis.

Conservative elites also used the Antifa dog whistle to delegitimize the hundreds of thousands of civil rights protestors who took to the streets across the United States following the murder of George Floyd. In response to the protests, Trump and his cabinet were quick to frame the protests as *riots* by focusing on rare instances of violence.[38] (In fact, research from Harvard's Radcliffe Institute finds that Black Lives Matter protestors were overwhelmingly peaceful.)[39] For example, Attorney General William Barr issued a press release on May 31, 2020, concluding that "the violence instigated and carried out by Antifa and other similar groups in connection with the rioting is domestic terrorism and will be treated accordingly." That same day, Trump stated on Twitter that "the United States of America will be designating ANTIFA as a Terrorist Organization." Two days later, the *Washington Examiner* published a piece titled "Trump Is Right: Antifa Is a Terrorist Group. It Always Was." The piece claims that only clueless commentators would think the label refers to people who protest fascism.

The same theme was furthered by *The Right View*, a Zoom-based talk show that was recorded live and distributed via various web-based channels including Trump's 2020 campaign app and Facebook. Funded by Donald J. Trump for President, Inc., *The Right View* mimicked the feel (and name) of ABC's *The View* with cohosts Lara Trump, Katrina Pierson, Kimberly Guilfoyle, and Mercedes Schlapp. In an episode shortly after the Black Lives Matter protests began to gain traction, the four women spent an entire episode inaccurately speculating about the role Antifa played in the Floyd protests. In Lara Trump's own words, it was tragic that "Antifa and other far-left anarchist groups are using this tragedy as an excuse to violently riot, burn down businesses and homes, and hurt the livelihoods of many Americans."[40]

As it turned out, white supremacists ran the social media accounts claiming to represent Antifa during the Floyd protests. Joan Donovan and Brian Friedberg, disinformation researchers at the Shorenstein Center on Media, Politics, and Public Policy at Harvard, refer to this practice of creating social media accounts specific to keywords or phrases as keyword squatting. Because the keyword "Antifa" is disproportionately used by accounts associated with troll accounts, or so-called sock puppet accounts (multiple accounts operated by one person or bot), the actual group is misrepresented and disinformation comes to further dominate social media searches and trends.[41]

Moreover, the FBI indicated that they found no intelligence linking Antifa to violence or looting during the protests of George Floyd's murder. Much like the inaccurate accusations that Antifa was to blame for the violence on August 12, 2017, in Charlottesville, conservatives claimed that the radical Left was tarnishing the memory of George Floyd. This served to vilify Black Lives Matter protestors while simultaneously evoking a need for more law and order (see Step Two). Framing Antifa as "dangerous" creates the perception that enhanced policing and the deployment of federal military force are needed against American citizens in cities like Portland and Chicago.

For more than four years, conservative elites were able to use the word *Antifa* to create a concerted disinformation campaign and distract constituents from racial injustice. The right-wing information ecosystem created a similarly misleading catchphrase to refute Trump's loss of the 2020 presidential election.

"STOP THE STEAL!"

During the 2020 election, the Trump administration repeatedly tried to undermine the legitimacy of mail-in voting. But disinformation surrounding a "stolen election," "ballot-harvesting," and "voter fraud" has been around long before Trump.

In the decade following the passage of the Reconstruction Act in March 1867, voters elected a record number of Black men to serve in the U.S. Congress.[42] As Black Americans used their voting rights to ascend the ranks of political office, conservative elites began circulating disinformation that African Americans had "abused their voting privileges, engaged in corruption, and stood generally unfit for democracy."[43] Despite redistricting efforts led by conservative politicians to group voters based on "moral issues" versus residential address, and to rig election outcomes, conservative elites spread propaganda that "others" were stealing their elections.[44]

In 1981, the Republican National Committee created the National Ballot Security Task Force, a group of armed, off-duty police officers hired to patrol polling sites in traditionally Black and Hispanic neighborhoods.[45] Similar to the language evoked by Trump in his efforts to recruit "election observers," the goal of these self-appointed armed watchers was to suppress the minority vote and affect electoral outcomes.

The keyword "Stop the Steal" first appeared back in 2016, when Trump supporters began circulating unverified information about the Clintons attempting to steal the presidential election. Based on Twitter archives, these posts evoked common themes already addressed in this book, that George Soros had paid to rig the election, that "illegal aliens" were voting, that voting machines were broken and unreliable, and that Trump supporters should get out and "poll watch." Roger Stone openly supported the Stop the Steal Movement in 2016 and encouraged groups in contested areas to talk with voters as they left the polls.[46] One tweet even included an advertisement for a company titled "Trump Ballot Security" with the email stopthesteal@gmail.com.[47]

Following Trump's win in 2016, the phrase stopped circulating. Looking at Google Trends data over time, there was a small peak of search traffic around the phrase "Stop the Steal" in 2016, but then it was dormant again until October 2020, when the curated keyword took off once more. The spike in "stop the steal" queries began shortly after Biden was declared the winner on November 7, 2020, and lasted for roughly a week following the outcome of the election. Trump did not concede. Instead, he continued to push the narrative of a stolen election. On social media, real Trump supporters and bot accounts began flooding platforms with disinformation calling for a recount and doubling down on claims that the election had been stolen. The phrase "stop the steal" began to peak again on Google Trends data in the days surrounding the Capitol insurrection (see Step Five for how to interpret Google Trends data).

On January 6, 2021, Trump stood on the Ellipse, just south of the White House, and addressed a sea of thousands gathered in Washington, DC, to protest what they believed was a stolen election. In his speech, Trump used the phrase "stop the steal" but incorrectly attributed the phrase to his supporters. He also signaled to keywords and phrases discussed elsewhere in this book (for example, "RINOS," the "Media," the "radical Left," and "taking back the country"), while framing his supporters as brave patriots and evoking the five f's of conservatism. Below I highlight specific instances in the speech where he promoted the narrative that conservatism is under attack and that the election was stolen:

> Turn your cameras please and show what's really happening out here because these people are not going to take it any longer . . . To use a favorite term that all of you people really came up with, *we will stop the steal* . . . After this, we're going to walk down and *I'll be there with you* . . . We will not be intimidated into accepting the *hoaxes* and the lies that we've been forced to believe over the past several weeks. We've amassed overwhelming evidence about a fake election . . . we had a lot of eyes watching one specific state, but they cheated like hell anyway . . . You will have an illegitimate president, that's what you'll have . . . I hope Mike has the courage to do what he has to do. *And I hope he doesn't listen to the RINOs* and the stupid people that he's listening to. It is also widely understood that the *voter rolls are crammed full of non-citizens*, felons, and people who have moved out of state and individuals who are otherwise ineligible to vote . . . We must *stop the steal* and then we must ensure that such outrageous election fraud never happens again . . . Looking out at *all the amazing patriots here today* . . . And we fight. We fight like Hell and if you don't fight like Hell, *you're not going to have a country anymore* . . . we're going to try and give them the kind of pride and boldness that they need to *take back our country.* So let's walk down Pennsylvania Avenue. I want to thank you all. *God bless you and God bless America.* Thank you all for being here, this is incredible. Thank you very much. Thank you.[48] [Emphasis added.]

Following the hour-long speech, the crowd left Trump's "Save America Rally" and, as encouraged by him to so so, walked to the U.S. Capitol. Unlike he promised, however, Trump did not join the protestors in their march along Pennsylvania Avenue.

Shortly after 1:00 pm, an altercation took place on the Capitol steps as people tried to enter the building. Perceiving imminent danger, Capitol police ordered an evacuation of the representatives who were there to count the certified electoral college ballots, the final step in confirming President-elect Joe Biden's victory. An hour later, people breached police lines and began scaling the walls.[49]

As Vice President Mike Pence was escorted out of the Senate chamber, Trump tweeted:

> Mike Pence didn't have the courage to do what should have been done to protect our Country and our Constitution, giving States a chance to certify a corrected set of facts, not the fraudulent or inaccurate ones which they were asked to previously certify. USA demands the truth!

At 2:44 pm, a Capitol police officer shot Air Force veteran and Trump supporter Ashli Babbitt in the neck as she attempted to break into the House legislative chambers through a window. Taking once again to Twitter, Trump posted a video saying:

> I know your pain. I know you're hurt. We had an *election that was stolen* from us. It was a landslide election and everyone knows it, especially the other side. But you have to go home now. We have to have peace. We have to have law and order . . . [Emphasis added.]

In addition to Babbitt, three other Trump loyalists and a Capitol police officer died the day of the insurrection, and two officers died of suicide after serving on active duty that day.[50] The official count stands at 140 officers injured as a result of the riot.[51]

Yet prominent conservative politicians and strategists used the same language as Trump, framing the insurrection as the work of "patriots" and defending the protestors' attempt to "stop the steal." Shortly after the attempted insurrection turned deadly, key players inside the right-wing information ecosystem spread the conspiracy theory that Antifa (that is, leftists/Black Lives Matter supporters) was behind the violence. Todd Herman began his episode of Rush Limbaugh's podcast by letting his audience in on a "tiny secret," telling listeners that Trump supporters would not have breached security on Capitol Hill and that "Antifa" and "BLM" were more inclined to incite violence. Claiming to monitor Antifa "chat channels," Herman said that members of Antifa planned to embed themselves into the protest to make it seem that Trump supporters were causing the problems.[52]

On Twitter, Candace Owens said that she guessed "Antifa thugs" were in the mix. On Fox News that night, Laura Ingraham repeated the same allegations, stating that "there are some reports that Antifa sympathizers may have been sprinkled throughout the crowd." Sean Hannity and Tucker Carlson made similar accusations, and an anchor on One America News Network described the chaos as "Antifa-like tactics." Speaking on Lou Dobbs's Fox Business show, Representative Mo Brooks (R-AL) said there were "two parts" to this event, that there were indications that "fascist Antifa elements" had embedded themselves in the Trump rally, and that these were the people who had stormed the Capitol.[53]

The *Washington Times* ran an article titled "Facial Recognition Identifies Extremists Storming the Capitol." In the original story, the reporter claimed that facial recognition software had "evidence" that Antifa infiltrators were among those inside the Capitol.[54] The next morning Representative Matt Gaetz (R-FL) took to the House floor and used the article as evidence to claim that some people who breached the Capitol "were members of the violent terrorist group antifa."[55] In a tweet still available on the platform as of June 2021, Representative Paul Gosar (R-AZ) shared the article and posted, "This [the storming of the Capitol] has all the hallmarks of Antifa provocation."[56]

The *Washington Times* removed the original tweet and later issued this correction:

> An earlier version of this story incorrectly stated that XRVision facial recognition software identified Antifa members among rioters who stormed the Capitol Wednesday. XRVision did not identify any Antifa members. The *Washington Times* apologizes to XRVision for the error.

As of January 2022, a Google search of "Washington Times antifa evidence" still showed this article as the top return. Under the headline "Facial Recognition Identifies Extremists Storming the Capitol," the recap inaccurately states: "Trump supporters say that Antifa members disguised as one of them infiltrated the protestors who stormed the U.S. Capitol on Wednesday." For conservatives practicing scriptural inference, the quick return incorrectly corroborates Antifa as the violent agitators on January 6, 2021.

Although the FBI found no evidence of Antifa involvement, disinformation surrounding the insurrection persists. According to a poll conducted between April 21 and 23, 2021, by the University of Massachusetts at Amherst, more than a fifth of Republican voters blamed Antifa for the violence at the Capitol on January 6, 2021. On Friday, May 14, 2021, when Democrats and Republicans on the House Homeland Security Committee struck a deal to create a bipartisan commission to investigate the January 6, 2021, attack on the Capitol, many conservative representatives expressed their disapproval of the commission because, in their view, it was designed only to advance partisan goals. Top Republicans insisted that any investigation of the lead-up to January 6, 2021, must also include an examination of violence from "far-left groups like Antifa during protests of police brutality last year."[57] On May 28, 2021, Senate Republicans blocked the plan for an independent commission. The measure fell short of the four votes it needed to proceed.[58]

The conservative narrative surrounding the attack on the Capitol on January 6, 2021, aligns with the response to the 2017 Unite the Right rally in Charlottesville. Akin to James Fields's legal defense strategy, conservatism is portrayed as being "under attack" from the supposedly dangerous Antifa. Time and again, civil rights protestors are framed as leftist threats to freedom. When advances toward equality are perceived as a menace to society, it becomes easier to justify the use of military force to neutralize and eliminate those so-called threats.

When conservatives are in fact breaking the law, as they were during the Unite the Right rally and the Capitol insurrection, focusing on Antifa deflects that blame. If the dangerous Left "staged" the removal of Confederate statues or "rigged" the election, the story goes, it seems likely that they were also the ones attempting to incite violence. Those on the "other side" that gathered on

August 12, 2017, or January 6, 2021, were simply patriots there
to defend law and order and protect their heritage or their vote.

Perhaps the most dangerous part of this loop is that it is often
promoted as an avenue for individuals to find out the "truth" for
themselves. Conservative programming sets the stage for voters
to rally around the five f's, and it employs scriptural inference to
make its case, but conservative media influencers also invite their
audiences to confirm what they are saying, challenging them to
do their own research (and to distrust the mainstream media).

Representative Marjorie Taylor Greene (R-GA) described this
process when she testified before Congress as the House debated
whether to remove her from her two committees. She explained
that her quest for more information was grounded in her support
for Trump and that she did not agree with how mainstream media
was portraying him. While doing her own research, Greene
stumbled across QAnon:

> I started seeing things in the news that didn't make sense
> to me, like Russian collusion, which are conspiracy theo-
> ries also, and have been proven so, these things bothered
> me deeply and I realized just watching CNN or Fox News,
> I may not find the truth and so what I did is I started
> looking up things on the internet. Asking questions. Like
> most people do every day. Using Google. And I stumbled
> across something and this is at the end of 2017, called
> QAnon. These posts were mainly about this Russian col-
> lusion information, a lot of it was some of what I would
> see on the news at night and I got very interested in it. So
> I posted about it on Facebook, I read about it, I talked
> about it, I asked questions about it, and then more and
> more information came from it.[59]

This strategy is important because it relies on the conservative
value of individualism. By inviting voters to do their own research
on a specific set of keywords or concerns (for example, Stop the
Steal, Antifa, the Black Lives Matter movement as communism),
conservative politicians and pundits are better able to control the

public narrative. While audiences believe that they are "fact-checking" and getting the information for themselves, they do not understand the way that information flows (see Step Four). Within the right-wing information ecosystem, thought leaders manipulate the web like a pinball machine, bouncing signals throughout their network of news programming, to the floor of the Senate, to hearings in the House, all while making it seem like the player is in control of the messages that they access and pass along themselves.

Designing a feedback loop anchored in self-discovery complicates calls for media literacy in order to combat misinformation. It is not that conservatives lack literacy. As my research demonstrates, they actively seek out information that both agrees and disagrees with their beliefs. They are grounded in a profound distrust of sourced materials and read carefully the content returned to them. They are in constant search of "the truth" but do not trust most sources that journalists rely on (for example, professors, government officials, or even doctors), let alone the publications that they write for.

Business scholars find that when consumers build their own merchandise, they value the product more than an already assembled item of similar quality: they feel more competent and happier with their purchase.[60] Conservative media producers draw on the same strategy: providing a tangible, do-it-yourself quality to the information they provide. This "IKEA effect of misinformation" makes audiences feel like they are drawing their own conclusions rather than being told what to think. But if conservative messaging is like a new table from IKEA, conservative elites are the engineers that design the furniture—making sure that the table goes together only one way, and with just the right amount of effort to give that perfectly satisfied feeling to the consumer (and encourage them to shop again soon). They suggest audiences go out and search for information on their own, but only after seeding the internet with problematic content and tagging information with keywords that are designed to keep their viewers following well-worn pathways within conservative ideology. This sophisticated marketing tactic empowers conservative voters with faux autonomy, making them think they came to propagandists' conclusions on their own.

EPILOGUE

RADICALISM IS NOT EXTREMISM

Too often, evidence of connections between conservative media personalities, Republican elected officials, and white supremacist leaders is quickly dismissed as "biased" because, as the story goes, the far Left is just as dangerous as the far Right with its manipulation of the media. According to this argument, groups on the far Left also spread propaganda, only theirs is about abolishing Immigration and Customs Enforcement (ICE), funding Medicare for all, and regulating gun ownership.

To be clear, the kinds of changes that congressional leaders like Cori Bush (D-MO), Alexandria Ocasio-Cortez (D-NY), Bernie Sanders (I-VT), and their peers advocate for may be radical, but they cannot be labeled extremism. Extremism involves messages or symbols that promote nationalism through prejudice and violence. Extremists frame "others" through a lens of subjugation, blaming them for perceived economic or cultural shortcomings, a rhetorical strategy to justify violent attacks against them.[1]

People who protest for progressive politicians or causes focus on federal protections for the environment and racial justice. They take to the streets to fight inequality. That is fundamentally different from creating a moral high ground that vilifies "nonwhite/non-Christian" others. Dismantling ICE may be a far-reaching policy, but that is not the same as advancing outdated claims used to justify eugenics. Increasing the scope of health care for all is different than spreading fears that an influx of foreign-born citizens leads to a decline in civilization.

In fact, conflating white supremacy with the radical Left is an extremist rhetorical strategy (Step Two). In this two-pronged approach, the Left is framed as a threat while conservatives are portrayed as under attack. Such logic justifies a defense of white supremacist ideas while pushing the idea that conservatives are the victims of oppression.

As communication scholar and internet researcher Rebecca Lewis notes, the rejection of language, policies, or measures intended to avoid offense is often the first step in a person's "red-pilling" journey toward embracing white supremacy.[2] By positioning "the Left" as too radical and "the media" as too biased, the alternative influence network advances a "freedom of expression" agenda aimed at dismantling "politically correct (PC) culture." Framing PC culture as "extremism" creates a logic whereby conservatives feel they need to "fight back" against perceived silencing and censorship. We can hear the effects of this logic in the offensive language and jokes that have re-entered the political arena. Trump's flippancy toward political correctness and safe spaces, after all, is one reason that many conservatives support him.

Consider how much has changed when it comes to politicians' use of racial epithets on the campaign trail. When Senator George Allen (R-VA) was running for reelection in 2006, he referred to a man of Indian American origin at his rally as "Macaca or whatever his name is." Continuing to evoke the racial slur, Allen encouraged his crowd of supporters to "Give a welcome to Macaca here. Welcome to America, and the real world of Virginia."[3] Not only did Allen's use of a racial epithet result in him losing his senate seat, but it also subsequently hurt his chances for a 2008 presidential bid.

Fast-forward eight years, when the United States elected a president whose grassroots conservative supporters were "thrilled by Trump's willingness to express their fears and angers with no regard for political correctness."[4] According to former House Speaker Paul Ryan (R-WI), President Trump routinely made "textbook" racist comments on his campaign trail, yet still won not only the primary but also the general election.[5] By framing "PC culture" as an example of how "the Left" has become too radical, the right-wing information ecosystem is able to normalize explicit racist discourse on the campaign trail and in the Oval Office.

Joseph P. Overton, like other conservative researchers, strategists, and politicians before and after him, wanted to study how the political middle ground was slowly widening to include more extreme positions. Nearly thirty years ago, he developed the concept of the "Overton Window" during his time at the Mackinac Center for Public Policy, a research and educational institute dedicated to reducing government intervention and promoting free market ideals.

Broadly speaking, the Overton Window is a tool for mapping the range of ideas that public discourse can tolerate. It is used by politicians to determine the rhetoric they can use or the policy they can champion without risking their political positions. The "window" is more of a model for understanding how public attitudes influence politics.[6] Historically, conservative pundits and politicians have used the concept to portray the Left as increasingly radical.

Consider *The Overton Window,* a political thriller that conservative media personality Glenn Beck published in 2010 under a genre he referred to as "faction" (fiction based on facts). In the novel, Beck and his co-authors fantasize that the U.S. government has orchestrated a terrorist attack against its own people in order to manipulate public perception that government control is no longer a radical idea. Beck then uses this concocted account of how the government works to back his claim that the Overton Window is opening. As he notes on his website:

"There is a powerful technique called the Overton Window that can shape our lives, our laws, and our future. It works by manipulating public perception so that ideas previously thought of as radical begin to seem acceptable over time. Move the Window and you change the debate. Change the debate and you change the country."

Some have taken to applying the same Overton Window analogy to the Right, arguing that conservative politicians are increasingly able to use white supremacist language and ideals without
damaging their careers or their agendas. But conservative elites
have espoused white supremacist concepts for over a hundred
years with the goal of limiting who is legally allowed to participate
in the democratic process. Conservatives are not becoming more
extreme; if anything, the right-wing information ecosystem is
becoming more covert, subtly and strategically retooling language,
laws, and policies to fit the culture du jour. When archaic and
overt white supremacist phrases have become unacceptable in
the modern political lexicon, conservative strategists have replaced
those keywords with others to attract voters invested in the perpetuation of white privilege (Step Two). It is not acceptable for
conservative personalities to discuss "white genocide," for instance, so they use other keywords to signal their belief in the
decline of Western civilization as a mythical ideal where "real
Americans" maintain control over social, cultural, and political
institutions. The Republican Party has always prioritized whiteness in order to make constituents think they are voting in their
own self-interest. Creating dog whistles that evoke racial fear and
signaling to the five f's of conservatism hide the fact that much of
the legislation passed by conservative politicians only supports
the interests of a small fraction of the public.[7]

Take Charlie Kirk's opening remarks at the 2020 Republican
National Convention, for example. Kirk is the founder and president of Turning Point USA, a conservative think tank that targets
college campuses. In his speech, Kirk signaled to the five f's of
conservatism when he stated that "Trump is the bodyguard of
Western Civilization [firearms]" because he "defends the American
way of life," in which "you follow the law [forces], you work hard
[free market], you honor God [faith], you raise your kids with
strong values [family], and you work to create a civil society."
Kirk's nod to protecting Western civilization—his claims that
Trump is the "bodyguard" and that Trump will create a nation
that "makes it easier to have many children" plays to fears of white
and Christian demographic decline (Step Six).

Applying the concept of an Overton Window to conservatism is inaccurate and misleading. Were conservative politicians still able to throw around racial epithets or openly deny the warming of the planet, political strategists like Lee Atwater and Frank Luntz would not have bothered to create a set of code words and signals.[8] Creating terms and phrases like "Antifa" or "climate change" allowed conservative politicians to promote white supremacy and spread conspiracy theories without damaging their political or financial interests. Pandering to white voters through "dog whistles" is a cornerstone of the Republican Party, which harnesses the government to protect the interests of the affluent by positioning whiteness as under attack.[9] Unfortunately the policies that Republicans create (tax cuts for the wealthy, limited labor oversights, slashes to social security safety nets) benefit only the owners of industry, not the millions who keep those businesses running.

The Overton Window implies that attitudes can and do "open" and "close." For the wealthy white people in power, policies and phrases like "tax cuts," the "border wall," or "law and order" are based on disinformation campaigns as old as the United States itself.[10] They are designed around a manufactured fear of the racialized other. The border wall is today's proverbial separate drinking fountain, a boundary enacted to protect whiteness based on the idea that "others" are subhuman, not worthy of equitable treatment. Trump's overt racist language and signaling to white supremacy was shocking only because not enough attention has been paid to how white supremacy is already woven into the American political fabric.

At the same time, conservative elites who repeatedly frame the Left as dangerous extremists must not be allowed to make this claim without explaining themselves. Are we to believe that policies and actions created to combat global warming and preserve human rights are *extreme*? Insinuating that groups fighting for equality are radicals, or dangerous, requires serious reflective pause.

The notion of defunding the police-state, for example, might seem radical to those with no historical knowledge of surveillance in the United States. But once we understand that these systems were designed to subjugate Black Americans so that whites could profit from their labor, it is easier to see why the oppressed are calling for a systematic change. In fact, arguing that dismantling the militaristic elements of the police would lead to chaos only reactivates the historical misunderstanding of nonwhite people as savage or a threat. The right-wing information ecosystem uses these curated keywords to scare conservative constituents into voting. By insinuating that the Left is akin to a terrorist group and evoking a threat to the five f's, conservatives use the concept of a dangerously shifting Overton Window to galvanize the vote in favor of those already in positions of power. Unsurprisingly, those who spread this propaganda stand to lose the most from a redistribution of wealth and services.

Accepting the idea of a sliding Overton Window is a media manipulation strategy. This is part of why "A Letter on Justice and Open Debate" published in *Harper's* in July 2020 is particularly concerning. In the opinion piece, the authors, self-identified cultural and creative leaders, state their need to "preserve the possibility of good-faith disagreement without dire professional consequences," and worry that "a new set of moral attitudes and political commit-ments" would weaken the possibility of "open debate and toleration of differences."[11] Such a logic is inextricably connected to the notion of an "intolerant Left" that refuses to engage in open dialogue with those who disagree with them, a concept created by the right-wing media ecosystem to shut down what they see as an attack on their form of "liberalism" (Step Two).

The *Harper's* op-ed buys into the conservative framing that the Left is intolerant and incapable of civilized discourse. It also redirects and misappropriates the meaning of "canceling" in a very misleading way. As media scholar Meredith Clark explains, "canceling" efforts in fact bring marginalized, less-powerful groups together through online networks in order to direct their anger toward a common social purpose. To complain that "cancel cul-ture" silences people in tremendous positions of power is to ignore that those doing the "canceling" are the underdogs in this fight. Instead it ignites a moral panic that twists the origin of the prac-tice, "associat[ing] it with an unfounded fear of censorship and silencing" and confirming conservative elites' power to define reality and frame the debate.[12] Even Noam Chomsky, a seminal thinker on how mass communication media is an effective and powerful propaganda machine, is not immune to the conservative disinformation. He is one of the signatories on the op-ed.[13]

Herein lies the true fear of conservative elites. It is not that progressive ideas will cause anarchy or chaos, but rather that social movements designed to improve access and inclusion will hamper their ability to maintain power.

While I have focused here on how conservative pundits and politicians manipulate conservative meaning-making practices, the strategies I have identified are not necessarily used exclusively by one political party, or even only in the United States. I centered my research around conservative voters because I wanted to know more about how these audiences determined what was "fake news." As I soon learned, much of the information that affected Trump voters was homegrown and spread across various media, not just shared on Facebook by Russian bots.

Successful propaganda campaigns in the United States have clearly been finely attuned to both the culture and practices of audiences and the ways in which these audiences use technology to find information.[14] Future research should continue where this book leaves off, to study other communities, especially non-Western ones—all to better understand how "deep stories," cultural logics, and information systems are used to spread propaganda and threaten the democratic process. Some questions to ask include, What role does siloed search play in democratic participation? Do other cultural groups have unique media literacy practices? Who might exploit these processes for monetary or political gain?

Another topic that is ripe for further research is how conservative politicians and pundits craft keywords that align with conservative dialects. Conservative elites exploit data voids to ensure that conservative content is returned when their audiences "do their own research," but so far it has proven nearly impossible to anticipate what these keywords will be before they circulate.

Social scientists could explore further how search engine optimization is connected to patterns of misinformation and how keywords are embedded in broader cultural narratives of distrust. Studying other platforms connected to search might provide insights into how misinformation is seeded before it sprouts. My preliminary research on Wikipedia revisions, for example, seems to indicate that keywords used in misleading ways are often contested and quickly deleted by Wikipedia editors. Studying how the community combats vandalism on their site could shed light on where pockets of misinformation are being spread elsewhere.

Researchers interested in the sociology of search could also apply the findings from my book to arenas other than politics. For example, how might the way anti-vaxxers see the world influence the kinds of queries they use in internet searches? Members of these groups are unlikely to seek out information regarding vaccine safety, because they already believe vaccines are unsafe, yet they might engage in broader questions like "how to get religious exemption for vaccines" that currently return a wealth of information on how to avoid vaccinating your child. Now that we know there is no such thing as a neutral internet search, we should pour more attention and resources into research that examines how epistemology shapes the who, what, where, when, and why of search. Without better insights in this area, propagandists like those mentioned in this book will continue to control the plays. That is because media manipulation practices are constantly evolving and, though often hiding in plain sight, are often invisible to those charged with programming the solution. By exposing the schemes behind the propaganda, my hope is that coders and information seekers alike will see the light. For we all need to advocate for greater transparency and verification in the sources we use to learn about our culture, our political candidates, and our world.

NOTES

PREFACE

1. N. K. Baym, *Personal Connections in the Digital Age* (Cambridge, UK: Polity, 2010); danah boyd, "Social Network Sites as Networked Publics: Affordances, Dynamics, and Implications," in Z. Papacharissi, ed., *A Networked Self: Identity, Community, and Culture on Social Network Sites* (New York: Routledge, 2011), pp. 39–58; T. Bucher, "The Algorithmic Imaginary: Exploring the Ordinary Effects of Facebook Algorithms," *Information, Communication & Society* 20, no. 1 (2016): 30–44; H. Postigo, "The Socio-Technical Architecture of Digital Labor: Converting Play into YouTube Money," *New Media & Society* 18, no. 2 (2016): 332–349.

2. To protect the confidentiality of those involved in this study, I do not list the names or cities where these groups are located. Individuals' names have also been changed.

3. The question of whether to capitalize or lowercase "white" has been the subject of much discussion over the past few years. It is now customary for all style guides to recommend capitalizing B when referring to a Black person. The decision to do so is predicated on the understanding that "Black" reflects a shared identity and community. It acknowledges the role that slavery played in deliberately stripping people of their ethnic/national ties and follows the same structure for capitalizing other identities united by race, geography, and culture (e.g., Asian or Indigenous). The capitalization of "white," however, is more contentious. Not doing so fails to account for the normative power of language and can naturalize the inner workings of racism. Yet capitalizing "white" risks following the lead of white supremacists and can insinuate symmetry when there are still deep inequalities driven by race (and whiteness in particular). Ultimately, I decided not to capitalize "white." A goal of this book is for readers to see whiteness, and

how whiteness is an often overlooked through line in misinformation campaigns, but I felt that capitalizing "white" throughout gave it too much power. Nonetheless, I wanted to call attention to the tension in this decision, because more effort is needed—especially by white people—to understand the role that whiteness plays as a race and to more deeply understand how whiteness functions in our social and political institutions. For more on this important issue, see Kristen Mack and John Palfrey, "Capitalizing Black and White: Grammatical Justice and Equity," MacArthur Foundation, August 26, 2020, https://www.macfound.org/press/perspectives/capitalizing-black-and-white-grammatical-justice-and-equity; Nell Irvin Painter, "Opinion: Why 'White' Should Be Capitalized, Too," *Washington Post*, July 22, 2020; Kwame Anthony Appiah, "The Case for Capitalizing the B in Black," *The Atlantic*, June 18, 2020, https://www.theatlantic.com/ideas/ar chive/2020/06/time-to-capitalize-blackand-white/613159/; and Mike Laws, "Why We Capitalize 'Black' (and Not 'White')," *Columbia Journalism Review*, June 16, 2020, https://www.cjr.org/analysis/capital-b-black-styleguide.php.

4. Harold Garfinkel, *Studies in Ethnomethodology* (Cambridge, UK: Polity Press, 1967).

5. Reece Peck, *Fox Populism: Branding Conservatism as Working Class* (Cambridge, UK: Cambridge University Press, 2018).

6. Elihu Katz and Paul F. Lazarsfeld, *Personal Influence: The Part Played by People in the Flow of Mass Communications* (Glencoe, IL: Free Press, 1955).

7. Stuart Hall, "Encoding, Decoding," in Simon During, ed., *The Cultural Studies Reader* (1973; London: Routledge, 1991), pp. 90–103.

8. Pertti Alasuutari, *Rethinking the Media Audience* (Thousand Oaks, CA: SAGE, 1999).

9. Tamar Liebes and Elihu Katz, "Patterns of Involvement in Television Fiction: A Comparative Analysis," *European Journal of Communication* 1, no. 2 (1985): 151–171; Andrea Lee Press, *Women Watching Television: Gender, Class, and Generation in the American Television Experience* (Philadelphia: University of Pennsylvania Press, 1991).

10. danah boyd, "Social Network Sites as Networked Publics."

11. Kathy Charmaz, *Constructing Grounded Theory: A Practice Guide through Qualitative Analysis* (Thousand Oaks, CA: SAGE Publications, 2006).

12. Claire Wardle and Hossein Derakhshan, *Information Disorder: Toward an Interdisciplinary Framework for Research and Policy Making*, Council of Europe report, January 2018, https://rm.coe.int/dgi-2018-01-spaces-of-inclusion/168078c4b4.

PROLOGUE

1. For the Festival of Cultures program, see http://www.festivalof cultures.org/2017-Event-Program.

2. Paul Duggan, "Charlottesville's Confederate Statues Still Stand— and Still Symbolize a Racist Legacy," *Washington Post,* August 10, 2019, https://www.washingtonpost.com/history/2019/08/10/charlottesvilles- confederate-statues-still-stand-still-symbolize-racist-past/. For updated local coverage, see also "Charlottesville's Confederate Statues Removed from Local Parks," NBC29, Charlottesville, Virginia, July 10, 2021, https:// www.nbc29.com/2021/07/10/charlottesvilles-confederate-statues-be- relocated/.

3. Ibid. The park was later renamed yet again, to Market Street Park. See Daily Progress staff, "Charlottesville City Council Changes the Names of Two Renamed Parks," *Daily Progress,* July 16, 2018, https:// dailyprogress.com/news/local/city/charlottesville-city-council-changes- the-names-of-two-renamed-parks/article_9ac64d52-8963-11e8-853a- a3864982745e.html.

4. Ethnographic observations were corroborated by an independent review of the 2017 protests. See Hunton & Williams, LLP, *Final Report: Independent Review of the 2017 Protest Events in Charlottesville, Virginia,* https://www.huntonak.com/images/content/3/4/v4/34613/final-report-ada- compliant-ready.pdf.

5. WVEC Staff, "Torch-Wielding Group Protests Confederate Statue Removal in Va," *13NewsNow,* May 14, 2017, https://www.13newsnow.com/ article/news/local/virginia/torch-wielding-group-protests-Confederate- statue-removal-in-va/291-439612397.

6. Hunton & Williams, LLP, *Final Report.*

7. Ibid.

8. Ibid., p. 46.

9. Jason Sokol, *There Goes My Everything: White Southerners in the Age of Civil Rights, 1945–1975* (New York: Knopf, 2006).

10. Ibid., p. 216.

11. Hunton & Williams, LLP, *Final Report.*

12. Hawes Spencer and Matt Stevens, "23 Arrested and Tear Gas Deployed after a K.K.K. Rally in Virginia," *New York Times,* July 8, 2017.

13. Lisa Provence, "Who's a Racist? Wes Bellamy and Jason Kessler Speak Out at City Council," *Cville,* December 6, 2016, https://www.c-ville. com/whos-racist-bellamy-kessler-speak-city-council.

14. Meredith Clark, "DRAG THEM: A Brief Etymology of So-Called 'Can- cel Culture,' " *Communication and the Public* 5, nos. 3–4 (2020): 88–92.

15. *The Daily Caller* removed the article from its website, but it is still accessible in this archive https://archive.fo/p72Qx#selection-1283.0-1314.0.

16. Facebook screenshots in author's possession.

17. Patrick J. Kiger, "How Ben Franklin's Viral Political Cartoon United the 13 Colonies," *History Channel News,* History.com, October 23, 2018, https://www.history.com/news/ben-franklin-join-or-die-cartoon-french- indian-war.

18. Twitter screenshots in author's possession.

19. Tim Stelloh, "Arrest Warrant Issued for Man Brutally Beaten at Charlottesville Rally," *NBC News,* October 9, 2017.

20. Rob Walker, "The Shifting Symbolism of the Gadsden Flag," *New Yorker,* October 2, 2016.

21. "Petition Urging Terror Label for Antifa Gets Enough Signatures for White House Response," Fox News, August 25, 2017.

22. "Trump Decried 'Alt-Left' in Charlottesville: 'Do They Have Any Semblance of Guilt?'" Fox News, https://www.foxnews.com/politics/trump-decries-alt-left-in-charlottesville-do-they-have-any-semblance-of-guilt.

23. Dan T. Carter, *The Politics of Rage: George Wallace, the Origins of the New Conservatism, and the Transformation of American Politics* (Baton Rouge: Louisiana State University Press, 2000); Sokol, *There Goes My Everything.*

24. Hunton & Williams, LLP, *Final Report.*

25. Leon Yin and Aaron Sankin, "How We Discovered Google's Hate Blocklist for Ad Placements on YouTube," *The Markup,* April 8, 2021, https://themarkup.org/google-the-giant/2021/04/08/how-we-discovered-googles-hate-blocklist-for-ad-placements-on-youtube.

INTRODUCTION

1. Pew Research Center, "Republicans and Democrats Move Further Apart in Views of Voting Access," April 2021, https://www.pewresearch.org/topics/political-polarization.

2. Ruth Braunstein, *Prophets and Patriots: Faith in Democracy across the Political Divide* (Berkeley: University of California Press, 2017); George Lakoff, *Moral Politics: How Liberals and Conservatives Think* (Chicago: University of Chicago, 2002); Andrea Lee Press, *Women Watching Television: Gender, Class, and Generation in the American Television Experience* (Philadelphia: University of Pennsylvania Press, 1991); Jen Schradie, *The Revolution That Wasn't—How Digital Activism Favors Conservatives* (Cambridge, MA: Harvard University Press, 2019).

3. Eli Pariser, *The Filter Bubble—How the New Personalized Web Is Changing What We Read and How We Think* (New York: Penguin Random House, 2012); B. D. Loader and D. Mercea, "Networking Democracy? Social Media Innovations in Participatory Politics," *Information, Communication and Society* 14, no. 6 (2011): 757–769, doi: 10.1080/1369118X.2011.592648; Cass R. Sunstein, *Echo Chambers: Bush v. Gore, Impeachment, and Beyond* (Princeton, NJ: Princeton University Press, 2001); Joshua A. Tucker, Yannis Theocharis, Margaret E. Roberts, and Pablo Barberá, "From Liberation to Turmoil: Social Media and Democracy," *Journal of Democracy* 28, no. 4 (2017): 46–59.

4. Benedict R. O'Gorman Anderson, *Imagined Communities: Reflections on the Origin and Spread of Nationalism*, rev. and exp. ed. (New York: Verso, 1991).

5. Zeynep Tufekci, *Twitter and Tear Gas: The Power and Fragility of Networked Protest*, reprint ed. (New Haven: Yale University Press, 2018).

6. M. Gentzkow and J. Shapiro, "What Drives Media Slant? Evidence from U.S. Daily Newspapers," *Econometrica* 78, no. 1 (2010): 35–71; R. Robertson, D. Lazer, and C. Wilson, "Auditing the Personalization and Composition of Politically Related Search Engine Results Pages," in *Proceedings of the 2018 World Wide Web Conference* (April 2018): 955–965, https://dl.acm.org/doi/10.1145/3178876.3186143.

7. Pariser, *Filter Bubble*; Sunstein, *Echo Chambers*.

8. Leading researchers in the field of dis/misinformation include (but aren't limited to) danah boyd, Emma Briant, Joan Donovan, Deen Freelon, Daniel Kreiss, Caroline Jack, Rebecca Lewis, Alice Marwick, Shannon McGregor, Ryan Milner, Whitney Phillips, Joshua Tucker, and Leon Yin.

9. Claire Wardle and Hossein Derakhshan, *Information Disorder: Toward an Interdisciplinary Framework for Research and Policy Making*, Council of Europe report, January 2018, https://rm.coe.int/dgi-2018-01-spaces-of-inclusion/168078c4b4; Caroline Jack, "Lexicon of Lies: Terms for Problematic Information," Data & Society report, 2017, https://datasociety.net/pubs/oh/DataAndSociety_LexiconofLies.pdf.

10. Yochai Benkler, Rob Faris, and Hal Roberts, *Network Propaganda: Manipulation, Disinformation, and Radicalization in American Politics* (Oxford, UK: Oxford University Press, 2018); Jack, "Lexicon of Lies."

11. Jack, "Lexicon of Lies, p. 8.

12. Samuel S. Wineburg, "On the Reading of Historical Texts: Notes on the Breach between School and Academy," *American Educational Research Journal* 28, no. 3 (1991): 495–519, esp. p. 498.

13. Kevin Kruse, *White Flight: Atlanta and the Making of Modern Conservatism* (Princeton, NJ: Princeton University Press, 2005).

14. Angela Saini, *Superior: The Return of Race Science* (Boston: Beacon Press, 2019).

15. Anthea Butler, *White Evangelical Racism: The Politics of Morality in America* (Chapel Hill: University of North Carolina Press, 2021).

STEP ONE. KNOW YOUR AUDIENCE

1. To protect the anonymity of those studied, all names of individuals, organizations, and geographic locations have been changed.

2. This inclusion of faith in God in a Republican creed is not exclusive to the State of Virginia. As recently as 2004, the Texas Republican Party platform stated, "The Republican Party of Texas affirms that the

United States of America is a Christian nation, and the public acknowl-
edgement of God is undeniable in our history. Our nation was founded
in the fundamental Judeo-Christian principles based on the Holy Bible."
Quoted in Michelle Goldberg, *Kingdom Coming: The Rise of Christian
Nationalism* (New York: W. W. Norton, 2006), p. 27.

3. Anne Nelson, *Shadow Network: Media, Money, and the Secret Hub
of the Radical Right* (London: Bloomsbury Publishing, 2019).

4. Katherine Cramer, *The Politics of Resentment: Rural Consciousness
in Wisconsin and the Rise of Scott Walker* (Chicago: University of Chicago
Press, 2016); Arlie Russell Hochschild, *Strangers in Their Own Land:
Anger and Mourning on the American Right* (New York: New Press, 2016).

5. Andrew L. Whitehead and Samuel L. Perry, *Taking America Back
for God: Christian Nationalism in the United States* (Oxford, UK: Oxford
University Press, 2021); Philip Gorski, *American Covenant: A History of
Civil Religion from the Puritans to the Present* (Princeton, NJ: Princeton
University Press, 2017).

6. Theda Skocpol and Vanessa Williamson, *The Tea Party and the
Remaking of Republican Conservatism* (Oxford, UK: Oxford University
Press, 2012); Deana A. Rohlinger, "Friend and Foe: Media, Politics, and
Tactics in the Abortion War," *Social Problems* 53, no. 4 (2006): 537–561;
Francesca Polletta and Jessica Callahan, "Deep Stories, Nostalgia Narra-
tives, and Fake News: Storytelling in the Trump Era," *American Journal
of Cultural Sociology* 5 (2017).

7. Martin Durham, *The Christian Right, the Far Right and the Boundaries of American Conservatism* (Manchester, UK: Manchester University
Press, 2001); Martin Durham, *White Rage* (New York: Routledge, 2007).

8. Dan T. Carter, *The Politics of Rage: George Wallace, the Origins of
the New Conservatism, and the Transformation of American Politics* (Baton
Rouge: Louisiana State University Press, 2000); Kevin Kruse, *White Flight:
Atlanta and the Making of Modern Conservatism* (Princeton, NJ: Princeton
University Press, 2005); Jason Sokol, *There Goes My Everything: White
Southerners in the Age of Civil Rights, 1945–1975* (New York: Alfred A.
Knopf, 2006).

9. Kruse, *White Flight*, p. 6.

10. Skocpol and Williamson, *Tea Party*, p. 7.

11. Kathy Charmaz, *Constructing Grounded Theory: A Practice Guide
through Qualitative Analysis* (Thousand Oaks, CA: SAGE Publications,
2006).

12. Kathy Charmaz and Robert Thornberg, "The Pursuit of Quality
in Grounded Theory," *Qualitative Research in Psychology* 18, no. 3 (2020).

13. Kristin Kobes Du Mez, *Jesus and John Wayne: How White Evangelicals Corrupted a Faith and Fractured a Nation* (New York: Liveright
Publishing, 2020), p. 253.

14. Ibid.

15. Durham, *Christian Right*.

16. Anthea Butler, *White Evangelical Racism: The Politics of Morality in America* (Chapel Hill: University of North Carolina Press, 2021); Carter, *Politics of Rage*; Du Mez, *Jesus and John Wayne*; Kruse, *White Flight*; Sokol, *There Goes My Everything*.

17. Carter, *Politics of Rage*; Durham, *Christian Right*.

18. Denise Lu et al., "Faces of Power: 80% Are White, Even as US Becomes More Diverse," *New York Times*, September 9, 2020, https://www.nytimes.com/interactive/2020/09/09/us/powerful-people-race-us.html.

19. Carter, *Politics of Rage*.

20. Kruse, *White Flight*, p. 232.

21. Ibid.; Ian Haney López, *Dog Whistle Politics: How Coded Racial Appeals Have Reinvented Racism and Wrecked the Middle Class* (Oxford, UK: Oxford University Press, 2014).

22. Will Drabold, "Mike Pence: What He's Said on LGBT Issues over the Years," *Time*, July 15, 2016.

23. Robert Barnes and Seung Min Kim, " 'Everything Conservatives Hoped for and Liberals Feared': Neil Gorsuch Makes His Mark at the Supreme Court," *Washington Post*, September 6, 2019.

24. Ruth Braunstein, *Prophets and Patriots: Faith in Democracy across the Political Divide* (Berkeley: University of California Press, 2017); Jen Schradie, *The Revolution That Wasn't—How Digital Activism Favors Conservatives* (Cambridge, MA: Harvard University Press, 2019); Skocpol and Williamson, *Tea Party*.

25. Derek Thompson, "Elite Failure Has Brought Americans to the Edge of an Existential Crisis," *The Atlantic*, September 5, 2019.

26. Molly Worthen, *Apostles of Reason: The Crisis of Authority in American Evangelicalism* (Oxford, UK: Oxford University Press, 2013).

27. Butler, *White Evangelical Racism*.

28. Randall Balmer, *Evangelicalism in America* (Waco, TX: Baylor University Press, 2016).

29. Matthew Avery Sutton, *American Apocalypse: A History of Modern Evangelicalism* (Cambridge, MA: Harvard University Press, 2014).

30. Nathan Hatch, *The Democratization of American Christianity* (New Haven: Yale University Press, 1989).

31. Ibid., p. 10.

32. Skocpol and Williamson, *Tea Party*.

33. Braunstein, *Prophets and Patriots*, p. 33.

34. Ibid., p. 57; Skocpol and Williamson, *Tea Party*.

35. Nelson, *Shadow Network*, p. 2.

36. Braunstein, *Prophets and Patriots*.

37. Skocpol and Williamson, *Tea Party*, p. 37.

38. Whitehead and Perry, *Taking America Back for God*, p. 36.

39. Braunstein, *Prophets and Patriots*.

40. Ibid., p. 31; Skocpol and Williamson, *Tea Party*.

41. British Broadcasting Company, "The Matrix Is a 'Trans Metaphor' Lilly Wachowski Says," *BBC News*, August 7, 2020.

42. Butler, *White Evangelical Racism*.

43. Du Mez, *Jesus and John Wayne*.

44. Lauren Egan, "Trump Becomes First Sitting President to Attend March for Life Rally," *NBC News*, January 24, 2020.

45. Pew Research Center, *Attitudes on Same-Sex Marriage*, May 14, 2019, https://www.pewforum.org/fact-sheet/changing-attitudes-on-gay-marriage.

46. Anna Brown, "Republicans, Democrats Have Starkly Different Views on Transgender Issues," *Pew Research Center*, November 8, 2017, https://www.pewresearch.org/fact-tank/2017/11/08/transgender-issues-divide-republicans-and-democrats.

47. Counsel's Office, Republican National Committee, "Resolution Condemning Governmental Overreach Regarding Title IX Policies in Public Schools," https://prod-cdn-static.gop.com/media/documents/Resolution_Title_IX%20_Overreach.pdf.

48. Greg Lacour and Emma Way, "HB2: How North Carolina Got Here," *Charlotte Magazine*, March 30, 2017.

49. Laurel Westbrook and Kristen Schilt, "Doing Gender, Determining Gender: Transgender People, Gender Panics, and the Maintenance of the Sex/Gender/Sexuality System," *Gender & Society* 28, no. 1 (2014): 32–57.

50. Du Mez, *Jesus and John Wayne*.

51. Butler, *White Evangelical Racism*; ibid.

52. Butler, *White Evangelical Racism*.

53. Stephanie Ritenbaugh, "Walmart to Stop Selling Handgun Ammunition," *Pittsburgh Post-Gazette*, September 3, 2019.

54. Jennifer Carlson, "Mourning Mayberry: Guns, Masculinity, and Socioeconomic Decline," *Gender & Society* 29, no. 3 (2015): 386–409; Jennifer Carlson, *Citizen-Protectors: The Everyday Politics of Guns in an Age of Decline* (Oxford, UK: Oxford University Press, 2015).

55. Martin Durhan, *The Christian Right, the Far Right and the Boundaries of American Conservatism* (Manchester, UK: Manchester University Press, 2000), p. 70.

56. Nelson, *Shadow Network*.

57. Saeed Ahmed, "2 of the 5 Deadliest Mass Shootings in Modern US History Happened in the Last 35 days," *CNN*, November 6, 2017.

58. Andrew O'Reilly, "Texas Church Shooting Not the First Time a Good Guy with Gun Takes Down Mass Shooter," *Fox News*, November 8, 2017.

59. Saeed Ahmed, Doug Criss, and Emanuella Grinberg, " 'Hero' Exchanged Fire with Gunman, Then Helped Chase Him Down," *CNN*, November 7, 2017.

60. Stockholm International Peace Research Institute (SIPRI) Military Expenditure Database (based on open sources only), https://www.sipri.org/databases/milex.

61. Steve Wyche, "Colin Kaepernick Explains Why He Sat during National Anthem," NFL.com, August 27, 2016.

62. Cindy Boren, "Trump Says He Directed Pence to Walk out of Game if 49ers Protested during National Anthem," *Washington Post,* October 8, 2017.

63. K. B. Turner, D. Giacopassi, and M. Vandiver, "Ignoring the Past: Coverage of Slavery and Slave Patrols in Criminal Justice Texts," *Journal of Criminal Justice Education* 17, no. 1 (2006): 181–195.

64. Carter, *Politics of Rage,* p. 249.

65. Dorothy Roberts, *Killing the Black Body: Race, Reproduction, and the Meaning of Liberty* (New York: Penguin Random House Press, 1997).

66. Kruse, *White Flight.*

67. Braunstein, *Prophets and Patriots*; Schradie, *Revolution that Wasn't*; Skocpol and Williamson, *Tea Party;* Whitehead and Perry, *Taking America Back for God.*

68. Nelson, *Shadow Network,* p. 209.

69. Butler, *White Evangelical Racism.*

70. Christopher Petrella has a PhD in African Diaspora Studies from UC Berkeley and is the associate director for advocacy at Boston University's Center for Antiracist Research. On November 3, 2017, he wrote "The Ugly History of the Pledge of Allegiance—and Why It Matters" for the *Washington Post.*

71. Nelson, *Shadow Network.*

72. Khadijah Costley White, *The Branding of Right-Wing Activism: The News Media and The Tea Party* (Oxford: Oxford University Press, 2018).

STEP TWO. BUILD A NETWORK

1. Yochai Benkler, Rob Faris, and Hal Roberts, *Network Propaganda: Manipulation, Disinformation, and Radicalization in American Politics* (Oxford, UK: Oxford University Press, 2018).

2. Khadijah Costley White, *The Branding of Right-Wing Activism: The News Media and The Tea Party* (Oxford: Oxford University Press, 2018).

3. Benkler, Faris, and Roberts, *Network Propaganda*, p. 79.

4. Anne Nelson, *Shadow Network: Media, Money, and the Secret Hub of the Radical Right* (London: Bloomsbury Publishing, 2019), p. 59.

5. Tom Rosentiel, "Fewer Voters Identify as Republicans. Democrats Now Have the Advantage." *Pew Research Center,* March 20, 2008.

6. Barbara Fister, "The Librarian War against QAnon," *The Atlantic,* February 18, 2021.

7. Antonio Gramsci, *Selections from Prison Notebooks: The Study of Philosophy* (London: ElecBook 1971), p. 641.

8. Nelson, *Shadow Network*, p. 80.

9. Benkler, Faris, and Roberts, *Network Propaganda*; Nicole Hemmer, *Messengers of the Right: Conservative Media and the Transformation of American Politics* (Philadelphia: University of Pennsylvania Press, 2018).

10. Matthew Sheffield, "Roy Moore, the *Federalist,* and the Decay of the Conservative Mind," *Salon,* December 1, 2017, https://www.salon.com /2017/12/01/roy-moore-the-federalist-and-the-decay-of-the-conservative-mind/.

11. Charles Bethea, "The *Federalist* as 'Medical Journal' in the Time of the Coronavirus," *New Yorker,* April 12, 2020.

12. Michael Levenson, "Twitter Blocks the *Federalist* for Promoting Coronavirus Parties," *New York Times,* March 5, 2020.

13. Lindsey Ellefson, " 'Morning Joe' Still Can't Topple 'Fox & Friends' Ratings, Even with Big Biden Interview," *The Wrap,* May 4, 2020.

14. Grace Guarnieri, "Trump Says 'Fox & Friends' Is the Most Influential News Show; That's Only Because He Watches It," *Newsweek,* December 21, 2017.

15. Justin Peters, "Joe Rogan's Galaxy Brain," *Slate,* March 21, 2019.

16. PragerU, www.prageru.com.

17. Eriq Gardner, "PragerU Headed to New Legal Defeat over 'Censorship' of Conservatives on YouTube," *Hollywood Reporter,* October 25, 2019.

18. PragerU Kids, www.prageru.com/prep.

19. Joe Concha, "Trump Dings CNN, 'Morning Joe' Rating as Tucker Carlson Sets Record," *The Hill,* July 1, 2020.

20. Derek Black, son of Stormfront creator Don Black, was interviewed by CNN on *The Van Jones Show* on March 30, 2019. In the interview, he revealed that his family would often watch and record Tucker Carlson's show so they could go back and refer to the content later. See http://transcripts.cnn.com/TRANSCRIPTS/1903/30/vjs.01.html.

21. Hemmer, *Messengers of the Right.*

22. Deana Rohlinger, *Abortion Politics, Mass Media, and Social Movements in America* (Cambridge, UK: Cambridge University Press, 2015).

23. Hemmer, *Messengers of the Right*, p. 65.

24. Ibid.

25. Nelson, *Shadow Network;* Jen Schradie, *The Revolution That Wasn't—How Digital Activism Favors Conservatives* (Cambridge, MA: Harvard University Press, 2019).

26. J. J. Gibson, "The Theory of Affordances," in R. Shaw and J. Bransford, eds., *Perceiving, Acting, and Knowing* (Hillsdale, NJ: Routledge, 1977); J. J. Gibson, *The Ecological Approach to Visual Perception* (Boston: Houghton Mifflin, 1979).

27. I. A. Ambalov, "Decomposition of Perceived Usefulness: A Theoretical Perspective and Empirical Test," *Technology & Society* 64 (February 2021).

28. N. K. Baym, *Personal Connections in the Digital Age* (Cambridge, UK: Polity, 2010); danah boyd, "Social Network Sites as Networked Publics: Affordances, Dynamics, and Implications," in Z. Papacharissi, ed., *A Networked Self: Identity, Community, and Culture on Social Network Sites* (New York: Routledge, 2011), pp. 39–58; T. Bucher, "The Algorithmic Imaginary: Exploring the Ordinary Effects of Facebook Algorithms," *Information, Communication & Society* 20, no. 1 (2016): 30–44; H. Postigo, "The Socio-Technical Architecture of Digital Labor: Converting Play into YouTube Money," *New Media & Society* 18, no. 2 (2016): 332–349.

29. Nelson, *Shadow Network*, pp. 237, 56.

30. Whitney Phillips and Ryan M. Milner, *You Are Here: A Field Guide for Navigating Polarized Speech, Conspiracy Theories, and Our Polluted Media Landscape* (Cambridge, MA: MIT Press, 2021).

31. Heather Hendershot, *What's Fair on the Air?: Cold War Right-Wing Broadcasting and the Public Interest* (Chicago: University of Chicago Press, 2011).

32. Nelson, *Shadow Network*.

33. Madison Trammel, "Making Airwaves," *Christianity Today*, January 26, 2007.

34. Nelson, *Shadow Network*, p. 168. Paul Matzko, "Talk Radio Is Turning Millions of Americans into Conservatives," *New York Times*, October 9, 2020.

35. Nelson, *Shadow Network*, p. 146.

36. Hemmer, *Messengers of the Right*.

37. Nelson, *Shadow Network*, p. 56.

38. Ibid.

39. Hemmer, *Messengers of the Right*, p. 50.

40. Ibid., p. 9. On early fact-checkers, see Merrill Fabry, "Here's How the First Fact-Checkers Were Able to Do Their Jobs before the Internet," *Time*, August 24, 2017, https://time.com/4858683/fact-checking-history.

41. Ibid., p. 270.

42. Benkler, Farris, and Roberts, *Network Propaganda*, p. 321.

43. Hemmer, *Messengers of the Right*.

44. Ian Haney López, *Dog Whistle Politics: How Coded Racial Appeals Have Reinvented Racism and Wrecked the Middle Class* (Oxford, UK: Oxford University Press, 2014).

45. Ryan Sit, "Trump Thinks Only Black People Are on Welfare, But Really, White Americans Receive Most Benefits," *Newsweek*, January 12, 2018.

46. Anthea Butler, *White Evangelical Racism: The Politics of Morality in America* (Chapel Hill: University of North Carolina Press, 2021).

47. Dan T. Carter, *The Politics of Rage: George Wallace, the Origins of the New Conservatism, and the Transformation of American Politics* (Baton Rouge: Louisiana State University Press, 2000); Kevin Kruse, *White Flight: Atlanta and the Making of Modern Conservatism* (Princeton, NJ: Princeton University Press, 2005); Haney López, *Dog Whistle Politics*.

48. The 1994 Contract with America is at https://global.oup.com/us/companion.websites/9780195385168/resources/chapter6/contract/america.pdf.

49. Ceci Connolly, "Consultant Offers GOP a Language for the Future," *Washington Post*, September 4, 1997, https://www.washingtonpost.com/archive/politics/1997/09/04/consultant-offers-gop-a-language-for-the-future/22445431-5687-458c-a727-3e13e86d73df/.

50. Frank I. Luntz, *Words That Work: It's Not What You Say, It's What People Hear* (New York: Hyperion, 2007), p. 70.

51. Jennifer 8. Lee, "A Call for Softer, Greener Language," *New York Times*, March 2, 2003, https://www.nytimes.com/2003/03/02/us/a-call-for-softer-greener-language.html.

52. Nelson, *Shadow Network*.

53. Luntz, *Words That Work*.

54. Phillips and Milner, *You Are Here*, refers to these conspiracies working in conjunction as the "Deep State."

55. "Candace Owens Rips Democrats as 'The Party of Hate, Intolerance, and Violence'—and Says America NEEDS to Vote Trump," *The Sun*, November 2, 2020, https://www.the-sun.com/news/1727763/candace-owens-democrats-hate-donald-trump-election-2020/.

56. Kim R. Holmes, "How the Left Became So Intolerant," *The Heritage Foundation*, December 12, 2017.

57. Fox News, *Tucker Carlson Tonight*, July 3, 2018.

58. Mary Douglas, *Purity and Danger: Mary Douglas Collected Works*, vol. 2 (London: Routledge, 1996).

59. Kristin Kobes Du Mez, *Jesus and John Wayne: How White Evangelicals Corrupted a Faith and Fractured a Nation* (New York: Liveright Publishing, 2020).

60. Nirmal Puwar, *Space Invaders: Race, Gender, and Bodies out of Place* (Oxford, UK: Berg Publishers, 2004).

61. Hemmer, *Messengers of the Right*, p. 33.

62. Ibid.

63. Ibid., p. 270.

64. Ibid.

65. Francesca Tripodi, "Google and Censorship through Search Engines," U.S. Senate Committee on the Judiciary Hearings, July 16, 2019, https://www.judiciary.senate.gov/meetings/google-and-censorship-though-search-engines; Francesca Tripodi, "Stifling Free Speech: Technological Censorship and the Public Discourse, United States Senate Committee

on the Judiciary," U.S. Senate Committee on the Judiciary Hearings, April 10, 2019, https://www.judiciary.senate.gov/meetings/stifling-free-speech-technological-censorship-and-the-public-discourse.

66. Quoted in Phillips and Milner, *You Are Here*, p. 15.

STEP THREE. ENGAGE IN THEIR FORM OF MEDIA LITERACY

1. Nathan Hatch, *The Democratization of American Christianity* (New Haven: Yale University Press, 1989).

2. Ibid.

3. Ibid., p. 45.

4. Ibid.

5. Anthea Butler, *White Evangelical Racism: The Politics of Morality in America* (Chapel Hill: University of North Carolina Press, 2021).

6. Hatch, *Democratization of American Christianity*.

7. Butler, *White Evangelical Racism*.

8. Ibid.

9. Ruth Braunstein, *Prophets and Patriots: Faith in Democracy across the Political Divide* (Berkeley: University of California Press, 2017).

10. Cain Hope Felder, *Race, Racism, and the Biblical Narratives* (Minneapolis: Fortress Press, 2002), p. 53.

11. Braunstein, *Prophets and Patriots*.

12. Felder, *Race, Racism, and the Biblical Narratives*, p. 89.

13. C. Wright Mills, *The Sociological Imagination* (Oxford, UK: Oxford University Press, 1959).

14. Felder, *Race, Racism, and the Biblical Narratives*.

15. Braunstein, *Prophets and Patriots*, pp. 45, 89.

16. Samuel S. Wineburg, "On the Reading of Historical Texts: Notes on the Breach between School and Academy," *American Educational Research Journal* 28, no. 3 (1991): 498.

17. Kristin Kobes Du Mez, *Jesus and John Wayne: How White Evangelicals Corrupted a Faith and Fractured a Nation* (New York: Liveright Publishing, 2020), p. 28.

18. Wineburg, "On the Reading of Historical Texts."

19. Cain Hope Felder, *Troubling Biblical Waters: Race, Class, and Family* (Maryknoll, NY: Orbis Books, 1990); Felder, *Race, Racism, and the Biblical Narratives*.

20. Felder, *Race, Racism, and the Biblical Narratives*, p. 42.

21. Butler, *White Evangelical Racism*.

22. Du Mez, *Jesus and John Wayne*.

23. Braunstein, *Prophets and Patriots*; ibid.; Theda Skocpol and Vanessa Williamson, *The Tea Party and the Remaking of Republican Conservatism* (Oxford, UK: Oxford University Press, 2012); Andrew L. Whitehead

and Samuel L. Perry, *Taking America Back for God: Christian Nationalism in the United States* (Oxford, UK: Oxford University Press, 2021).

24. Skocpol and Williamson, *Tea Party*, p. 50.

25. Braunstein, *Prophets and Patriots*, pp. 61, 63.

26. Ibid., p. 93.

27. Du Mez, *Jesus and John Wayne*, pp. 108–109.

28. Texts specifically referenced in this study include the Constitution, the Federalist Papers, the Affordable Care Act, the Massachusetts Bill of Rights, letters between Thomas Jefferson and the Danbury Baptists, the Northwest Ordinance, the Virginia Declaration of Rights, and several U.S. Supreme Court Hearings.

29. Braunstein, *Prophets and Patriots*, p. 91.

30. Whitehead and Perry, *Taking America Back for God*.

31. PragerU, "What Does Separation of Church and State Mean?" video posted May 25, 2020.

32. Butler, *White Evangelical Racism*.

33. Ibid.

34. Ibid.

35. Ibid.

36. Steve Benen, "Group Quietly Boasts about Crafting GOP's Voter-Suppression Bills." *MSNBC*, May 14, 2021, https://www.msnbc.com/rachel-maddow-show/group-quietly-boasts-about-crafting-gop-s-voter-suppression-bills-n1267339.

37. "Madison's Theory of the Republic," Online Library of Liberty, https://oll.libertyfund.org/page/madison-s-theory-of-the-republic.

38. James Madison, "The Conformity of the Plan to Republican Principles for the Independent Journal," Federalist Papers 39, January 16, 1788.

39. Katherine Cramer, *The Politics of Resentment: Rural Consciousness in Wisconsin and the Rise of Scott Walker* (Chicago: University of Chicago Press, 2016); Arlie Russell Hochschild, *Strangers in Their Own Land: Anger and Mourning on the American Right* (New York: New Press, 2016).

40. Michael Rothfeld and Joe Palazzolo, "Trump Lawyer Arranged $130,000 Payment for Adult Film Star's Silence," *Wall Street Journal*, January 12, 2018, https://www.wsj.com/articles/trump-lawyer-arranged-130-000-payment-for-adult-film-stars-silence-1515787678; "U.S. Election: Full Transcript of Donald Trump's Obscene Videotape," BBC News, October 9, 2016; https://www.bbc.com/news/election-us-2016-37595321.

41. Du Mez, *Jesus and John Wayne*; Butler, *White Evangelical Racism*.

42. Du Mez, *Jesus and John Wayne*; Whitehead and Perry, *Taking America Back for God*.

43. Butler, *White Evangelical Racism*.

44. See the WallBuilders' website at www.wallbuilders.com.

45. Anne Nelson, *Shadow Network: Media, Money, and the Secret Hub of the Radical Right* (London: Bloomsbury Publishing, 2019).

46. Denis Prager, "In Defense of Pro-Trump Christians," *National Review,* October 18, 2016, https://www.nationalreview.com/2016/10/pro-trump-christians-unfairly-criticized/.

47. Nelson, *Shadow Network,* p. 197.

48. Bill Hoffmann, "Rick Perry Likens Trump to King David as 'Chosen Man of God.' " *Newsmax,* August 2, 2017, https://www.newsmax.com/newsmax-tv/rick-perry-trump-king-david/2017/08/02/id/805313/.

49. Nicole Hemmer, *Messengers of the Right: Conservative Media and the Transformation of American Politics* (Philadelphia: University of Pennsylvania Press, 2018).

50. The story this respondent was referring to was written on May 11, 2017, by Dan Merica of CNN with a headline that ran "Trump Gets 2 Scoops of Ice Cream, Everyone Else Gets 1—and Other Top Lines from This *Time* Interview," http://www.cnn.com/2017/05/11/politics/trump-time-magazine-ice-cream/index.html.

51. Eli Pariser, *The Filter Bubble—How the New Personalized Web Is Changing What We Read and How We Think* (New York: Penguin Random House, 2012), p. 64.

52. Gregory Korte and Alan Gomez, "Trump Ramps Up Rhetoric on Undocumented Immigrants: 'These Aren't People. These Are Animals.'" *USA Today,* May 16, 2018.

53. Tucker Carlson, "The Left Doesn't Think MS-13 Is a Problem Because Trump Thinks They're 'Animals,' " *Fox News,* May 24, 2019.

54. Ian Haney López, *Dog Whistle Politics: How Coded Racial Appeals Have Reinvented Racism and Wrecked the Middle Class* (Oxford, UK: Oxford University Press, 2014).

55. Rich McKay, "Georgia Bans Giving Water to Voters in Line under Sweeping Restrictions," *Reuters,* March 25, 2021.

56. Faith Karimi, "It's Now Illegal in Georgia to Give Food and Water to Voters in Line," *CNN,* March 26, 2021.

57. Ariane Datil and Mauricio Chamberlin, "Yes, It's Illegal to Give Water, Food to Georgia Voters in Line for Polls," *WCNC-Charlotte,* March 31, 2021.

58. Tim Carman, "New Limits on Food and Water at Georgia's Polls Could Hinder Black and Low-Income Voters, Advocates Say," *Washington Post,* April 9, 2021.

59. Georgia Senate bill SB202, 2021, p. 73. The full text of the bill is available from the *New York Times* at https://int.nyt.com/data/documenttools/georgia-sb-202/8f7976cadb0bcb56/full.pdf.

60. Ibid., p. 74.

61. The Heritage Foundation, "Heritage Foundation Releases Fact-Check on Election Reform Law," Heritage.org, April 16, 2021.

62. Sam Wineburg and Sarah McGrew, "Why Students Can't Google Their Way to the Truth," *Education Week* 36, no. 11 (2016): 22–28; Sam Wineburg and Sarah McGrew, "Lateral Reading: Reading Less and Learning More When Evaluating Digital Information," *Social Science Research Network*, October 6, 2017, https://papers.ssrn.com/abstract=3048994; Sam Wineburg and Sarah McGrew, "Lateral Reading and the Nature of Expertise: Reading Less and Learning More When Evaluating Digital Information," *Teachers College Record* 121, no. 11 (2019): 1–40.

63. J. Breakstone, M. Smith, P. Connors, T. Ortega, D. Kerr, and S. Wineburg, "Lateral Reading: College Students Learn to Critically Evaluate Internet Sources in an Online Course," *Harvard Kennedy School Misinformation Review* 2 no. 1 (2021): 1–17, https://doi.org/ 10.37016/ mr-2020-56.

64. Wineburg and McGrew, "Lateral Reading: Reading Less and Learning More"; Michael Caufield, "Info-Environmentalism: An Introduction," *Educause Review* 52, no. 6 (2017): 92–93.

65. For more on trickle-down economics, see David Hope and Julian Limberg, "The Economic Consequences of Major Tax Cuts for the Rich," International Inequalities Institute Working Paper, no. 55 (London: London School of Economics and Political Science, 2020).

66. Claire Wardle and Hossein Derakhshan, *Information Disorder: Toward an Interdisciplinary Framework for Research and Policy Making*, Council of Europe report, January 2018, https://rm.coe.int/dgi-2018-01-spaces-of-inclusion/168078c4b4.

STEP FOUR. UNDERSTAND HOW INFORMATION FLOWS

1. Lawrence Page, Sergey Brin, Rajeev Motwani, and Terry Winograd, "The PageRank Citation Ranking: Bringing Order to the Web," 1999, http://ilpubs.stanford.edu:8090/422.

2. Eli Pariser, *The Filter Bubble—How the New Personalized Web Is Changing What We Read and How We Think* (New York: Penguin Random House, 2012); Cass R. Sunstein, *#Republic: Divided Democracy in the Age of Social Media* (Princeton, NJ: Princeton University Press, 2018); Cass R. Sunstein, *Echo Chambers: Bush v. Gore, Impeachment, and Beyond* (Princeton, NJ: Princeton University Press, 2001).

3. Even though Google is a noun, the act of "googling" is a verb. When it is used as an action, I do not capitalize it.

4. Daniel Kreiss and Shannon C. Mcgregor, "The 'Arbiters of What Our Voters See': Facebook and Google's Struggle with Policy, Process, and Enforcement around Political Advertising," *Political Communication* 36, no. 4 (2019): 499–522; Frank Pasquale, *The Black Box Society—Frank Pasquale* (Cambridge, MA: Harvard University Press, 2015); Siva Vaid-

hyanathan, *The Googlization of Everything*, 1st ed. (Berkeley: University of California Press, 2011).

5. Virginia Eubanks, *Automating Inequality: How High-Tech Tools Profile, Police, and Punish the Poor* (New York: St. Martin's Press, 2018); Safiya Umoja Noble, *Algorithms of Oppression* (New York: NYU Press, 2018).

6. Shoshana Zuboff, *The Age of Surveillance Capitalism: The Fight for a Human Future at the New Frontier of Power* (New York: PublicAffairs, 2019).

7. Siva Vaidhyanathan, *Antisocial Media: How Facebook Disconnects Us and Undermines Democracy* (Oxford, UK: Oxford University Press, 2018).

8. Zuboff, *Age of Surveillance Capitalism*.

9. Ruha Benjamin, *Race after Technology: Abolitionist Tools for the New Jim Code* (Cambridge, UK: Polity Press, 2019); Manuel Castells, *Communication Power* (Oxford, UK: Oxford University Press, 2011); Kate Crawford and Tarleton Gillespie, "What Is a Flag For? Social Media Reporting Tools and the Vocabulary of Complaint," *New Media & Society* 18, no. 3 (2016): 410–428; Tarleton Gillespie, "The Politics of 'Platforms,' " *New Media & Society* 12, no. 3 (2010): 347–364; Lucas D. Introna and Helen Nissenbaum, "Shaping the Web: Why the Politics of Search Engines Matters," *Information Society* 16, no. 3 (2000): 169–185; Safiya Umoja Noble and Sarah J. Roberts, "Through Google-Colored Glass(es): Design, Emotion, Class, and Wearables as Commodity and Control," *Media Studies Publications* 13 (2016): 25; Cathy O'Neil, *Weapons of Math Destruction* (Harlow, UK: Penguin Books, 2017).

10. Nicholas Negroponte, *Being Digital* (New York: Alfred A. Knopf, 1995).

11. Sunstein, *#Republic*; Emily Thorson, "Changing Patterns of News Consumption and Participation," *Information, Communication & Society* 11, no. 4 (2008): 473–489.

12. Sunstein, *Echo Chambers*.

13. Robert D. Putnam, *Bowling Alone: The Collapse and Revival of American Community* (New York: Simon & Schuster, 2000).

14. Kevin G. Barnhurst and John Nerone, *The Form of News: A History* (New York: Guilford Press, 2001).

15. Charles Simmons, *The African American Press: A History of News Coverage during National Crises, with Special Reference to Four Black Newspapers, 1827–1965* (Jefferson, NC: McFarland, 2006).

16. Zuboff, *Age of Surveillance Capitalism*.

17. Ibid., p. 67.

18. Ibid.

19. A. W. Geiger, "Key Findings about the Online News Landscape in America," *Pew Research Center,* September 11, 2019, https://www.pewresearch.

org/fact-tank/2019/09/11/key-findings-about-the-online-news-landscape-in-america/.

20. This speech was not recorded and is based on field notes taken during the speech.

21. Richard Oppel, "Steelers' Villaneuva Takes a Stand, But Might Agree with Kaepernick's Mission," *New York Times*, September 25, 2017.

22. Vaidhyanathan, *Googlization of Everything*.

23. Jutta Haider and Olof Sundin, *Invisible Search and Online Search Engines* (Oxfordshire, UK: Taylor & Francis, 2019), p. 108.

24. Laura Granka, "The Politics of Search," *Information Society* 6 (2010): 364–374, https://www.tandfonline.com/doi/abs/10.1080/0197224 3.2010.511560.

25. Lawrence Page, Sergey Brin, Rajeev Motwani, and Terry Winograd, "The PageRank Citation Ranking: Bringing Order to the Web," 1999, retrieved October 30, 2019 (http://ilpubs.stanford.edu:8090/422/); Pariser, *The Filter Bubble*.

26. Taina Bucher, "Want to Be on the Top? Algorithmic Power and the Threat of Invisibility on Facebook," *New Media & Society* 14 (2012): 1164–1180; Gillespie, "Politics of 'Platforms' "; Introna and Nissenbaum, "Shaping the Web"; Granka, "Politics of Speech."

27. Noble, *Algorithms of Oppression*.

28. Kristen Grind, Sam Schechner, Robert McMillan, and John West, "How Google Interferes with Its Search Algorithms and Changes Your Results," *Wall Street Journal*, November 15, 2019.

29. Min Jiang, "The Business and Politics of Search Engines: A Comparative Study of Baidu and Google's Search Results of Internet Events in China," *New Media & Society* 16, no. 2 (2013): 212–233.

30. Grind et al., "How Google Interferes with Its Search Algorithms."

31. Vaidhyanathan, *Antisocial Media*.

32. Andrew Orlowski, "Google Stabs Wikipedia in the Front: Is Knowledge Graph Killing Its Readership?" *The Register*, January 13, 2014, https://www.theregister.com/2014/01/13/google_stabs_wikipedia_in_the_front.

33. Adrianne Jeffreis and Leon Yin, "Google's Top Search Result? Surprise! It's Google," *The Markup*, July 28, 2020, https://themarkup.org/google-the-giant/2020/07/28/google-search-results-prioritize-google-products-over-competitors.

34. Robert Epstein and Ronald E. Robertson, "The Search Engine Manipulation Effect (SEME) and Its Possible Impact on the Outcomes of Elections," *Proceedings of the National Academy of Sciences of the United States of America* 112, no. 33 (August 2015); Eszter Hargittai and Heather Young, "Searching for a 'Plan B': Young Adults' Strategies for Finding Information about Emergency Contraception Online," *Policy & Internet* 4, no. 2 (2012); Ahmed Allam, Peter Johannes Schultz, and Kent Nakamoto, "The Impact of Search Engine Selection and Sorting Criteria on

Vaccination Beliefs and Attitudes: Two Experiments Manipulating Google Outputs," *Journal of Medical Internet Research* 16, no. 4 (2014).

35. Arlie Russell Hochschild, *Strangers in Their Own Land: Anger and Mourning on the American Right* (New York: New Press, 2016).

36. David Mikkelson, "Rumors about Target," Snopes.com, November 4, 2002, https://www.snopes.com/fact-check/rumors-about-target/.

37. D. Bilal and J. Kirby, "Differences and Similarities in Information Seeking: Children and Adults as Web Users," *Information Processing & Management* 38, no. 5 (2002): 649–670; M. Hearst, *Search User Interfaces* (Cambridge, UK: Cambridge University Press, 2009); H. L. O'Brien, R. Dickinson, and N. Askin, "A Scoping Review of Individual Differences in Information Seeking Behavior and Retrieval Research between 2000 and 2015," *Library & Information Science Research* 39, no. 3 (2017): 244–254; R. Robertson, D. Lazer, and C. Wilson, "Auditing the Personalization and Composition of Politically Related Search Engine Results Pages," in *Proceedings of the 2018 World Wide Web Conference* (April 2018): 955–965, https://dl.acm.org/doi/10.1145/3178876.3186143; M. L. Wilson, "Search User Interface Design," *Synthesis Lectures on Information Concepts, Retrieval, and Services* 3, no. 3 (2011): 1–143.

38. Eszter Hargittai, "Open Portals or Closed Gates? Channeling Content on the World Wide Web," *Poetics* 27, no. 4 (2000): 233–254; Eszter Hargittai, "Do You 'Google'? Understanding Search Engine Use Beyond the Hype," *First Monday* 9, no. 3 (2004); Eszter Hargittai, "Hurdles to Information Seeking: Spelling and Typographical Mistakes during Users' Online Behavior," *Journal of the Association for Information Systems* 7, no. 1 (2006): 52–67.

39. Hargittai and Young, "Searching for a 'Plan B.' "

40. Gary Marchionini, "Exploratory Search: From Finding to Understanding," *Communications of the ACM* 49, no. 4 (2006): 41–46.

41. Noble, *Algorithms of Oppression*: p. 118; Jutta Haider and Olof Sundin, *Invisible Search and Online Search Engines* (Oxfordshire, UK: Taylor & Francis, 2019).

42. Page et al., "PageRank Citation Ranking."

43. Introna and Nissenbaum, "Shaping the Web."

44. Casey Newton, "Google Tweaks Image Search to Make Porn Harder to Find," CNET.com, December 12, 2012, https://www.cnet.com/tech/services-and-software/google-tweaks-image-search-to-make-porn-harder-to-find/.

45. Michael Buckland, *Information and Society* (Cambridge, MA: MIT Press, 2017), p. 6.

46. Jiang, "Business and Politics of Search Engines."

47. Hargittai and Young, "Searching for a 'Plan B.' " Andrei Zavadski and Florian Toepfl, "Querying the Internet as a Mnemonic Practice: How

Search Engines Mediate Four Types of Past Events in Russia," *Media Culture & Society* 42, no. 2 (2018).

48. Erving Goffman, *The Presentation of Self in Everyday Life* (New York: Anchor Books, 1959); Peter L. Berger and Thomas Luckmann, *The Social Construction of Reality: A Treatise in the Sociology of Knowledge* (New York: Penguin, 1966).

49. An exception to this would be Eszter Hargittai. See Hargittai, "The Social, Political, Economic, and Cultural Dimensions of Search Engines: An Introduction," *Journal of Computer-Mediated Communication* 12, no. 3 (2007): 769–777.

50. Haider and Sundin, *Invisible Search*; Noble, *Algorithms of Oppression*.

51. Erving Goffman, *Frame Analysis: An Essay on the Organization of Experience* (Cambridge, MA: Harvard University Press, 1974).

52. Karl Marx, *Das Capital*, in Robert Tucker, ed., *Marx-Engels Reader* (New York: W.W. Norton, 1978), vol. 1, chap. 25, https://genius.com/Robert-c-tucker-the-marx-engels-reader-chap-25-capital-volume-one-annotated.

53. Eviatar Zerubavel, "Islands of Meaning," in J. O'Brien, ed., *The Production of Reality: Essays and Readings on Social Interaction*, 5th ed. (Thousand Oaks, CA: Pine Forge Press, 1991), 11–27.

54. Eviatar Zerubavel, "The Five Pillars of Essentialism: Reification and the Social Construction of an Objective Reality," *Cultural Sociology*, November 20, 2015. "Eternalism" is the concept that what is real or true now will "always" stay the same—we tend to regard the historically specific world we currently exist in as if it has always been that way.

55. Sandra Harding, "Rethinking Standpoint Epistemology: What Is 'Strong Objectivity'?," in Linda Alcoff and Elizabeth Potter, eds., *Feminist Epistemologies* (London: Routledge, 1993).

56. "Why Isn't the Sky Blue?" *RadioLab*, May 21, 2012, https://www.wnycstudios.org/podcasts/radiolab/segments/211213-sky-isnt-blue.

57. NASA Science Space Place, https://spaceplace.nasa.gov/blue-sky/en/.

58. Indiana Public Radio, "Why the Sky Is Not Blue," January 26, 2012, https://indianapublicmedia.org/amomentofscience/sky-blue.php.

59. Noble, *Algorithms of Oppression*.

60. Felix Stalder and Christine Mayer, "The Second Index: Search Engines, Personalization and Surveillance," in Konrad Becker and Felix Stalder, eds., *Deep Search: The Politics of Search beyond Google* (Vienna: Studien Verlag, 2009), pp. 98–115.

61. Eszter Hargittai has been calling for this kind of interdisciplinary work since the early 2000s.

62. Noble, *Algorithms of Oppression*.

63. Jessie Daniels, "Cloaked Websites: Propaganda, Cyber-Racism and Epistemology in the Digital Era," *CUNY Academic Works* (Summer 2009), https://academicworks.cuny.edu/hc_pubs/271.

64. Rebecca Hersher, "What Happened When Dylann Roof Asked Google for Information about Race?" *The Two-Way,* NPR, January 10, 2017.

65. Noble, *Algorithms of Oppression.*

66. Annie Y. Chen, Brendan Nyhan, Jason Reifler, Ronald E. Robertson, and Christo Wilson, "Exposure to Alternative and Extremist Content on YouTube," *Center for Technology & Society—The Belfer Fellowship Series,* https://www.adl.org/resources/reports/exposure-to-alternative-extremist-content-on-youtube.

67. M. Gentzkow and J. Shapiro, "What Drives Media Slant? Evidence from U.S. Daily Newspapers," *Econometrica* 78, no. 1 (2010): 35–71.

68. Francesca Tripodi, "Searching for Alternative Facts," Data & Society report, May 2018, https://datasociety.net/wp-content/uploads/2018/05/Data_Society_Searching-for-Alternative-Facts.pdf.

69. Zavadski and Toepfl, "Querying the Internet as a Mnemonic Practice."

70. Haider and Sundin, *Invisible Search.* See their discussion of Brian Vickery (1961) on p. 15.

71. Gillespie, "Politics of 'Platforms' "; Introna and Nissenbaum, "Shaping the Web."

STEP FIVE. SET THE TRAPS

1. Lucas D. Introna and Helen Nissenbaum, "Shaping the Web: Why the Politics of Search Engines Matters," *Information Society* 16, no. 3 (2000): 169–185.

2. Deirdre K. Mulligan and Daniel S. Griffin, "Rescripting Search to Respect the Right to Truth," *Georgetown Law Technology Review* 557 (2018).

3. Introna and Nissenbaum, "Shaping the Web."

4. Judi Bar-Ilan, "Google Bombing from a Time Perspective," *Journal of Computer-Mediated Communication* 12, no. 3 (2007): 910–938; ibid.

5. Introna and Nissenbaum, "Shaping the Web"; Bar-Ilan, "Google Bombing."

6. Marshall McLuhan, *Understanding Media: The Extensions of Man* (New York: McGraw-Hill, 1964).

7. Victoria Chemko, "Content Seeding & Your Marketing Strategy," Umami Marketing, December 20, 2019, https://umamimarketing.com/blog/content-seeding-marketing-strategy/.

8. Francesca Tripodi, "Google and Censorship through Search Engines," U.S. Senate Committee on the Judiciary Hearings, July 16, 2019,

https://www.judiciary.senate.gov/meetings/google-and-censorship-though-search-engines.

9. Eli Pariser, *The Filter Bubble—How the New Personalized Web Is Changing What We Read and How We Think* (New York: Penguin Random House, 2012), p. 142.

10. Ibid., pp. 142–143.

11. Michael Golbiewski and danah boyd, *Data Voids: Where Missing Data Can Easily Be Exploited*, Data & Society report, October 29, 2019, https://datasociety.net/library/data-voids/.

12. Kate Starbird, Ahmer Arif, and Tom Wilson, "Disinformation as Collaborative Work: Surfacing the Participatory Nature of Strategic Information Operations," *Proceedings of the ACM on Human-Computer Interaction* 3, no. 127 (November 2019).

13. Ibid.

14. See FusionGPS at https://fusiongps.com/.

15. Starbird, Arif, and Wilson, "Disinformation as Collaborative Work."

16. The full text of Nunes's memo can be found at Wikipedia, "Nunes Memo," https://en.wikipedia.org/w/index.php?title=File:Nunes_Memo.pdf.

17. Tarleton Gillespie, "Algorithmically Recognizable: Santorum's Google Problem, and Google's Santorum Problem," *Information, Communication & Society* 20, no. 1 (2017): 63–80.

18. Bar-Ilan, "Google Bombing."

19. This analysis is drawn primarily from Michel Foucault's 1972 book *The Archaeology of Knowledge: And the Discourse on Language* and Foucault's 1977 book *Discipline & Punish*.

20. Nikol G. Alexander-Floyd, "Disappearing Acts: Reclaiming Intersectionality in the Social Sciences in a Post-Black Feminist Era," *Feminist Formations* (2012): 1–25; Sirma Bilge, "Doing Critical Intersectionality in an Age of Popular and Corporate Diversity Culture," paper presented at the International Colloquium on Intersecting Situations of Domination, from a Transnational and Transdisciplinary Perspective, Université de Paris, June 8, 2011; Sirma Bilge, "Developing Queer Solidarities: A Plea for Queer Intersectionality," in Malinda Smith and Fatima Jaffer, eds., *Beyond the Queer Alphabet: Conversations in Gender, Sexuality, and Intersectionality* (Alberta, Canada: University of Alberta Press, 2012); Kimberlé Crenshaw, "Beyond Racism and Misogyny: Black Feminism and 2 Live Crew," in Mari J. Matsuda, Charles R. Lawrence III, Richard Delgado, and Kimberlé Williams Crenshaw, eds., *Words That Wound: Critical Race Theory, Assaultive Speech and the First Amendment* (Boulder, CO: Westview Press, 1993), pp. 111–132; Patricia Hill Collins, "The Social Construction of Black Feminist Thought," *Signs* 14, no. 4 (1989): 745–773.

21. Bailey Troia, " 'You're the One That Put Me in a Box': Integration, Cultural Constraints, and Fluid LGBTQ+ Millennial Identities," paper presented at the 113th Annual Meeting of the American Sociological Association, Philadelphia, 2018.

22. Lauren Garcia, "Deep Roots: Mapping the Networks of the Old, New, and Alt-Right," *Eastern Sociological Society Annual Conference,* February 22–25, 2018.

23. "Herstory," Black Lives Matter, https://blacklivesmatter.com/herstory/.

24. The original website this language was taken from, https://bluelivesmatter.blue/organization, is no longer in service, but an archive of the website is available at https://web.archive.org/web/diff/201706141 05638/20170617231543/https://bluelivesmatter.blue/organization. The original website now redirects to a new organization called the *Police Tribune,* "a law enforcement news publication staffed by journalists and columnists with family in law enforcement." Similar language, however, is still available under the mission statement of Blue Lives Matter NYC; see https://bluelivesmatternyc.org/pages/frontpage.

25. This language was originally taken from the "history" section of the Blue Lives Matter website, bluelivesmatter.blue. This website is no longer active and now redirects to the *Police Tribune,* but an archive of these statements is available at https://web.archive.org/web/diff/2016061 8013508/20170614105638/https://bluelivesmatter.blue/organization.

26. On Black Americans being the group most likely to be killed by police, see Jon Swaine, Oliver Laughland, Jamiles Lartey, and Cirara McCarthy, "The Counted: People Killed by Police in the US," *Center for Victim Research Repository,* 2016, https://ncvc.dspacedirect.org/handle/20.500.11990/1182.

27. Loren Collingwood and Benjamin Gonzales O'Brien, *Sanctuary Cities—The Politics of Refuge* (Oxford, UK: Oxford University Press, 2019); Angela S. García, "Hidden in Plain Sight: How Unauthorized Migrants Strategically Assimilate in Restrictive Localities," *Journal of Ethnic and Migration Studies* 40, no. 12 (2014): 1895–1914.

28. Collingwood and O'Brien, *Sanctuary Cities.*

29. Ibid.

30. Starbird, Arif, and Wilson, "Disinformation as Collaborative Work."

31. Ibid.

32. Abby Ohlheiser, "How Googling It Can Send Conservatives Down Secret Rabbit Holes of Alternative Facts," *Washington Post,* May 25, 2018, https://www.washingtonpost.com/news/the-intersect/wp/2018/05/25/how-googling-it-can-send-conservatives-down-secret-rabbit-holes-of-alternative-facts/.

33. Juan González and Joseph Torres, *News for All the People: The Epic Story of Race and the American Media* (New York: Verso, 2011).

34. Ibid.; Dan T. Carter, *The Politics of Rage: George Wallace, the Origins of the New Conservatism, and the Transformation of American Politics* (Baton Rouge: Louisiana State University Press, 2000).

35. Sandra Haarsager, "Choosing Silence: A Case of Reverse Agenda Setting in Depression Era News Coverage," *Journal of Mass Media Ethics* 6 (2009): 35–46.

36. Sarah Stillman, "The Missing White Girl Syndrome: Disappeared Women and Media Activism," *Gender and Development* 15, no. 2 (2007): 491–502.

37. Whitney Phillips, "The Oxygen of Amplification: Better Practices for Reporting on Extremists, Antagonists, and Manipulators," *Data & Society Research Institute*, 2018, https://datasociety.net/library/oxygen-of-amplification/.

38. Joan Donovan and danah boyd, "Stop the Presses? Moving from Strategic Silence to Strategic Amplification in a Networked Media Ecosystem," *American Behavioral Scientist* 65, no. 2 (2019).

39. Ibid.

40. Phillips, "Oxygen of Amplification"; Whitney Phillips and Ryan M. Milner, *You Are Here: A Field Guide for Navigating Polarized Speech, Conspiracy Theories, and Our Polluted Media Landscape* (Cambridge, MA: MIT Press, 2021).

41. Nicole Hemmer, *Messengers of the Right: Conservative Media and the Transformation of American Politics* (Philadelphia: University of Pennsylvania Press, 2018).

42. Phillips and Milner, *You Are Here*.

43. Ibid.

44. Ibid.

45. Starbird, Arif, and Wilson, "Disinformation as Collaborative Work."

46. "Schiff Outed Eric Ciaramella in Transcript Release," *The Rush Limbaugh Show*, November 7, 2019, https://news.iheart.com/featured/rush-limbaugh/content/2019-11-07-pn-rush-limbaugh-schiff-outed-eric-ciaramella-in-transcript-release/.

STEP SIX. MAKE OLD IDEAS SEEM NEW

1. On the interconnectedness of the web, see Tim Berners-Lee, *Weaving the Web: The Original Design and Ultimate Destiny of the World Wide Web* (New York: HarperCollins, 2000).

2. Galen Stocking et al., "YouTube News Consumers about as Likely to Use the Site for Opinions as for Facts," Pew Research Organization, September 28, 2020, https://www.pewresearch.org/journalism/2020/09/28/

youtube-news-consumers-about-as-likely-to-use-the-site-for-opinions-as-for-facts/.

3. Rebecca Lewis, *Alternative Influence: Broadcasting the Reactionary Right on YouTube*, Data & Society report, September 18, 2018, https://datasociety.net/library/alternative-influence/.

4. Ibid.; Alice Marwick and Rebecca Lewis, *Media Manipulation and Disinformation Online*, Data & Society report, May 15, 2017, https://datasociety.net/library/media-manipulation-and-disinfo-online/; Whitney Phillips and Ryan M. Milner, *You Are Here: A Field Guide for Navigating Polarized Speech, Conspiracy Theories, and Our Polluted Media Landscape* (Cambridge, MA: MIT Press, 2021).

5. Lewis, *Alternative Influence*.

6. Felix Harcourt, *Ku Klux Culture: America and the Klan in the 1920s* (Chicago: University of Chicago Press, 2017).

7. Michelle Alexander, *The New Jim Crow: Mass Incarceration in the Age of Colorblindness* (New York: New Press, 2010).

8. Cynthia Miller-Idriss, *The Extreme Gone Mainstream: Commercialization and Far Right Youth Culture in Germany* (Princeton, NJ: Princeton University Press, 2017), p. 18.

9. Robert Mejia, Kay Beckermann, and Curtis Sullivan, "White Lies: A Racial History of the (Post)Truth," *Communication and Critical/Cultural Studies* 15, no. 2 (2018): 109–126; Linda Villarosa, "Myths about Physical Racial Differences Still in Use Today," *The 1619 Project, New York Times,* August 14, 2019, https://www.nytimes.com/interactive/2019/08/14/magazine/racial-differences-doctors.html.

10. Federal Bureau of Investigation and Department of Homeland Security, Joint Intelligence Bulletin, *White Supremacist Extremism Poses Persistent Threat of Lethal Violence*, May 10, 2017, https://www.documentcloud.org/documents/3924852-White-Supremacist-Extremism-JIB.html.

11. Michael Omi and Howard Winant, *Racial Formation in the United States: From the 1960s to the 1990s* (New York: Routledge, 1994).

12. Anthea Butler, *White Evangelical Racism: The Politics of Morality in America* (Chapel Hill: University of North Carolina Press, 2021).

13. Jason Sokol, *There Goes My Everything: White Southerners in the Age of Civil Rights, 1945–1975* (New York: Alfred A. Knopf, 2006).

14. Mejia, Beckermann, and Sullivan, *White Lies*.

15. F. James Davis, *Who Is Black? One Nation's Definition* (College Park: Penn State University Press, 1991). Mejia, Beckermann, and Sullivan, *White Lies*.

16. Eduardo Bonilla-Silva, *Racism without Racists: Color-Blind Racism and the Persistence of Racial Inequality in America* (Lanham, MD: Rowman & Littlefield, 2003); Victor Ray, "A Theory of Racialized Organizations," *American Sociological Review* 84, no. 1 (2019): 26–53.

17. Miller-Idriss, *Extreme Gone Mainstream*.

18. Ibid.

19. Ibid.

20. Joe R. Feagin, *Racist America: Roots, Current Realities, and Future Reparations* (New York: Routledge, 2010).

21. For "polluted" information, see Whitney Phillips and Ryan M. Milner, *You Are Here: A Field Guide for Navigating Polarized Speech, Conspiracy Theories, and Our Polluted Media Landscape* (Cambridge, MA: MIT Press, 2021).

22. Kevin Roose, "The Making of a YouTube Radical," *New York Times*, June 8, 2019, https://www.nytimes.com/interactive/2019/06/08/technology/youtube-radical.html.

23. Johannes Baldauf, Julia Ebner, and Jakob Guhl, eds., "Hate Speech and Radicalisation Online: The OCCI Research Report," *ISD*, 2019, https://www.isdglobal.org/wp-content/uploads/2019/06/ISD-Hate-Speech-and-Radicalisation-Online-English-Draft-2.pdf.

24. Noah A. Rosenberg, Jonathan K. Pritchard, James L. Weber, Howard M. Cann, Kenneth K. Kidd, Lev A. Zhivotovsky, and Marcus W. Feldman, "Genetic Structure of Human Populations," *Science* 298 (2002): 2381–2385.

25. National Human Genome Project, National Institutes of Health, "The Human Genome Project," https://www.genome.gov/human-genome-project.

26. "Race: The Power of an Illusion," PBS, https://www.pbs.org/race.

27. W. E. B. Du Bois, "Dusk of Dawn: An Essay toward an Autobiography of a Race Concept," in H. L. Gates Jr., ed., *The Oxford W. E. B. Du Bois*, vol. 8 (1940; New York: Oxford University Press, 2007); Michael Omi and Howard Winant, *Racial Formation in the United States from the 1960s to the 1990s* (London: Routledge, 1994); Ginetta Candelario, *Black behind the Ears: Dominican Racial Identity from Museums to Beauty Shops* (Chapel Hill, NC: Duke University Press, 2010); Wendy D. Roth, "The Multiple Dimensions of Race," *Ethnic and Racial Studies* 39, no. 8 (2016): 1310–1338.

28. Jennifer Patrice Sims, Whitney Laster Pirtle, and Iris Johnson-Arnolds, "Doing Hair, Doing Race: The Influence of Hairstyle on Racial Perceptions across the US," *Ethnic and Racial Studies* 43, no. 12 (2020): 2099–2119.

29. Matt Perez, "YouTube Bans White Supremacists Stefan Molyneux, Richard Spencer, David Duke," *Forbes*, June 29, 2020, https://www.forbes.com/sites/mattperez/2020/06/29/youtube-bans-white-supremacists-stefan-molyneux-richard-spencer-david-duke/?sh=76bde1665ff1.

30. Lewis, *Alternative Influence*.

31. For a classic rebuttal to the book's premise, see the editorial page of the *New York Times*, October 24, 1994, https://timesmachine.nytimes.com/timesmachine/1994/10/24/622443.html?pageNumber=16.

32. Episode 396 (September 2013) and Episode 436 (January 2014) are still on Spotify as of September 23, 2021. Episode 538 (August 2014) is not.

33. Claude S. Fisher, Michael Hout, Martin Sanches Jankowski, Samuel R. Lucas, Ann Swidler, and Kim Voss, *Inequality by Design: Cracking the Bell Curve Myth* (Princeton, NJ: Princeton University Press, 1996); Ned Block, "How Heritability Misleads about Race," *Cognition* 56 (1995): 99–128.

34. Mejia, Beckermann, and Sullivan, *White Lies.*

35. Lisa Powell, "Eugenics and Equality: Does the Constitution Allow Policies Designed to Discourage Reproduction among Disfavored Groups? *Yale Law & Police Review* 20, no. 2 (2002): 481–512.

36. Ibid., p. 502.

37. This statistic is from the Disability Justice website, www.disabilityjustice.org.

38. Ibid.

39. Kathryn Paige Harden, *The Genetic Lottery: Why DNA Matters for Social Equality* (Princeton, NJ: Princeton University Press, 2021).

40. Eric K. Ward, "Skin in the Game: How Antisemitism Animates White Nationalism," PoliticalResearch.org, June 29, 2017, http://www.politicalresearch.org/2017/06/29/skin-in-the-game-how-antisemitism-animates-white-nationalism#sthash.xyKGl7XX.s8lwywIo.dpbs.

41. Fisher et al., *Inequality by Design.*

42. Daniel Karell and Michael Freedman, "Rhetorics of Radicalism," *American Sociological Review* 84 (2019): 726–753.

43. Anthea Butler, *White Evangelical Racism: The Politics of Morality in America* (Chapel Hill: University of North Carolina Press, 2021).

44. Episode 3709, "The Morality Crisis," available online at PodChaser, https://www.podchaser.com/podcasts/freedomain-with-stefan-molyneu-82402/episodes/3709-the-morality-crisis-denni-18155071.

45. Nirmal Puwar, *Space Invaders: Race, Gender, and Bodies out of Place* (Oxford, UK: Berg Publishers, 2004); J. Cheney, "Truth, Knowledge and the Wild World," *Ethics & the Environment* 10, no. 2 (2005): 101–135; Shana Almeida, "Face-Based Epistemologies: The Role of Race and Dominance in Knowledge Production," *Wagadu* 13 (Summer 2015).

46. Adam Serwer, "White Nationalism's Deep American Roots," *The Atlantic*, April 2019, https://www.theatlantic.com/magazine/archive/2019/04/adam-serwer-madison-grant-white-nationalism/583258/. *The Passing of the Great Race* (color illustrated edition) is available on Walmart.com for purchase. Currently it arrives within a week and boasts a lone five-star review on the site (as of September 24, 2021).

47. Thomas Chatterton Williams, "The French Origins of 'You Will Not Replace Us,' " *New Yorker*, December 4, 2017, https://www.newyorker.com/magazine/2017/12/04/the-french-origins-of-you-will-not-replace-us.

48. Nellie Bowles, " 'Replacement Theory,' a Racist, Sexist Doctrine, Spreads in Far-Right Circles," *New York Times,* March 18, 2019, https://www.nytimes.com/2019/03/18/technology/replacement-theory.html.

49. Bruce Haring, "Fox News Host Laura Ingraham Clarifies Remarks on Immigration," *Deadline,* August 9, 2018, https://deadline.com/2018/08/fox-news-host-laura-ingraham-clarifies-remarks-on-immigration-1202443557/.

50. Ibid.

51. Paulina Firozi, "GOP Lawmaker: 'We Can't Restore Our Civilization with Somebody Else's Babies,' " *The Hill,* March 12, 2017, https://thehill.com/blogs/ballot-box/323606-gop-lawmaker-invokes-far-right-dutch-politician-in-retweet.

52. Emile Durkheim, *The Elementary Forms of Religious Life,* trans. Carol Cogman, ed. Mark Cladis (Oxford, UK: Oxford University Press, 2001).

53. Miller-Idriss, *Extreme Gone Mainstream*; Phillips and Milner, *You Are Here.*

54. Miller-Idris, *Extreme Gone Mainstream,* looks at ambiguity in physical symbols like clothing; Phillips and Milner, *You Are Here,* studies ambiguity in online symbols such as memes.

55. Ibid.

56. Phillips and Milner, *You Are Here.*

57. Michael Thomsen, "Guilt, Shame, and Quiet: Women in 'Metal Gear Solid,' " *Forbes,* September 6, 2015, https://www.forbes.com/sites/michaelthomsen/2015/09/06/guilt-shame-and-quiet-women-in-metal-gear-solid/#fa405174a6cf.

58. Tom Bartlett, "What's So Dangerous about Jordan Peterson?," *Chronicle of Higher Education* (2018), https://www.chronicle.com/article/What-s-So-Dangerous-About/242256.

59. Fox News Facebook post featuring Candace Owens on *Watters' World,* September 24, 2017, https://www.facebook.com/FoxNews/photos/on-%22watters'-world-%22-candace/10156034491031336/.

60. Elizabeth Ames, "Liberals Sick of the Alt-Left Are Taking 'the Red Pill,' " Fox News, September 13, 2017, https://www.foxnews.com/opinion/liberals-sick-of-the-alt-left-are-taking-the-red-pill.

61. Berners-Lee, *Weaving the Web.*

62. This data-pollution imagery was inspired by Phillips and Milner, *You Are Here.*

63. In the 2020 election, at least twenty-five congressional candidates that publicly espoused QAnon conspiracy theories appeared on ballots in November (all Republicans). See Joseph Stepansky, "In QAnon-Linked US Candidates, Populism Meets Conspiracy," *Al Jazeera,* October 16, 2020, https://www.aljazeera.com/news/2020/10/16/in-qanon-linked-us-candidates-populism-meets-conspiracy.

64. It is worth noting that since the removal of the flag in 2015, the South Carolina Secessionist Party has been permitted to fly the flag on the same day (July 10) at 10:00 am for the past three years to "mark the anniversary" of the flag's removal. See Bristow Marchant, "3 Years Later, Confederate Flag Casts Shadow Again over SC State House," *The State*, July 20, 2018, https://www.thestate.com/news/politics-government/article214555950.html.

65. In a series of mini-documentaries produced by the Center for Christian Study, Louis Nelson, professor of Architectural History at the University of Virginia, provides a walking tour of the city's monuments and the history behind them. The virtual tour is available at https://www.studycenter.net/race-and-place-episodes.

66. Ava Duvernay, director, and Jason Moran, composer, *13th* (film), USA, 2016.

67. Dan T. Carter, *The Politics of Rage: George Wallace, the Origins of the New Conservatism, and the Transformation of American Politics* (Baton Rouge: Louisiana State University Press, 2000).

68. Miller-Idriss, *Extreme Gone Mainstream*.

69. Kevin Kruse, *White Flight: Atlanta and the Making of Modern Conservatism* (Princeton, NJ: Princeton University Press, 2005).

70. Cain Hope Felder, *Troubling Biblical Waters: Race, Class, and Family* (Maryknoll, NY: Orbis Books, 1990), p. 103.

71. Ian Haney López, *Dog Whistle Politics: How Coded Racial Appeals Have Reinvented Racism and Wrecked the Middle Class* (Oxford, UK: Oxford University Press, 2014).

72. Arlie Russell Hochschild, *Strangers in Their Own Land: Anger and Mourning on the American Right* (New York: New Press, 2016).

73. Katie Reilly, "Here Are All the Times that Trump Insulted Mexico," *Time*, August 31, 2016, https://time.com/4473972/donald-trump-mexico-meeting-insult/.

74. Francesca Polletta and Jessica Callahan, "Deep Stories, Nostalgia Narratives, and Fake News: Storytelling in the Trump Era," *American Journal of Cultural Sociology* 2017, https://cpb-us-e2.wpmucdn.com/faculty.sites.uci.edu/dist/2/432/files/2011/03/Deep-Stories-Polletta-and-Callahan.pdf.

75. Michael Paarlberg, "Transnational Militancy: Diaspora Influence over Electoral Activity in Latin America," *Comparative Politics* 49, no. 4 (2017).

76. Kavitha Surana, "How Racial Profiling Goes Unchecked in Immigration Enforcement," *ProPublica*, June 8, 2018, https://www.propublica.org/article/racial-profiling-ice-immigration-enforcement-pennsylvania.

77. Theda Skocpol and Vanessa Williamson, *The Tea Party and the Remaking of Republican Conservatism* (Oxford, UK: Oxford University Press, 2012), p. 76.

78. Kruse, *White Flight*.

79. Charles W. Mills, *The Racial Contract* (Ithaca, NY: Cornell University Press, 1997); Charles W. Mills, "White Ignorance," in Shannon Sullivan and Nancy Tuanas, eds., *Race and Epistemologies of Ignorance* (Albany: SUNY Press, 2007), 11–39.

80. Butler, *White Evangelical Racism*; Puwar, *Space Invaders*; Almeida, "Face-Based Epistemologies."

81. Karolin Schwarz and Josef Holnburger, "Disinformation: What Role Does Disinformation Play for Hate Speech and Extremism on the Internet and What Measures Have Social Media Companies Taken to Combat It?," in Johannes Baldauf, Julia Ebner, and Jakob Guhl, eds., *Hate Speech and Radicalisation Online: The OCCI Research* Report (London: Institute for Strategic Dialogue, 2019).

STEP SEVEN. CLOSE THE LOOP

1. Yochai Benkler, Rob Faris, and Hal Roberts, *Network Propaganda: Manipulation, Disinformation, and Radicalization in American Politics* (Oxford, UK: Oxford University Press, 2018).

2. Nicole Hemmer, *Messengers of the Right: Conservative Media and the Transformation of American Politics* (Philadelphia: University of Pennsylvania Press, 2018).

3. Joseph Bernstein, "How PragerU is Winning the Right-Wing Culture War without Donald Trump," *BuzzFeedNews*, March 3, 2018

4. Claudia Goldin, Sari Pekkala Kerr, Claudia Olivetti, and Erling Barth, "The Expanding Gender Earnings Gap: Evidence from the LEHD-2000 Census," *American Economic Review* 107, no. 5 (2017): 110–114.

5. Alice Marwick and William Partin, "QAnon Shows That the Age of Alternative Facts Will Not End with Trump," *Columbia Journalism Review*, October 5, 2020.

6. Ibid.

7. NAACP, "The 1963 March on Washington," NAACP.org, https://naacp.org/find-resources/history-explained/1963-march-washington.

8. Ian Haney López, *Dog Whistle Politics: How Coded Racial Appeals Have Reinvented Racism and Wrecked the Middle Class* (Oxford, UK: Oxford University Press, 2014).

9. L. G. Carr, *"Color-Blind" Racism* (Thousand Oaks, CA: Sage Publications, 1997); Stephanie M. Wildman, *Privilege Revealed: How Invisible Preference Undermines America*, 6th ed. (New York: New York University Press, 1996); Eduardo Bonilla-Silva, *Racism without Racists: Color-Blind Racism and the Persistence of Racial Inequality in America* (Lanham, MD: Rowman & Littlefield, 2003).

10. Haney López, *Dog Whistle Politics*.

11. Kimberlé Crenshaw, "Demarginalizing the Intersection of Race and Sex: A Black Feminist Critique of Antidiscrimination Doctrine, Feminist Theory, and Antiracist Politics," *University of Chicago Legal Forum* 1, no. 8 (1989): 139–167, https://chicagounbound.uchicago.edu/cgi/viewcontent.cgi?article=1052&context=uclf; Cornel West, Kimberlé Crenshaw, Neil Gotanda, Gary Peller, and Kendall Thomas, *Critical Race Theory: The Key Writings That Formed the Movement* (New York: New Press, 1995).

12. Victor Ray, "A Theory of Racialized Organizations," *American Sociological Review* 84, no. 1 (2019): 26–53.

13. These words were used in the *title* of Trump's executive order. After Trump lost the election, the executive order was taken down from whitehouse.org, but you can still access it, as of May 26, 2021, at https://www.crowell.com/NewsEvents/AlertsNewsletters/all/Trump-Executive-Order-Barring-Race-and-Sex-Stereotyping-and-Scapegoating-Poses-Special-Challenges-for-Universities-and-Colleges.

14. Christopher F. Rufo, "Radicals of the State," ChristopherRufo.com, July 15, 2020, https://christopherrufo.com/radicals-of-the-state/.

15. Kreiss, Daniel, Alice Marwick, and Francesca Tripodi, "The Anti-Critical Race Theory Movement Will Profoundly Affect Public Education," *Scientific American*, November 10, 2021.

16. "Tomi Lahren Torches Lori Lightfoot," *Fox News* video, https://www.youtube.com/watch?v=oRPNFnJZkOs.

17. Peter Rainer, "Dr. King Was Tracked by the FBI. In 'MLK/FBI,' Filmmakers Explore Why," *Christian Science Monitor*, January 14, 2021.

18. Jason Sokol, *There Goes My Everything: White Southerners in the Age of Civil Rights, 1945–1975* (New York: Alfred A. Knopf, 2006); quote on p. 83. For how the misguided belief that Blacks have less intellectual ability than whites has been used in disinformation campaigns, see Step Six.

19. The President's Advisory 1776 Commission, *The 1776 Report*, p. 16. The full report is available at https://trumpwhitehouse.archives.gov/wp-content/uploads/2021/01/The-Presidents-Advisory-1776-Commission-Final-Report.pdf.

20. Haney López, *Dog Whistle Politics*.

21. Dan T. Carter, *The Politics of Rage: George Wallace, the Origins of the New Conservatism, and the Transformation of American Politics* (Baton Rouge: Louisiana State University Press, 2000), 217.

22. Sokol, *There Goes My Everything*.

23. Pierre Lemieux, "Similarity between Socialism and Facism: An Illustration," Library of Economics and Liberty, n.d., https://www.econlib.org/similarity-between-socialism-and-fascism-an-illustration/.

24. The pronunciation varies by ideological dialect. Conservative elites and voters I interviewed pronounced it as "an-TEE-fuh," whereas progressives tend to pronounce it "*ANTI*-fa."

25. Rachael Levy, "What Is Antifa?" *Wall Street Journal*, January 7, 2021, https://www.wsj.com/articles/q-a-what-is-antifa-11598985917.

26. Throughout this section, quotations from social media have been documented by screenshots in the author's possession.

27. Alice Marwick and Rebecca Lewis, "Media Manipulation and Disinformation Online," Data & Society report, 2017, https://datasociety.net/wp-content/uploads/2017/05/DataAndSociety_ExecSummary-MediaManipulationAndDisinformationOnline.pdf.

28. Robert Mejia, Kay Beckermann, and Curtis Sullivan, "White Lies: A Racial History of the (Post)Truth," *Communication and Critical/Cultural Studies* 15, no. 2 (2018): 109–126.

29. Tess Owen, "How Boston's Massive 'Free Speech' Rally Fell Apart," *Vice*, August 19, 2017, https://www.vice.com/en_ca/article/zmy8be/how-bostons-massive-free-speech-rally-fell-apart.

30. Max Marcilla, "Charlottesville City Council Votes to Remove Two Confederate Statues after Hearing from Public," NBC29.com, June 7, 2021, https://www.nbc29.com/2021/06/07/charlottesville-city-council-votes-remove-two-Confederate-statues-after-hearing-public/.

31. Laura Smith, "In 1965, the City of Charlottesville Demolished a Thriving Black Neighborhood," *Timeline*, August 15, 2017, https://timeline.com/charlottesville-vinegar-hill-demolished-ba27b6ea69e1; Erica L. Green and Annie Waldman, "You Are Still Black: Charlottesville's Racial Divide Hinders Students," *New York Times*, October 16, 2018.

32. Sokol, *There Goes My Everything*, p. 78.

33. Fox News Facebook post, https://www.facebook.com/FoxNews/videos/it-has-become-socially-acceptable-at-uc-berkeley-for-conservatives-to-be-physica/10156131981831336/.

34. The independent report did not find any direct evidence of such an order. See Hunton & Williams, LLP, *Final Report: Independent Review of the 2017 Protest Events in Charlottesville, Virginia*, https://www.huntonak.com/images/content/3/4/v4/34613/final-report-ada-compliant-ready.pdf.

35. Ibid.

36. Elizabeth R. Varon, "UVA and the History of Race: The Lost Cause through Judge Duke's Eyes," *UVAToday*, September 4, 2019.

37. "Jason Kessler," Southern Poverty Law Center website, https://www.splcenter.org/fighting-hate/extremist-files/individual/jason-kessler.

38. Francesca Tripodi and Yuanye Ma, "You've Got Mail: How the Trump Administration Used Legislative Communication to Frame His Last Year in Office," *Information, Communication and Society*, 2022, https://doi.org/10.1080/1369118X.2021.2020873.

39. Erica Chenoweth and Jeremy Pressman, "Black Lives Matter Protesters Were Overwhelmingly Peaceful, Our Research Finds," *Harvard Radcliffe Institute*, October 20, 2020, radcliffe.harvard.edu/news-and-ideas/

black-lives-matter-protesters-were-overwhelmingly-peaceful-our-research-finds.

40. Alice Wilder, "Trump Team Online," *Trump, Inc.*, WNYC Radio, https://www.wnycstudios.org/podcasts/trumpinc/episodes/trump-inc-campaign-media.

41. Joan Donovan and Brian Friedberg, "Source Hacking: Media Manipulation in Practice," Data & Society report, September 4, 2019, https://datasociety.net/library/source-hacking-media-manipulation-in-practice/.

42. Sarah Pruitt, "When Did African Americans Actually Get the Right to Vote?" History.com, April 15, 2021, https://www.history.com/news/african-american-voting-right-15th-amendment.

43. Sokol, *There Goes My Everything*, p. 238.

44. Anthea Butler, *White Evangelical Racism: The Politics of Morality in America* (Chapel Hill: University of North Carolina Press, 2021).

45. Joseph F. Sullivan, "Florio's Defeat Revives Memories of G.O.P. Activities in 1981," *New York Times*, November 11, 1993.

46. John Kruzel, "Controversial Pro-Trump Group Warns Members to Avoid Election Day Meddling: Stop the Steal Issued New Guidance to Its Network of Volunteer Poll Monitors," *ABC News*, November 7, 2016, https://abcnews.go.com/Politics/controversial-pro-trump-group-warns-members-avoid-election/story?id=43372037.

47. Archived tweets are available at https://archive.li/UiiQI.

48. "Transcript of Trump's Speech at Rally before US Capitol Riot," AP News, January 13, 2021, https://apnews.com/article/election-2020-joe-biden-donald-trump-capitol-siege-media-e79eb5164613d6718e-9f4502eb471f27.

49. A timed account of the events was recorded by *USA Today* and is available at https://www.usatoday.com/in-depth/news/2021/01/06/dc-protests-capitol-riot-trump-supporters-electoral-college-stolen-election/6568305002/.

50. Peter Hermann, "Two Officers Who Helped Fight the Capitol Mob Died by Suicide: Many More Are Hurting," *Washington Post*, February 11, 2021, https://www.washingtonpost.com/local/public-safety/police-officer-suicides-capitol-riot/2021/02/11/94804ee2-665c-11eb-886d-5264d4ceb46d_story.html.

51. Tom Jackman, "Police Union Says 140 Officers Injured in Capitol Riot," *Washington Post*, January 27, 2021.

52. *The Rush Limbaugh Show* podcast, January 6, 2021, transcript available at https://www.happyscribe.com/public/the-rush-limbaugh-show/the-rush-limbaugh-show-podcast-jan-06-2021.

53. "Representative Mo Brooks Responds to Capitol Riot, Urges No Finger-Pointing," *Fox Business* video, January 7, 2021, https://video.foxbusiness.com/v/6220803869001#sp=show-clips.

54. Rowan Scarborough, "Facial Recognition Identifies Extremists Storming the Capitol," *Washington Times,* January 6, 2021.

55. Ryan Bort, "A Guide to the Right's Unhinged Conspiracy Theories about Jan. 6." *Rolling Stone*, January 6, 2022, https://www.rollingstone.com/politics/politics-news/jan-6-conspiracy-theories-capitol-riot-antifa-1278597/.

56. See the tweet at https://twitter.com/drpaulgosar/status/13469408 16514813953?lang=en.

57. Jeremy Herb, Ryan Nobles, and Annie Grayer, "House Strikes Deal to Create Independent January 6 Commission," CNN, May 14, 2021.

58. Brian Naylor, "Senate Republicans Block a Plan for an Independent Commission on Jan. 6 Capitol Riot," NPR, May 28, 2021.

59. "House Debate on Removal of Representative Greene from Committees," C-SPAN, February 4, 2021, https://www.c-span.org/video/?c4943639/house-debate-removal-representative-greene-committees.

60. Michael I. Norton, Daniel Mochon, and Dan Ariely, "The IKEA Effect: When Labor Leads to Love," *Journal of Consumer Psychology* 22 (2012): 453–460.

EPILOGUE

1. Cynthia Miller-Idriss, *The Extreme Gone Mainstream: Commercialization and Far Right Youth Culture in Germany* (Princeton, NJ: Princeton University Press, 2017).

2. Rebecca Lewis, *Alternative Influence: Broadcasting the Reactionary Right on YouTube*, Data & Society report, September 18, 2018, https://datasociety.net/library/alternative-influence/.

3. Jake Tapper and Betsy Kulman, "The Macaca Heard Round the World," *ABC News*, August 17, 2006, https://abcnews.go.com/Nightline/story?id=2322630&page=1.

4. Theda Skocpol and Vanessa Williamson, *The Tea Party and the Remaking of Republican Conservatism* (Oxford, UK: Oxford University Press, 2012), p. 215.

5. "Paul Ryan Denounces Donald Trump's 'Textbook Racism,' " BBC News, June 7, 2016, https://www.bbc.com/news/av/world-us-canada-36474325.

6. "The Overton Window," Mackinac Center for Public Policy, n.d., https://www.mackinac.org/OvertonWindow.

7. Ian Haney López, *Dog Whistle Politics: How Coded Racial Appeals Have Reinvented Racism and Wrecked the Middle Class* (Oxford, UK: Oxford University Press, 2014).

8. Ibid.

9. Ibid.

10. Robert Mejia, Kay Beckermann, and Curtis Sullivan, "White Lies: A Racial History of the (Post)Truth," *Communication and Critical/Cultural Studies* 15, no. 2 (2018): 109–126.

11. "A Letter on Justice and Open Debate," *Harper's,* July 7, 2020, https://harpers.org/a-letter-on-justice-and-open-debate.

12. Meredith Clark, "Drag Them: A Brief Etymology of So-Called 'Cancel Culture,'" *Communication and the Public* 5, nos. 3–4 (2020): 88–92.

13. Noam Chomsky's book *Manufacturing Consent* explains how effective ideological institutions are at propaganda.

14. Deen Freelon and Chris Wells, "Disinformation as Political Communication," *Political Communication* 37, no. 2 (2002): 145–156.

INDEX